BECOMING ON

Alan

CONTENTS

1

INTRODUCTION

There are several questions behind this account of my five years at the Dragon School Oxford. One concerns who I was and how I came to be as I am. So this is the autobiographical quest for personal roots and identity. A second question concerns my family and its history. It seems that I come from a well-documented and interesting family whose tentacles spread across the world and can be traced in detail from the later seventeenth century.

A third question concerns England and Britain. I came back from India when I was six and encountered a new land. I needed to start to understand its distinctive history and culture. My final question concerns the British Empire. Britain was just the small hub of a great empire for more than a century. The British created this empire, but equally it created Britain. It has a very distinctive character which makes it different from other empires in the way it worked and imagined itself. I am particularly interested in what held it together and how the identity of those who were involved with it, such as my ancestors, was constructed.

Knitting all these questions together is an interest in how we are educated, in the broadest sense. So this book is part of a larger project to understand in a comparative way how education works around the world, and in particular in England and China.

*

I seem to have been interested in the evocation of memory from a relatively early period in my life. This partly explains why I have been reluctant to throw anything away. From my teens I had the idea that I would try to construct an 'archive' of my life and perhaps that of my relatives. So I hoarded toys, photographs, letters, writings, anything I could. This desire to hold on to the past is shown in an essay that I wrote when I was eighteen entitled 'The past'. I shall just include the first paragraph to show my awareness, even then, of the importance of memory.

'People often find tremendous pleasure in reliving the pleasures of past events, partly as I have already explained, because they are surveying it from a safe peak of knowledge. It is only when we are not fully conscious, however that we can be truly transported there again and feel every emotion that we once felt. We must not worship the past. It is dangerous to idealise it, and useless to live continually in it. It can be utilized as a springboard to the future, and for those who have had an unhappy life it may be the dim backcloth to the glorious future, but that is all.'

There is a comment by my teacher in red ink at the end: 'One angle left out – the aged. What does it feel like, I wonder when all the major experiences of one's life lie in the past? The sole adventure left, death.' As I read this fifty years later it seems a pertinent remark.

*

In constructing this book I first wrote down everything I thought I could remember about this period when I was aged six to thirteen. I then checked this against the diaries, letters and school reports. This has thrown some light on the way in which my memory works. It shows that for this period, or at least before I was ten, without supporting documentation almost everything would be irretrievable. There would be just a very few lightning flashes of memory, usually moments of high excitement or pain or effort. A.C. Benson beautifully describes these isolated moments.

'Early impressions are like glimpses seen through the window by night when lightning is about. The flash leaps out without visible cause or warning, and the blackness lifts for a second revealing the scene, the criss-cross of the rods of rain, the trees shining with moisture.... So it is with memory; my early blinks are exceedingly vivid, but they are sundered, and though the passage of time does not dim them, as it dims the more fading impressions of later life, they do not form part of a continuous picture.'[2]

A second thing I have found is how faulty memory is, not usually in the experience itself, but in the surrounding details of when or where the event occurred or who was involved. I have re-contextualized many memories, when I caught my first fish at Oxford, when I learnt to cycle, when I stole from my grandfather. I have also had to revise my whole assessment of the degree to which I was unhappy at the Dragon School.

What I regret is that even with the detail in the documents, so little new memory has been triggered. I have sometimes managed to capture again the ambient smells, sounds and feelings surrounding a photograph or a letter. Yet very often I feel I may be forcing or imposing memories now that I know an event happened. For, on the whole, I can recall very little of even major events of that time, like going to India for my eleventh birthday holiday, or singing in 'Iolanthe' when I was twelve.

Yet gazing at my past as it unrolls in photos and comments it seems mainly to be the life of a slightly familiar stranger. I feel a little affinity, some ghostly overlap. Yet mostly it seems to be a different person. I recognize the little boy as someone I knew a very long time ago but have almost now forgotten. The past is not just a foreign country where they do

---

[2] A.C. Benson, *As We Were: a Victorian Peepshow* (Penguin edn., 2001), 67.

6

things differently; it is inhabited by half-familiar ghosts of one's younger self who seem disconnected strangers, yet are also part of oneself

This again emphasizes the good fortune of having the photographs, letters and other documents. There are clearly some people who seem to be able to remember their early years in vivid detail – Lord Berners, Roald Dahl, W.H. Hudson, Naomi Mitchison, Muriel Spark to name but a few. I cannot do this and would never have felt it worth attempting this study of a growing boy if it had not been for the chance survival of these documents, the 'paper trail' as it is now called in our audit-ridden culture.

Without the contemporary photographs, letters, diaries, school reports and other materials, I would be like an anthropologist who had done fieldwork in another society some sixty years ago and had destroyed all the fieldnotes. It would be an impossible task to write the ethnographic and anthropological account without the primary materials.

Yet even with these sources, one needs constantly to remember that each of them is biased. Just to take one example, an over-riding first impression is of how insular the letters were. While Indian Independence and its aftermath rocked India, the Cold War and the Korean War rekindled fears of nuclear war in the late 1940s and early 1950s. These events, let alone the two elections which took place in Britain, there is only a small amount in the documents suggesting that they impinged on us.

Yet I soon realized that, along with a slightly head-in-the-sand attitude which my mother admits to, there were also good reasons for this. Personal letters and diaries are not usually where you will find discussion of international or national politics or events – unless they directly impinge on plans. This is worth remembering. The sources I have, like all historical documents, create a bias - in this case away from the general to the particular.

Another bias lies in the letters that I wrote to my parents and grandparents. Addressing an adult, especially when one is still learning to control language, can lead into a kind of writing which conceals as much as it shows. How much of my own views and voice comes out of the letters, especially those written within the scrutiny of the Dragon School? I don't notice much difference in my letters from home and from school to my parents.

*

The English preparatory school is a very unusual institution and it is difficult to analyze it from within. Though a number of authors have used a scattering of letters and diaries of preparatory school children, these are usually used illustratively and from a wide variety of different children, different schools and different periods in order to create a collage. This is a useful approach, but it is different from this account.

In searching through my papers I have found over a hundred letters I wrote from the Dragon to my parents and grandparents. We were required to write each week, so there should have been at least 150 letters. To still have perhaps two thirds of those I wrote (there are only five for my first year, but thereafter they are fairly complete) was encouraging. These were supplemented by another source which has seldom been integrated into a systematic study of letters from a boarding school. These are the letters from parents and grandparents. The letters were written mainly by my mother between 1950 and 1955. They are supplemented by her detailed and observant letters to my father when they were apart (he was a tea planter in Assam) about her visits to me and my progress.

My mother's letters and other sources also allowed me to reconstruct the context of home life while I was at the Dragon. I realized that we cannot understand children in their boarding context without also understanding their family and home life, as well as their earlier childhood. My life in the period between six and thirteen in the periods when I was not at the Dragon dovetailed with the school experience. It is described in a companion volume to this, Dorset Days, which shows how much my experience and imagination bridged the two parallel worlds, as well as my parents' life in India.

These letters allowed me to re-enter the mind of the growing child, filtered, of course, by convention, reticence, assumptions about the interests of the receivers of the letters, yet nevertheless recording much of the daily life of childhood in a detail which it would be impossible to remember. They allowed me to examine what struck me <u>at the time</u>, what was significant, the biases and assumptions of childhood.

The contemporary letters in two directions are supplemented by several other contemporary sources which give depth to the analysis. School reports are occasionally referred to in the literature on preparatory schools, but I know of no systematic analysis of an almost complete series relating to a child. The Dragon school took reports seriously. I have the full termly reports for all but one of the fifteen terms I was at the school and also several dozen of the less detailed, but revealing, fortnightly reports which we sent home.

A further source of relevant background is the unusually detailed accounts published in the termly school magazine, The Draconian. In particular, the Term Notes by C.H. Jacques, which he later used as the basis for his 'Centenary History of the Dragon', are insightful and amusing. They constitute a diary of the school while I was there. The 'Term Notes' are complemented by much else in the 'Draconian'. For example, there are accounts of debates, sermons, visits, plays, films, games, many of them extremely detailed, although they are, of course, written by and reflect the perceptions of the staff and not the Dragons. The magazine also contained some photographs, which complement some early picture postcards of the school as it was in my time. For the first two years of my time there, there are also our weights, and throughout there is a complete inventory of all the boys and their classes, sets and even home addresses.

*

The book is based on letters all of which are in italics. Extracts from these letters are often relevant in more than one context. I have tried to eliminate multiple uses of the same extract, but I have allowed some repetition in the interests of providing as rich a contemporary basis for the book as possible. I have also tried to eliminate as much overlap between the world of the school and my independent account of home life. Occasionally, however, it is necessary to repeat material in the two different contexts.

My letters were written between the ages of seven and thirteen. They are not always easy to interpret. There is much strange spelling, omitted punctuation and odd grammar, though some readers have noted that my spelling is much improved when I am writing about games, perhaps because I really enjoyed that part of my letters.

I have attempted to steer a middle course between making the letters comprehensible through the correction, insertion or expansion of some words [in square brackets], and leaving them as much as possible in the form that they reached our parents. This, it is hoped, will give a feeling for schoolboy writing of the time. Frequently, for example, 'the' should be 'there', 'one' and 'won' are interchangeable and there are very often omissions of a comma or full stop. Often, when a word looks strange, it is a good idea to say it aloud, for it is phonetically correct, even if the spelling is not standard. I have also in quite a few cases inserted an editorial dash [–] where a passage in the original letter is innocent of all punctuation

*

One particular difficulty is that of reinterpreting the contemporary materials with the use of hindsight and hence distorting the meaning. It is easy to be wise after the event and to allocate praise or blame, to smooth out contradictions or to find premonitions of later events. I have tried as far as possible to refrain from retrospective speculations. And I have also tried to refrain from the anachronistic practice of judging past times by the values of the present. It would be easy to condemn casual snobbery or racism expressed at times, or just smugness and complacency. This is unhelpful and often unfair unless we fully think ourselves back into a different age with its special pressures and assumptions.

Yet the text needs some framework of interpretation, some hypotheses to lift it above the level of merely a narrative of loosely connected pieces of information. I have tried to do this within the context of the two major over-arching changes of those years. One is the huge societal shift of the 1950s as the effects of the Second World War diminished. My infancy was lived in the war and our life at the Dragon was still under the shadow of that war. The second is the rapid dismemberment of the British Empire begun in the decade after 1947. The largest empire in history was set free in an amazingly short time. This also altered the type of schooling I was starting to receive.

*

The book I have written is a period piece and also an account of a rather special school. This has both advantages and disadvantages. It means that the school cannot be held to be representative of preparatory boarding establishments of that time. On the other hand, the Dragon appears to us to be interesting both in the way it was run and in the kind of pupils it recruited and what it made of them.

The school was founded on concepts which went against much of the educational philosophy of late Victorian imperial education, even if it also retained some of an earlier Edwardian tradition of boarding schools in which our teachers had been reared. Unlike St. Cyprian's of the early twentieth century as described by some of its old boys, including Cyril Connolly and George Orwell, the school tried to overcome some of the traumas of this kind of socialization. It formed a bridge between the muscular Christian, imperialist, attitudes of the aftermath of Thomas Arnold through to our modern, post-imperial, world.

It is also an interesting school because of the later distinction of a considerable number of its former pupils in a wide variety of fields. The Dragon has helped to shape our national life and it is now helping to educate new elites who are sending their children to it from China, Japan, India and elsewhere.

*

This is a shortened version of parts of Dragon Days, a book written jointly with Jamie Bruce Lockhart and published in 2012. That work is over twice the length of this account, for it contains the letters of two other boys, Jamie and his brother Sandy. Those who would like the full and detailed account and analysis of the school through the eyes of three boys can use that account.

When it was necessary to re-publish the book in 2013 it occurred to me that it might be helpful to split off my writing. Some have found the immense detail of the full account somewhat overwhelming. Furthermore, it becomes a book about a school, rather than any one individual. By focusing on just my account, this version fits into my more personal, ongoing, autobiographical project. My five years at the Dragon School is only a part of a more general autobiographical and biographical account. The period before we came back to England will be dealt with in a volume provisionally titled 'Indian Infancy'. The parallel life at home from 1947-1955 is published in Dorset Days. I hope to continue the story through my years at Sedbergh (1955-60) and Oxford University (1960-66) in later volumes.

*

This is a collaborative project and I would like to thank those who have helped. I would e would particularly like to thank Jamie and the late Flip Bruce Lockhart, Sarah Harrison and Loulou Brown for their very careful and constructive comments. Three Dragon contemporaries read all or much of the book and made numerous useful comments: Jake Mermagen, John and Harry Machin. Various other Dragon friends, including Anna Biddle, Christopher Penn, Stephen Grieve, Tom Stanier and Patrick Lepper, made helpful observations. Gay Sturt, archivist at the Dragon, supplied much advice and material. I also thank the headmaster of the Dragon School for kind permission to publish material from the school archive. The work is part of a wider project comparing high quality education in China and England, kindly supported by the Kai Feng Scholars Program.

ORIGINS

Alan (seated on the ground, right) and his family in 1951

1 WHENCE I CAME

My ancestors seem to have been at the outward edge of many of the waves of predatory expansion of the British Empire. My eleventh generation James ancestors were among the first to settle in Jamaica and Colonel Richard James was supposedly the first English child to be born there in 1655. The James family prospered on Jamaica and a distant branch still owned an estate there until the 1920s. My own fourth generation great grandfather was a Chancery lawyer in Jamaica. He finally left for England in 1837, three years after the ending of slavery. His children were sent home with his wife to be educated in England and essentially to become English.

He invested in land in the newly opened settlement of South Australia on behalf of his three sons, and one of his grandsons went to India where my grandfather, William Rhodes-James, was born in 1886 in Coonor amidst the Nilgiri coffee estates. After school in England and Sandhurst, my grandfather was commissioned into the Indian Army. By the time he met my grandmother Violet Swinhoe, he was working as an Intelligence Officer on the Burma-China frontier.

The Swinhoe branch was reputedly descended from Viking raiders in Northumbria, where there is a village of that name. We have traced them back to the eighteenth century when they were lawyers in Calcutta. I have visited their impressive graves in the Old Park Street graveyard in Calcutta and seen the street named after them in that city. One distant cousin went to China in the middle of the nineteenth century and a Chinese pheasant is named after him. In the later nineteenth century Rodway Swinhoe discovered a potentially lucrative niche in a new frontier of Empire, upper Burma, where he practised as a lawyer in Mandalay for over thirty years. It was in upper Burma that my grandmother was born in 1896.

Much of British life from the eighteenth to twentieth centuries was essentially a system of what anthropologists might call cyclical nomadic predation. This depended on two poles. Britain was the base, the emotional, social and political core, and the family home. Here the children were sent to school and perhaps on to university or at least to some kind of finishing or training institution. It was also here that those from the colonies would retire and become grandparents and carers for the young sent home from abroad. Going abroad was a stage. Some stayed on in remote hill stations and elsewhere, but the great majority came back to

13

what they considered to be their real home.

In such cyclical movements, the boarding school became an essential mechanism. Such schools were part of an internal system for encouraging social mobility by converting money into status and training the middle classes for professions within Britain. They were also a mechanism for indoctrinating, disciplining and training those who would become the colonizers to make their fortunes around the world. My family participated in this pattern from the eighteenth century onwards, various branches sending their children home to school to learn how to be English. My being sent to the Dragon was one of the last instances of this many-generational pattern.

*

I was born in Shillong, Assam in December 1941. My first five years were spent in India as the Second World War rolled to the edges of Assam and I ended my time in India for a few brief months on a tea estate. In an autobiographical essay written at the age of eighteen I commented that 'My first recollections are of a slightly unhappy childhood. My parents were in India, my father in the army, and so we did not live a settled life. There always seemed to be something wrong with my tummy (later I learnt it was acidosis) and once I broke my arm. At the age of five I came home to England, and then I did not remember much, except that I was seasick most of the way home, and that my youngest sister was given a little stove for her birthday.' My mother later told me that I formed a strong friendship with the sweeper's son in Assam but the Urdu I spoke and ability to swim were to vanish almost immediately I returned to England with my father, mother and my two younger sisters, Fiona and Anne, in April 1947.

The warmth, both physical and emotional, the brilliance of the landscape and the freedom which I think I remember from those first five years made the shock of coming home to North Oxford at the end of the coldest winter of the twentieth century, with wartime rationing and very limited coal supplies, all the greater. My mother stayed in England for eighteen months and then left me and my elder sister Fiona at home when I was aged six and three quarters.

I remember that parting vaguely as one of those Kiplingesque moments – the delight I felt as I woke the morning after she had kissed me to sleep and discovered a small present at the foot of the bed quickly evaporating into a desperate feeling of loneliness and separation which has remained with me ever since. The incident is described in a letter written shortly after my parent's departure, with the soothing initial words of my grandmother contradicted by her description of my reaction to a phone call and letter. *My darling Iris – You must not be hurt when I tell you that neither of the*

14

children have shed a tear – it was a brilliant notion of yours to leave the presents and Alan has lived as a conductor ever since. He turned white after hearing you on the telephone and again when your letter came this morning as we waited for the postman before he went to school...

*

My progress at kindergarten in the two-and-a-half years before I went to the Dragon is described in the companion volume, Dorset Days, based largely on termly reports and my mother's letters. The over-all impression from the reports is that I enjoyed my school, tried hard, was generally liked, was enthusiastic and not too miserable. There is no talk of any problems or sadness, some cheerfulness and helpfulness and popularity. It is a different picture to that of my mother on her first return two years later, for she found me very difficult, if endearing, at times. For example, in the July before I went to the Dragon she wrote: *Alan is my chief headache, noisy rude and disobedient, bullying Fiona incessantly and yet the fear of parting from him is haunting me. He is so frightfully sensitive and is going to suffer so at school.*

It is clear that in the two years of preparation for the Dragon I was covering quite a wide range of the subjects I would then go on to study there. What were missing were languages, particularly Latin and French. That was the largest change academically in content. It is also clear that I was just about average in ability. The reports were moderately good, but I was always at least half a year older than the average age, and I seem to have stayed in transition – with a brief move up. Early signs of mathematical ability, which my mother hopefully noted, were not borne out in later reports. My best subjects were geography and nature study. My worst were, as my mother noted, that I was very slow in reading and writing.

The best way to introduce my family is by analysing the photograph reproduced at the start of this chapter. This shows the important relatives in my life at the end of my first year at the Dragon in summer 1951. Starting at the top left, it shows my Uncle Robert, Uncle Richard, Father, Grandfather, Grand-mother, Uncle Billy, sister Anne, Mother, Sister Fiona, Alan.

My grandparents, with whom I spent much of my time in England before coming to the Dragon, and the majority of my school holidays while there, were neither of them formally academically inclined. Yet they had a number of qualities and experiences which meant that they could support me well. My grandfather, William Rhodes-James had been a distinguished army officer in Burma and India and had won a Military Cross and an O.B.E. He was an excellent linguist, a lover of poetry, an avid reader and a lovely gentleman who encouraged me in every way.

My grandmother Violet was a force of nature. She was highly intelligent, strong willed, perennially optimistic, warm and imaginative, an excellent artist (one of the youngest ever students at the Academy Schools) and a very good actress and singer. They had themselves both been away in boarding schools when young and had supported my three uncles through boarding preparatory schools and then public schools, so they knew that world well. They looked after me excellently, playing with me, encouraging me in every way, and gave me much love and support, and I owe an enormous amount to them. I never remember that they were ever cruel, unjust or unpleasant to me.

My parents were very different from each other but equally supportive. My father Donald Macfarlane was born in El Paso, Texas, in 1916. He had been sent back to boarding school at Dollar in Scotland at the age of twelve and had been miserably homesick for his first two years. He never took to the school, despite being a first-rate athlete and rugger player, and left without any Higher School Certificates to be apprenticed to the engineering firm of John Brown on the Clyde. At the age of about twenty he was sent out to be an engineer on a tea plantation in Assam. During the war he joined the Assam Rifles and raised troops to fight against the Japanese. He met my mother when he was twenty-four and very soon married her.

My father was a good role model – tall, very handsome, an excellent games player, a keen fisherman, very strong but also gentle and kind. He adored my mother and was excellent with children as I noted in later years. He was not academic, but quite a keen reader and a good painter.

My mother complemented him. She had been born in Quetta, now in Pakistan, in 1922 and sent home very young. She was small, with a polio-damaged leg, good-looking and highly gifted. She was sent to six or seven schools before the age of sixteen. She won an open scholarship to Oxford when she was in her last school but was not allowed to take it up and was sent out to India. There, at the age of eighteen, she met and married my father. She was an excellent poet, novelist, philosopher and a reasonable painter. She wrote me wonderful letters and short stories and gave me enormous encouragement and love. I never doubted her love despite the fact that she kept being forced to leave me, and much of what I am stemmed from learning from her.

My three uncles, my mother's brothers, were the other major force in my life. The oldest, Billy, I did not see much as he was in the army. But the middle one, Richard, spent part of several holidays with us. He was a gentle, thoughtful, a devout Christian, a housemaster at Haileybury and a brave soldier in the war in Burma about which he wrote a book. He was always kind and encouraging to me and his car and presence enlivened my holidays.

The younger brother, Robert, was only eight years older than me and still at Sedbergh during these years. So he was at home for school holidays with me and my sister Fiona. He became a distinguished academic and politician, a Fellow of All Souls, a Member of Parliament for Cambridge, and the author of many books. When young he was keen on sports and before I went to the Dragon taught me how to play football, cricket and other skills which made a huge difference when I went to the school. He taught me how to lose at games, how to try my hardest, how to sing musicals. He was highly imaginative and had a wide range of toys which he generously shared with me. He never bullied or put pressure on me, despite the fact that I and my sister Fiona took away much of his mother and father's time and energy. He was a constant inspiration, and having a much older but non-threatening 'brother' was an enormous benefit for me. He made holidays wonderful and helped me to cope with boarding school through his example.

I was also lucky in my siblings. Fiona was with me for the time when my mother first left, until I was ten. She is a remarkable person; highly intelligent, a very gifted artist, a great reader and a remorseless thinker. She was great fun, enormously plucky and determined, and a real friend through much of my life. Of course we quarrelled and my mother notes that I bullied her in a mild way. But she stood up to me and I was always aware, as was my mother, that she was more mature and intellectually gifted than I. So I had a good younger sparring partner from whom, together with my grandmother and mother I learnt to appreciate in a non-threatening way the virtues of able women. My sister Anne was four years younger than me and I saw much less of her at this time, really only for the year in 1951 when my mother brought her back on leave, and again for my last year at the Dragon. She was less academic than Fiona, but a keen sportsperson and close to my father. I seem to have got on with her fine.

*

A few features of our life away from school are particularly relevant to my time at the Dragon. First, there was our class background. The family were basically upper middle class: my grandmother's father had been a lawyer in upper Burma; my grandfather was a Lt Colonel in the Indian army, my uncles were schoolmasters, army officers; and one became an MP. Further back the family had been professionals – lawyers, doctors, military officers – and before that adventurers and slave-owners in Jamaica.

My father, on the other hand, though coming from a family of Scottish clergyman, followed his own father in training as an engineer. He then became manager of various tea plantations. Taken as a whole, though struggling, my parents, grandparents and uncles had social connections and expectations which were well in line with the kind of boys who went to the Dragon. What we talked about at home, the films we went to, the interests in sports and art, were complementary to the kind of things I learnt in school. Yet there was something about me that was slightly different from many Dragon boys because our family had lived for much of their past outside England. I think this contributed to a slight feeling of being an outsider when I went to the school.

Another problem was our financial position. In my account of Dorset Days I have uncovered the fact that, like many middle class families after the war, we were very short of money. The kind of upper middle class life my grandparents and parents would like to have aspired to – a pony, a car, reasonable holidays on the Continent, even a television set – were beyond us. My parents on their pay, and grandparents on an insufficient pension, were constantly worrying about money. This combined with post-war austerity made our life something of a physical struggle. Perhaps, however, this was not a bad background for going to the Dragon since the kind of material life in terms of food, heating, clothing and other things I experienced at the Dragon was not much different from that at home, though my grandmother in particular ensured that we were pretty well fed.

Two particular features of our family are worth noting. One is the Scottish connection. My father was proud of his Scottish ancestry and nostalgic about parts of his upbringing. We spent summer holidays, and I spent one Christmas, in Scotland and was equally proud of my Scottish roots. This again gave me a sense of self-confidence and despite other incapacities, being small and not particularly gifted in academic work, arts and other things, I was at least a descendant of the Macfarlane clan.

Another was the connection to Assam. Children live in many parallel worlds simultaneously. They may be shut away in the intense atmosphere of a boarding school, but this does not mean that they cannot remember or draw sustenance from other worlds. I drew much strength from the vibrant world of my grandparents' home in Dorset, the games, fun, hobbies, expeditions, animals and gardening. I also drew support from the world of India that I had known until I was five and which remained alive through my mother's vivid letters, the relics of India around me at home, and my visit at the age of eleven for the Christmas holidays. I knew that, however cold and grey and hard the world at school might sometimes seem, there was another world of colour, exotic smells, strange animals and wonderful fish-filled rivers which existed for my parents and my sisters and which, one day, I might re-visit.

This is important since, for me, like many at British boarding schools, the experience was one which was meant to make us British, but not designed to crush our desire, one day, to follow our many ancestors and even our parents back to foreign lands. So we were encouraged to learn about the places where we might well end up as missionaries, doctors, lawyers, civil servants, district commissioners, or even tea planters. For me the constant allusions to India through artefacts, paintings, food, words, letters and my memories of infancy and a re-visit, meant that the Dragon was part of a far greater experience where space and time were stretched out over the whole planet and Oxford was only a tiny speck, along with Dorset and Scotland, in a greater adventure.

GOING TO SCHOOL

The Old Hall, where we assembled each morning for prayers. It was also the scene of many concerts, games and other activities. Classrooms opened off to the right and left.

2 LANDSCAPES

'There was one evening in the hall of late golden light and the unmistakable noise of the marbles ringing and rolling on the wood floor, hundreds of them, and the voices of my school mates, all in a state of pleasure and purposeful activity, and I was running round, not even, I think, playing He, just swinging up onto the platform off the parallel bars. I looked down the hall and I thought in a flash, I will remember this all my life. It came to me as a certainty on one running foot before the other touched the ground, and then I was off again. But it was true.'[3]

The distinguished writer Naomi Mitchison, who went to the Dragon school aged five, remembered this moment seventy years later, as we do a number of such moments at the same school. It was an extraordinary environment which has shaped our lives. How to capture what was special about it?

Let us start with a little history. The Dragon School is an English preparatory school situated in North Oxford. The school was founded in 1877. At that time there were many thousands of preparatory boarding schools in the country. Half a century earlier, in 1830, there were said to be over 10,000 such schools.[4] What was special about the Dragon school was that it was specifically set up for a particular group, the children of Oxford (and Cambridge) dons who had recently been allowed to marry and were producing children.

It started as a small school with a few boarders and dayboys, but quite quickly rented a larger area of playing fields and potential school premises at the bottom of Bardwell Road, on the edge of the Cherwell. The first headmaster was Mr Clarke who died within ten years and then C.C. Lynam (the Skipper), who was already teaching at the school, bought the school from Mrs Clarke.[5] Numbers grew fairly rapidly. By 1891 there were 62 pupils, by 1893 some 76 and by August 1905 the numbers had exceeded 100. By the time I went to the school in the 1950s there were well over 400 pupils.

The Skipper's direct influence lasted for eighty years. He was

---

[3] Naomi Mitchison, *Small Talk: Memoirs of an Edwardian Childhood* (1973), 63–4.

[4] Vyvyen Brendon, *Preparatory School Children: A Class Apart Over Two Centuries* (2009), 29.

[5] *The Skipper*, 11.

headmaster from 1887 to 1921 and lived on with an active involvement until 1938. He was succeeded by his younger brother A.E. Lynam ('Hum') who was sole headmaster from 1921 to 1942. Hum then became senior headmaster with his own son J.H.R. Lynam, known as 'Joc', from 1942. Joc continued as headmaster from 1942 to 1965. So two generations (three individuals) of the family were headmasters from 1887 to 1965.

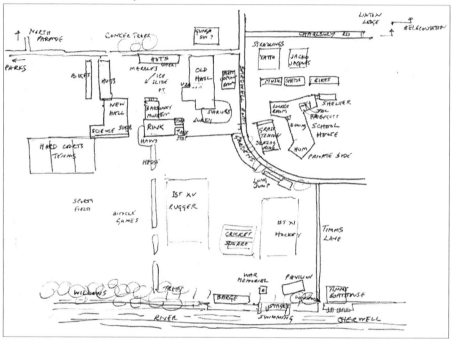

Sketch map of the school and grounds: by Jamie Bruce Lockhart from memory

Of course, it is the emotions and feelings in this landscape that are the most important rather than the stage, but the stage, that of a rather unusually spacious and well-equipped boy's school for its time, is part of it all. I never felt it was a prison, for we were at liberty to wander, and, of course, there were many expeditions – to the Parks for cricket, to Port Meadow for skating, up the river in canoes and boats for picnics, and down the river to the edge of the mysteriously named nude bathing places, Dames Delight and Parson's Pleasure.

*

Our social, intellectual and cultural lives are all influenced by our material world. I see this as an area which is particularly interesting for several reasons. One is that it is something which is remembered best. I have completely forgotten most of my teachers' faces (until I see their portraits), or my friends at that age except for their names. But the shape of the playing fields and School Hall, some of the highs and lows of food, the illnesses and the cold, these we remember.

A second reason for pursuing this is the particular period of my childhood, the ten years after the war. This was a really low period, the age of austerity. It is very difficult for younger people to know how bleak those days were – perhaps as bleak as the war itself, but without any excitement. England was grim, particularly after India, and there was full rationing until almost the end of my schooling at the Dragon.

The freezing classrooms, the thin diet and importance of tuck, the struggle to find clothes and shoes, the constant minor illnesses, all are part of the background. My sense of moving from Purgatory to Paradise at the Dragon may, in part at least, be a reflection of the material improvements which, even in the five years at the Dragon between 1950 and 1955, had occurred. Rationing was ending, television was arriving, and things were not as tight.

The story of the material world is thus complementary to other descriptions of this period and helps to explain how the toughness and hard work which were inculcated into us in sports and elsewhere were not so much at odds with it. Revisiting the Dragon makes me realize how much improved everything is in material terms. The pupils and their parents would be horrified at the relatively thin, diseased, shivering, little things which we were in those days, and it is worth showing how, even in one of the best boarding schools in the country, life was hard.

This material deprivation has also entered into my soul. Unlike modern children I find it difficult to throw away useful things, deplore parts of our wasteful consumer society, and find a grim satisfaction in the return to austerity which looks likely as global warming threatens us.

*

My first house, Plummer's, at 6 Bardwell Road, is near the start of the road. My mother describes it as having a yard and a locker room. I just remember it vaguely as similar to other North Oxford houses. I remember the dining room where I sat for long hours over unfinished food and that is really all. I was in this house, which must have had about twenty to thirty boys I suppose, for two years.

From Plummer's, I then went to School House opposite the main school for a year: on the corner near it was the pillar-box where I awaited my mother's return in 1954, and it was approached by a sweeping drive round a lawn where in the summer we played tennis and in the winter skated on frozen newspaper. There was a lane between Gunga Din (another boarding house), where I spent my fourth year (which The Draconian describes as being dug up for two of the five years I was at the

Dragon). Here were conker trees – now I find there is only one – and the lane led on by way of several of the quintessentially North Oxford roads and past a women's college to the Parks.

I remember the dormitories vaguely, but particularly sitting swinging my legs in one of the locker rooms or 'boys' rooms in the evenings where we sang folk songs together. I also remember that a road led off to Linton Lodge where my mother took me when she came to visit. Across the road from School House was the main school which consisted of a number of buildings and a large expanse of playing fields down to the river Cherwell.

*

I started in a class on the ground floor of the New Hall. Recently I met Nick Bullock who confirmed this, and said that he remembered sitting next to me in our first lesson in the school. I remember the room was crowded with chairs and there seemed to be shutters or windows on the right which could be fully opened in the summer. A lady teacher taught us and she tried to teach me Latin. Later I moved to a much bigger classroom in the Old Hall. I ended up in one of the classrooms in the huts on the left – behind which there were bicycle sheds. In the middle of the yard was the old Museum from which marbles were hurled; underneath was the woodworking classroom.

The Old Hall was where we had school assemblies and end of term concerts took place and we played our torch games at night. An old postcard of the interior of the Hall suddenly brought it back to my mind. Another vivid memory was of the far end of the New Hall (much associated with ballroom dancing, film shows, plays etc) where there was the School Library which I remember for chess, books and my first sex education talk, and beyond it the science block and Gerd Sommerhoff.

A number of photographs which I and others have taken bring this large expanse back to my mind. It all seemed huge to me as a small boy, leading down to the river and places where we played many of our games and had our firework displays.

I remember most of the physical classrooms I was in. I started with Mrs Owens and Miss Mumford in the right-hand classroom on the ground floor in the New Hall. I think I then moved to the other end of the same building for a while. So I suspect these were the classes for the Lower School. Then when I went up to the Middle School we went into the Old Hall. Here I started on the left hand end looking up towards the stage. Then with Oof we were in the top right-hand classroom which I seem to remember enjoying. (Oof was the nickname of F.R. Wylie). He used to come into the classroom in the coldest of weather and say 'Oof' there is a dreadful fug in here, please open the windows. This memory is corroborated by a note on the unseasonably warm weather of the Christmas term 1953 in the Term Notes: 'Even North side classroom windows were flung wide throughout, so that classroom four for once looked no different from the rest'.

Then when I moved to Upper School we went to the huts round the playground, probably starting in Upper IVA in one facing the Museum, and then in 2B I distinctly remember being in one which has now been covered over with new buildings, but at the far end. The science class was held near where the new swimming pool is built, and woodwork under the Museum. A sudden memory of the desks is brought back by Naomi Mitchison's description: 'The desks of course were copiously carved with initials and the soft wood gouged out for railways. Some were good enough to run small marbles along.'[6] The desks became palimpsests of previous generations, engraved totemic objects to which we added our initials or wisdom. I gather that only recently, and regretfully, have the last of these old desks been replaced.

*

---

[6] Mitchison, *Small Talk*, 60.

3 MATERIAL LIFE

It is perhaps not surprising that many school memoirs concentrate on the physical experience of school. Food, drink, clothing, heating and periods of pain seem to be most indelibly fixed in our memories.

*

As far as food goes at the Dragon, I hardly remember anything: I vaguely remember being forced to eat things which I still hate – tapioca pudding ('frogspawn'), beetroot, prunes, porridge, and lumps of fat or gristle. We were forced, I think, in normal fashion, to sit over the cold food until we had finished it – or it would come back at the next meal. There were no doubt things I really liked, for instance Kraft dairy slices of cheese, and Marmite and, of course, sweets. I don't recall that the food rationing which covered almost all of this period at school had much obvious effect on us. Somehow the school coped and only the butter ration was once mentioned in the Term Notes.

There is a great deal in most schoolboy reminiscences of this period about the Tuck Box and the Tuck Shop and the importance of extra food. I don't remember having a tuck box at the Dragon (though I did have one at Sedbergh) and certainly when I am pictured setting off on my first trip to school there is no tuck box. The arrangement seems to have been that we were given some pocket money to spend on tuck (that is mainly sweets) and also sent what seem to have been more or less weekly parcels. Given the cost of postage and the difficulties of collecting and packing weekly parcels, this seems strange, but the little evidence I have from letters suggests that this was the case.

It also seems that at some point the headmaster either accumulated all the sweets sent back with the boys, or else was given the ration books and bought the sweets. Something like this occurred, for in the Term Notes for Easter 1952 there is reference to the Headmaster's Study having 'a solid wall of cartons containing the term's sweet ration'. A later arrangement in the 1970s is described by Watkins 'Along with the tuck shop, there was a padlocked tuck cupboard back at the dormitory. Boys arrived at school each term with boxes of chocolate which were stored in the tuck cupboard. The cupboard was opened each day after lunch...'[7]

---

[7] Paul Watkins, *Stand, Before Your God* (1993), 46.

At the end of my time at the Dragon, on 6 February 1955, my mother wrote to my father about the expenses of school. She mentions the cost of *socks, hankies, gloves, tuck and pocket-money for school, and rail fares of course.* My only references to tuck during the whole of my correspondence at the Dragon came in the following few weeks. On about 20 February I wrote *Dear Mummy, Thank you for your letter. The tuck didn't come last week.* I added *P.P.S. Don't forget the tuck.* A couple of weeks later, in an undated letter, I mentioned that *I am not spending any money on the tuck shop and so I am nearly out of tuck (just dropping a hint).* Dayboys, no doubt, also brought in tuck and, as described under marbles, within the internal economy of the Dragon one could exchange chocolate for other things. I certainly didn't develop an obsession with sweets, though I did collect chocolate covers. Looking through them brings back the sudden taste of Swiss chocolate to the mouth.

There are scattered references to sweets in the letters. Writing to Father Xmas on 25 November 1949, shortly before my eighth birthday, I asked for an ambitious list of things, including *sum sweets.* I wrote in a letter from school in early March 1951 *Thank you very much for the lovely sweets you sent me.* This looks like a special present. My mother, however, was economizing on such things and in outlining her expenses in a letter to my father on 15 May of that year she mentions *Sweets. One ration book (I never use all three).* Yet we seem to have managed. For example, she makes mention of the large amounts of chocolate we ate when we went to the pantomime on 11 January 1951 even when rationing was still present: *We got home eventually over-tired, over-excited and stuffed with chocolate in the time-honoured fashion.*

The rationing of sweets continued until 1953, for I wrote somewhat wistfully on 22 February to my parents *I suppose you know sweets are off ration but that will not make any difference to you as they were off all the time.* A few years later when my mother came to visit me at the Dragon to see 'Iolanthe' she described on 14 November 1954: *Then set out to buy Alan some sweets and was met with the usual ghastly Saturday afternoon crowds, went to Woolworths and was nearly suffocated, eventually fought my way out and when I got to the door flung the entire contents of my purse onto the pavement.* I returned the kindness apparently, for my mother describes how that Christmas (in a letter written two days after the event) *Alan gave me an enormous box of chocolates which must have cost the earth!*

It does not seem to have been rationing alone which made sweets so important. Roald Dahl's obsession with the subject in his 'Boy' was before the Second World War. Paul Watkins is writing about the 1970s, and long after rationing, he wrote 'For us, the only things worth eating were sweets. Sweets were as good as money at the Dragon School. In a way, they were better than money, and the way you showed that you were friends with

27

someone was to share your chocolate with them. You could buy chocolates at the tuck shop. It was a brown hut with a tar-paper roof in the middle of the playground.[8] 'Sharing chocolate' with a friend could also be instrumental, as well as expressive. One memory I have is of encouraging a friend, towards whom I felt a physical attraction, to give me a kiss in return for a piece of chocolate.

What I don't remember is ever being seriously hungry at the Dragon – I remember being much hungrier later at Sedbergh. Somehow the school seem to have fed us reasonably, given rationing, and my very slow physical growth at the school cannot have been due to under-feeding, especially as I made up for any deficiency in the holidays.

I don't remember what we drank at the Dragon. There was 'Government milk'; we all received a third of a pint of milk a day as did all schools in this period. I suppose that we mainly drank water, perhaps with squash of some kind on special occasions such as the Leaver's Picnic. Whether we had hot drinks, certainly not coffee, but perhaps a little tea, Ovaltine, Bovril and such drinks, I am not sure.

*

Most of the Dragon's top competitor schools had very elaborate uniforms – if they were in the queue to get their boys into Eton this would often be based on Eton collars. Again the Dragon school was different – the uniform was practical, relatively cheap, and unostentatious. Thus Peter Snow describes it as 'famously and scruffily successful', and notes that 'Attitudes towards dress are relaxed'.[9]

This started in the early days, though others later began to follow. 'In the 1920s, the Dragon's open-necked shirts worn over dark blue shorts were considered cranky. Yet by the mid-thirties its smart Oxford rival, Summer Fields, had replaced its Eton suits with jerseys and plus-fours for everyday wear.'[10] Even here, however, there is a strong difference – most young boys wore shorts at this period, only a select few wore plus-fours.

Even the teachers were relaxed and sometimes eccentric in their clothes. I remember that Bruno always seemed to be in an aertex shirt, and Joc wore scarlet braces. A hint of this is given in the Term Notes which described the Sports Day in 1954 where 'any masters who are visible at, or near, this function are probably wearing trousers of roughly the same material as their jackets, which is quite enough to draw from any Dragon an admiring "Coo! Spiv!"'

I certainly don't remember much dissonance between what I wore at home and at school. Furthermore, my parents, who were short of money

---

[8] Watkins, *Stand*, 46.
[9] Peter Snow, *Oxford, Observed: Town and Gown* (1991), 167.
[10] Brendon, *Preparatory School*, 94.

and frequently lamenting costs, do not make much of the costs of my school uniform until near the end when my mother tried to make a saving by not buying me two of everything.

*

I remember the cold: perhaps this was exacerbated in my case by the contrast with my infancy in Assam. But it has to be set within the context of a world before the central heating revolution of the 1960s. Much of the time between October and March seemed to revolve around trying to move from one small pool of heat to another. There were just coal fires, gas fires perhaps, and apparently rather inefficient radiators (at school). The nearest an affluent western person can now get to the situation is perhaps to go to an old church or cathedral where the huge coke-fired heaters are still kept operating.

Yet the cold was so much an accepted part of life that I only mentioned it once in one of my letters, and that a rather particular event, describing on 2 February 1954 that *we have had freezing weather. And I have not played any games (except ice hockey). We have had a wizard time except for the cold as I have lost my gloves.*

The bedrooms (and school dormitories) were perhaps the worst, often with little or no heating. That awful moment of getting out of bed and into one's clothes, or the reverse of entering an icy bed, is an indelible memory, and my pleasure in hot water bottles and central heating has never diminished. There were no hot water bottles at school, as I recall.

I imagine that we all wore as many layers as possible, but feeling cold and huddling round radiators at the Dragon was usual. When it was particularly cold it was permitted to wear extra clothes at night, as was reported in the Term Notes for Easter 1954. It was a time of blankets and sheets and, of course, the wonders of the duvet had not been imported, though the covering or eiderdown was probably present – at least at home.

*

According to a now out-dated kind of psychology, our characters are partly determined by our bodily functions – hence the fact that I have hoarded my past so carefully is a sign of my anal-retentive streak. The theory, unfortunately, looks quite plausible.

Whether it was the various tummy problems I had in India, or my mother's apprehensions about potty training, I seem to remember that even at the time we moved when I was aged six to Dorset, I was having difficulty in controlling my bowels – a mixture of constipation and leaking. I seem to remember my grandmother giving me advice and instruction then, and my sitting for hours in the loo in the hope that something would

29

come. I found peeing was fine and probably at this time first encountered the joy of peeing in the water when swimming in the sea, and peeing in the wild wood in our garden.

Certainly the problem of bowel control was a major nightmare at the Dragon. While a number of literary accounts attest to the widespread problem of bed-wetting, which was clearly partly psychological, my problem was 'biggies' as I think they were then called. I still remember the agony of soiled and caked underpants, which had to be secretly buried down in the communal laundry basket to evade shameful discovery. But I think matrons did occasionally notice and not unkindly ask what the problem was. I still don't know what it was, but it continued through Sedbergh, where the system of having toilets with no doors aggravated the problem. Even to this day, if I go away from home it seriously disturbs my rhythms.

All this is no doubt strange and significant, whether mainly physical or psychological. But it is clear that some anxiety about the way my body turns food into evil-smelling matter is a shock I remember consciously recognising when I was about eight – and has affected me considerably.

As far as I recall the toilets at the Dragon were adequate. For example, I am pretty sure that the toilets had doors to them. John Machin remembers that 'there were lavatories at the West end of the New Hall – infinitely preferable to the Old Hall ones'. The ones in the houses were also adequate.

This contrasted with other elite boarding schools. For example, Summer Fields in the 1930s, the lavatories had no doors.[11] When George Orwell was at St Cyprian's he describes 'the row of filthy, dilapidated lavatories, which had no fastenings of any kind on the doors, so that whenever you were sitting there someone was sure to come crashing in.'[12] Partly as a consequence of this, 'It was common to remain constipated for days together. Indeed, one was hardly encouraged to keep one's bowels open, since the only aperients tolerated were castor oil or another almost equally horrible drink called liquorice powder.[13] The 'Compulsory Constipation' which John Betjeman noted in his poetic autobiography is referred to in relation to his public school rather than the Dragon.[14]

Things may have improved at the Dragon by the time I arrived there, and there have certainly been changes since then. The old central toilet near the Old Hall is now an office, but still the same building with the weather vane, must have had doors since wandering visitors would easily encounter it. This is rather delightfully described in the Term Notes for Summer 1954: Visitors asked 'what is that interesting-looking building with

[11] Brendon, *Preparatory School*, 106.
[12] George Orwell, *Essays*, (2000), 432.
[13] Orwell, *Essays*, 433.
[14] John Betjeman, *Summoned by Bells* (1960), 66.

the weather-vane? – a question to which there are only two possible answers, a sudden attack of deafness or the truth.'

*

It is worth considering the growth of my body during this period. When I first went to the Dragon, the weight of each boy was given in The Draconian. When I arrived at the age of eight-and-three-quarters I was four stone and two ounces. The following term I had dropped to four stone. There is no measurement in summer 1951 but by the Christmas report 1951 I was four stone seven pounds. In a year I had just managed to put on seven pounds – which does not seem much. By the following Easter term I had lost weight again and was only four stone, four pounds and four ounces. By the end of the summer term I was back to four stone six ounces. Thus in two years I had managed to put on only four ounces.

If the earlier figures are correct (for The Draconian in Easter 1952 mentioned that the weighing machine was inaccurate and had been replaced) then I was indeed very small, and according to modern theories, my failure to put on weight at this point may be an outward indication of my psychological distress.

My mother noted my small size when I was near the end of my time at the Dragon, writing to my father on 3 April 1955 that *Fiona now weighs 5 st 12 lbs and Anne not much less. Alan doesn't seem to alter at all!* In fact, from the measurements which were taken when I had been a term at Sedbergh, Fiona and I were probably roughly the same weight, even though she was over two years younger than me and certainly the photographs of that time shows her to be, if anything, slightly taller than me.

There are no further measurements until I go to Sedbergh. My measurements are given at the start of my first term, when I was thirteen-and-three-quarters, three months after leaving the Dragon. By then I weighed six stone seven pounds and two ounces. So I had put on two stone in my last three years at the Dragon. I was still small, though, measuring four feet ten and three quarter inches. My girth was 32 inches.

My small size is shown in the photographs I have of me at the end of my time at the Dragon alongside other boys in the team photos in all four of the organized games. I am always the smallest in the team (perhaps alongside Jake Mermagen my cousin). And my small size is noted in comments on my rugger playing, described elsewhere but also worth noting here. In The Draconian account of the rugger season for 1954 it is stated: 'Nor was the size of our full-back much of a deterrent to the opposition. He was, in fact, smaller and lighter than any three-quarter ...'

The only other aspect of my physical development worth noting at this point is puberty. I had my first ejaculation in the summer of 1954, but this was a one-off event and did not happen again for another fifteen months or so. But I was obviously sexually mature from the age of about twelve-and-a-half.

My mother's account of meeting me after an absence of two years gives another insight into my physical growth. When she left I was six-and-three-quarters; when she came to visit me at the Dragon I was nearly nine. She was shocked at the change, as described more fully elsewhere.

The school holidays seem to have transformed me back into something closer to my mother's hopes. On 29 April 1951 she wrote *Anne is her blooming self again. Neither she nor Alan has Fiona's really lovely skin, but they all look very brown and freckled.* Then on 6 May 1951 my mother wrote *He was looking so well when he left, fat rosy cheeks and his hair bright and curly. When I take him out from school he has dark lines under his eyes and the little hair they leave him is plastered to his head and he looks awful.*

*

4 SICKNESS AND HEALTH

Our memories seem to be inhabited by moments of excess – either of happiness, or, more often, of pain. Many of the schoolboy reminiscences I have read particularly dwell on pain – the loneliness, the bullying, the beating and the sickness. Although I do not remember the one beating my mother gave me, or any beatings or other painful punishments of a physical kind at the Dragon, there is a great deal both in my memory and in the letters about sickness.

The diseases overlapped between home and school, so it is only possible to make a rough distinction between them. Here I shall deal with those illnesses which were ones I mainly remember in relation to school. The holiday illnesses – particularly dentistry, ear treatments and tonsillitis – I shall deal with under home life.

This pattern of illness seems to be one of the greatest differences between the post-war years and now. Looking back, we lived in a world where the new miracle drugs and improved dentistry and hospitals were just coming in. It was exactly on a mid-point between the high insecurities and levels of perennial pain that I have examined as a historian of illness in Japan and England, or as an anthropologist in a mountain village in Nepal, and the privileged part of the world I inhabit. It was not as bad as the pre-industrial and pre-Koch and Pasteur world, but it was far more difficult than now.

The number of days when I missed school, almost always from illness provides a preliminary statistical picture of the incidence of disease in one boy's life. The tally of days missed was as follows.

	1950–51	1951–52	1952–53	1953–54	1954–55
Winter	0	0	0	0	0
Spring	13	7	1	0	3
Summer	NA	0	0	0	1

[NA = not available]

Two observations can be made here. Clearly the spring term, which accounts for twenty-four of the total of twenty-five days of absence recorded for the Dragon, was the sickly term. Secondly, as I had the diseases, or built up resistance, the absences dramatically decreased. Twenty out of twenty-five absences occurred in the first two years.

33

There is a certain amount in the letters about diseases which spread particularly quickly in schools at this time – influenza, measles, mumps and chicken pox – and disrupted lives and schedules, though they were no longer, on the whole, mortal threats. We were vaccinated against that deadly disease of childhood including smallpox.

The Term Notes for Easter 1953 mentioned the arrival of the first cases of measles. Though the victims were comparatively few in number, the sickrooms began to fill up. I wrote on 2 February to my parents that *Auk and Bearmoth our dorm and another have been evacuated and I have moved into dodo wich is a big dorm and has about 14 people instead of auks 6.* Having had the disease before arriving at the Dragon, I could write quite calmly from the Dragon on 18 February 1953, *There are about 35 out of 80 in school house who are in the sick room and there are a few cases of measles.* I don't seem to have succumbed to anything, however, as I was only absent for one day in the term.

The first epidemic disease I caught at the Dragon was chicken pox, which I got in my second term. My grandfather's diary on 22 March 1951 mentioned 'Alan has chicken pox' and on 28 March that 'Alan arrives with chicken pox'. On that same day my mother wrote to my father that

> *Alan has complicated our plans somewhat by getting chicken pox. He got it about 8 days ago but after a rather hectic correspondence the school have sent him back to-day and Mummy has taken him back with her for the night until I can get him to our doctor to be vetted. He's only had a mild attack, but still has "pox" on his face, otherwise he looks alright after the journey. I don't want to throw the girls into quarantine so shall leave him with Mummy until he's free I think. All rather bothering.*

I dimly remember the unpleasantness of finding one's face temporarily pock marked and coming home a little early from school.

One curious episode to do with this which I do not remember now, but I suspect I may have told my parents, is recounted in my mother's autobiographical 'Daughters of the Empire'.[15] She describes of me 'When he got chickenpox and was sick his housemaster made him eat it as a punishment for making a mess. This of course, we only learnt later.' I seem to remember either I or other boys were made to eat their own sick for some offence, but can't remember what.

This outbreak of chicken pox was briefly mentioned in the Term Notes, where it was stated that 'when the flu began to weaken, the torch

---

[15] Iris Macfarlane, *Daughters of the Empire* (2006), 134.

was flung from failing hands to a chicken-pox germ, which had been maturing quietly in the background and which now moved purposefully through the ranks of the vulnerable...'

The fact that I had chicken pox meant that when there was another outbreak in my last spring term, I was able to write back with some reassurance in March 1955 that *At the moment there is a slight epidemic of chicken pox and about* [blank] *people are ill.* Interestingly the disease seems to have either lost its virulence or been seen as less of a threat, or both, for the Term Notes for Easter 1955 mentions a chicken-pox germ, but 'as a major scourge, for the plain fact is that he is no longer taken very seriously. A day or two in the sick-room, and his victims are back at their desks, spots and all.'

In my first summer term, 1951, the Term Notes stated that 'the School had Mumps'. My mother wrote to my father on 25 June 1951 *Have just heard Alan's school has mumps – I suppose he'll get it just at the last moment and dish our Scottish holiday – but at least you'll be here to make decisions.* Unfortunately this is the one term where I have no school report so do not know if I missed school. I seem to remember the odd and unpleasant feeling of one's neck swelling up with mumps, but this may be a false memory. Some boys stayed on with the illness, but there is no record in my family papers that I caught mumps. There was a case or two of mumps at the start of my last summer term in 1955, according to the Term Notes, but I do not mention this.

The most widespread epidemic during my time at the Dragon was influenza. The first outbreak occurred in Britain after Christmas in 1951 and was a serious world pandemic (A.H1N1), which caused a considerable number of deaths according to contemporary reports. This hit our family at home, where all members caught it. It also raced through the Dragon.

The Term Notes for Easter 1951 describe this particular epidemic visitation in more detail than any other illness during my time at the Dragon. The tone is vaguely facetious, but nevertheless shows the gravity of the situation.

'The Authorities were frankly defeatist from the start. The pre-term circular, including 'flu in the list of diseases that you didn't return if you had been in contact with, was followed by an announcement on the Common Room board that we would all shortly have flu, that no one who felt ill must go near anyone who felt well, and vice versa, in fact that nobody must go near anybody, and that victims on the Staff must inform the Headmaster, or (sinister touch) his deputy, then mark a cross on the bedroom doors and wait for the end. It was almost a relief when, about the ninth day, the epidemic got going.' The epidemic 'followed its usual course. Sickroom territory expanded along the top landing, took over Dodo and nosed into Phoenix.'

At the end of my second term, in March 1951 when I was nine years three months, the termly report showed that I had been quite ill, absent for thirteen days, by far the largest number of any term at the Dragon. On 1 February my mother wrote to my father, *Alan has been in the sick-room at school but is out again now, it's a dreadfully unhealthy year.* On 19 February she wrote again to my father. *I'm going to see Alan next week-end before or after my visit to London, did I tell you he had had flu and spent another week in bed poor little scrap, I hope he won't be looking too run down when I see him next week...* In the same letter she mentions that *I'm still streaming, and coughing and have been since my flu but everyone tells me it's the worst winter they ever remember and its certainly the wettest for over eighty years.*

The following Easter 1952 the Term Notes took a jaunty attitude to the disease. 'Flu and rumours of 'flu were ignored, quarantine-breaking connived at, and health certificates thrown away unopened...' The plan apparently worked well and there was only a little illness, unspecified, in the seventh week. Again during the following Easter term 1953 there was only 'a solitary flu germ'.

The other major outbreak of flu at the Dragon occurred in my last winter term. The Term Notes for the Christmas term mention that 'the press was full of news of a flu epidemic sweeping through schools, but it was hoped to avoid it'. In the last few days of term people started to get temperatures. This was confirmed as 'flu, but the headmaster was torn between warning parents, and wanting to finish the term properly, so 'in the end he compromised with a pink notice to parents sanctioning evasive action but listing all the end-of-term entertainments that a fugitive would miss.' We are told that 'As the week ended, sick rooms began to encroach on dormitories' and that the end of term dance was sparsely attended.

On 10 December 1954 my mother wrote

> *I had a letter from the Dragon this morning to say they have 'flu at the school, so wired them to put Alan on the train to-morrow, he's not due back till Tuesday and will probably be livid at missing end-of-term activities but if he gets 'flu at the last moment it'll mean endless complications. He'll probably give it to us all here instead, but we'll have to meet that when it comes.*

I did return home and on 15 December my mother wrote

> *Alan came back on Saturday, as I think I told you, in good form and very chatty, but yesterday morning (Tuesday) he started feeling low, and to-day has been in bed with 'flu – so I'm relieved I got him back in time to nurse him here. It's a childish variety, so I trust we shan't all succumb – he is running a temp. of 100.8 which is nothing much and has read two detective novels to-day and listened to the wireless without a pause*

36

and is no trouble.

There is no evidence that any of the rest of the family caught this variant of flu, but the Term Notes were right that 'For a good many Dragons the Christmas holiday seemed to have carried on where the term left off, with 'flu and rumours of flu".

My final spring term was marked by illness and I wrote in an undated letter in March to my mother *I hope you have not got any illness. At the moment there is a slight epidemic of chicken pox and about* [blank] *people are ill.* I was sick with something for on about 17 March I wrote with mock humour to my mother. *This is the last letter I will be writing this term. By some bad luck I am in the sick-room because I was sick on Friday morning but I have been perfectly alright since but the old hags (Three witches from Macbeth) have been trying their foul concoctions on us in the form of many coloured gargolls (of course I have not got a sore throat).* My mother also wrote to my father two days later *I got a card yesterday to say he was in the san with sickness and temp. So immediately visualized the worst sort of appendicitis but hope it turns out to be a chill. There always seems to be a crisis about his return and I'll be relieved when he doesn't have to come so far.*

*

My mother's letters describing home life in detail; there is a good deal about endemic pain, the whole horrendous saga of ear, nose, throat and teeth which deeply affected us. It is well to remember, however, that in school holidays and even before I went to the Dragon I had been subjected to levels of pain which are now unfamiliar to many children in Britain and had learnt something about how to face suffering with fortitude. All this tends to have been forgotten in the improvements since that distant period.

Likewise, the constant background of minor pain from various forms of skin disease or irritation is easy to overlook. They are too trivial for me to note in letters and descriptions, though they constantly lowered the quality of my life. I tended to accept them and only really notice its absence when they stopped. Since I mainly associate this kind of minor pain with boarding school rather than home life, I shall deal with it here.

One sign of the interaction between sub-optimum feeding, perhaps defective hygiene, and the absence of central heating and hence the seeking of warmth near radiators, as well as the primitive state of medicines, was the widespread affliction of minor debilitating sores. It is difficult now to recall how much suffering we had as children from various forms of skin irritation. There were the chaps which fired great sore patches behind the knees and on the hands, rubbing red and painful and sometimes bleeding.

There were the chilblains often erupting and bursting on our fingers and toes.

There was also that disgusting, strange, sponge-like disintegration of the end of one's fingers called impetigo for which as I recall gentian violet (or dipping one's hands in vinegar?) was a sovereign remedy. Putting cold wet hands on radiators was, no doubt, behind much of this. There were also things that had to be cut out – like verukas. We also had some really horrible boils – I still bear the scars of two of them on my legs and these sometimes had to be lanced (though not in such an unpleasant way without any anaesthetic as described by Dahl in 'Boy').

Colds must have been very frequent, though again they are seldom mentioned. An exception is when, on 11 January 1951, I wrote to my parents *I have not had to go into bed yet though I have had a cold.* But the following month on 25 February I apologised *I am sorry that this letter is such a short one I have been in bed just about a weak So I have not much to say we started hocky on Saturday but I was in bed.*

There were also frequent minor injuries. On 3 February 1951 I wrote from the Dragon, *Dear Granny and Grandpa, I had a game of hokey in wich I hurt my ne but I scored a goal and it was a very nice game.* The next injury I record is over two years later on 18 May 1953 when I write, *I have been off games for a week because I was hit on the eye by a cricket ball.* I did not miss any days that term, so it could not have been too serious.

*

5 DORMITORY LIFE

We spend approximately a third of our lives asleep. In the other two-thirds, children often spend considerable periods in the places where they sleep. Their bedrooms are often their main playrooms and in boarding schools the life of the dormitory is one of the most private and influential. It is where other boys can exert their pressure and where the unhappiness of leaving home strikes most forcefully.

Suddenly being thrown into a dormitory at the age of eight is quite a shock. Paul Watkins has written about his first night in a Dragon dormitory and the throwing out of his teddy bear in an initiation ceremony. Whether I took any toy to the Dragon I cannot remember, nor do I remember many of the events. But I did consider the dormitory I was in to be an important place. Such dormitories seem to have been graded by age and contained between four and fourteen boys on average. Younger boys were in domestic houses and older ones in School House or Gunga Din.

At the start of my second year in Plummer's House I wrote to my mother on 7 October *Actually there are 6 new people in our house and one of them are in our dorm.* The following summer I went to a seaside resort with some connection to the Dragon at Milford on Sea. In my short letter to my parents on 20 April I bothered to tell them that *We have four people in our dormatory. Joseph sanders, Crispin Marshàll, Greggary sanders, and Me.*

When I returned for the start of my third year, I had been moved from Plummer's to the more senior School House. I mentioned in my first letter on 28 September 1952 *I am in school house know and I am in a dorm called Auk some of the other ones are Doddo, Phenix, Levaithen, Bearmoth, Icksorias, emu, unicorn, Ptrodactyll.* This was a real advance, as I recall. On 18 January 1953 I wrote that *I am in the same form and dorm but I have up to 4th from 6th in soccer.* This hints at the three main ladders I was climbing – social (dorm and house), academic (form and sets) and games.

It is clear that the dormitories were not just places for social life and sleeping, midnight feasts, rags, and so on. They were also sporting entities, at least the larger ones were at the top of the school. On 15 March 1953 I wrote that *There is going to be a dodo v Phenix match. Dodo and Phenix are two big dorms and they are going to have hockey match.*

Then in the summer term I was moved again, writing on 3 May that *I am in a dorm called Pheonix wich is a big dorm and I am having jolly good fun.* It is implied that social life in the dormitory was important and the

39

importance I attached to it is shown in the fact that I bothered to draw a sketch plan of the dormitory with my bed marked (included in the visual section at the end of the book). I wrote *Here is a sketch of our Dorm. That is Roughly what it looks like Except Everything is closer together.*

At the start of my fourth year I was moved again to another, smaller, house, which I only dimly remember, if at all. Again I place the various hierarchies next to each other in a letter of 27 September *I am in a new hous called Gunga. And my dorm is Hugh Sedgewick.* (Hugh Sedgwick was a brilliant young scholar and poet who died in the First World War). Whether I stayed in Gunga or returned, as I seem to recall, to School House for my last year, I do not accurately recall.

Unlike many other memoirs of dormitory life, I cannot remember particular raids, rags, midnight feasts, reading in bed, sexual hanky-panky or anything else. But I do seem to remember vaguely where in School House the senior dormitories were, and that they were important for our sense of identity. Learning to sleep in a communal space was an important art we learnt, alongside the communal eating, bathing and other such things. As someone has previously pointed out, ending up in a prison for a boy who had been through this experience was almost home from home.

DRAGON ALCHEMY

The Headmasters in the 1950s

A.E. Lynam (Hum) and J.H.R. Lynam (Joc)

6 PHILOSOPHY

When the Dragon was founded in the late nineteenth century, and as it expanded through the first half of the twentieth, there were huge pressures to create a boarding school with an ethic like that of its top competitors. The Lynam headmasters could have made it like Summer Fields, which was already in existence. The Summer Fields' philosophy was geared to taking the children of rich parents, giving them a strict and formal education, particularly in Latin, and winning top scholarships to Eton, Winchester and elsewhere.

Two writers on Oxford wrote about Summer Fields. Jan Morris described it as 'a famous breeding-ground for Eton, going in for admirals, judges and Mr Harold Macmillan'.[16] Peter Snow likewise describes it as 'an Etonian feeding factory ... which serves a few select areas of Belgravia. "Very Pimm's-on-the-lawn", according to one member of staff.'[17]

Or the Dragon could have modelled itself on St Cyprians, which later merged with Summer Fields. Though Orwell's account may be a little extreme, it is worth describing what the Dragon *might* have been like in terms of its physical state and its aspirations.

Orwell also points to a deep contradiction in the school's philosophy, which is different from what I encountered in the Dragon, but shows how fierce tides tend to meet in these small educational pools.

'The various codes which were presented to you at St Cyprian's – religious, moral, social and intellectual – contradicted one another if you worked out their implications. The essential conflict was between the tradition of the nineteenth-century asceticism and the actually existing luxury and snobbery of the pre-1914 age. On the one side were low-church Bible Christianity, sex Puritanism, insistence on hard work, respect for academic distinction, disapproval of self-indulgence, on the other, contempt for "braininess", and worship of games, contempt for foreigners and the working class, an almost neurotic dread of poverty, and, above all, the assumption not only that money and privilege are the things that matter, but that it is better to inherit them than to have to work for them'.[18]

Orwell was aware that there was a danger of distortion. Yet he felt that his boarding experience was awful – and the accounts of a good number of those quoted in Vyvyen Brendon's book on preparatory schools is not

---

[16] James Morris, *Oxford*, (1965), 160.
[17] Snow, *Oxford*, 65–6.
[18] Orwell, *Essays*, 440.

dissimilar. Orwell writes 'Whoever writes about his childhood must beware of exaggeration and self-pity.... But I should be falsifying my own memories if I did not record that they are largely memories of disgust. The overcrowded, underfed, underwashed life that we led was disgusting, as I recall it.'[19]

*

Instead, the Dragon followed another path, and much of this developed out of the personality and philosophy of its first, and perhaps greatest, headmaster. The Skipper (C.C. Lynam) was born in 1858 and went to King William's College, Isle of Man, 'a romantic place in those days, with few of the traditions or restrictions of the modern Public School'.[20] This gave him an alternative pattern of education, where he learnt to roam freely and let his imagination develop. When he went to Hertford College, Oxford he was good enough to read mathematics, which he later taught at the Dragon, but found it dry and changed to history. He was a radical, almost an agnostic, anti-war and played rugger for the university for three years. He then followed two parallel careers, as a great schoolmaster and as a passionate and expert sailor.

He was, we are told by Frank Sidgwick, 'a keen player of bridge and chess; an indefatigable sketcher in pencil, watercolour, or oils; a most voracious reader of fiction; a capable plain cook. For thirty years he annually "produced" a play of Shakespeare at the school... often painting the scenery...'[21] To produce these difficult plays with little boys all aged thirteen or less from 1888 to 1919 is no mean achievement. His views on how the plays should be produced reveal other sides of his character.

In 1904 he wrote about the preparations. 'I always prefer that they should form their own ideas, even if not quite accurate ones, than that I should give them mine, I believe the boys take the greatest interest and delight in it, and, as far as their experience and imagination allow, appreciate its motive and action.' After he had handed over the productions, he reminisced further about his methods in 1927: '... you know I have always preferred the haphazard to ordered method, anachronism to dull accuracy, impossible attempts at beauty to any limits of audacity; and, if you like, fiction to truth, credit to cash in hand, faith to fact. And I am afraid I must confess that I have always tried to make the most of outstanding genius rather than to aim at the high level for mediocrity.'

The difference between the Dragon and its chief rival, Summer Fields, came out when the Skipper met a little boy from that school who said he

---

[19] Orwell, *Essays*, 432.
[20] *The Skipper; A Memoir of C.C. Lynam 1858–1938* (1940), 5.
[21] *The Skipper*, 96.

envied the freedom of the young Dragons. The Skipper explained in telling a joke against himself that 'Now our Summer Fields boys were great friends – or foes – of the Dragons whenever they met at games, but were rather jealous about the liberty the said Dragons were allowed, liberty denied to themselves. For instance, they saw them occasionally riding about on bicycles, a joy not permitted to any other Preparatory School in those days; or they came across heaps of them swarming up the Cherwell, unattended by masters, ragging about in four-oared boats or canoes as they passed through our bathing-place.'

A final assessment of his encouragement of the independence and originality of his pupils reveals some of the elements. Frank Sidgwick writes: 'One of the most brilliant of his old pupils speaking at an Old Boys' dinner, put the rhetorical question: What was the distinctive character of the school and its training? And found the answer in the Skipper's refusal to force his boys into conventional moulds, in his active encouragement of originality, in his affording them every opportunity to discover and develop each his own interest and genius. The Skipper attached great importance to leaving boys free to do what they liked with their spare time, instead of forcing them into a scheduled programme out of school as well as in school.'[22]

*

It is difficult to cast one's mind back to the prevailing educational philosophy in the 1880s when the Skipper took over the Dragon. C.P. Harvey, who had been four years at a conventional school and then went to the Dragon, contrasts the Skipper's views with the philosophy of Dr Arnold of Rugby.

He asks what Dr Arnold would 'have thought of a Headmaster who arranged strawberry feasts for his pupils at the Trout Inn; who played cards with them out of school hours; who encouraged them to write English verses rather than Latin verses; who laid bets with them in the classroom; who kept live-stock in his study; and who did not wear a neck-tie?' He continues that 'for me, the Skipper stands for the enfranchisement of schoolboys from the yoke of Arnold and for the final debunking of the system of conventional austerity which Arnold left behind him'.

'The Skipper by his own character and example gave the lie to a number of precepts and principles which had previously seemed inseparable from educations such as:

(1) That religion consisted of a devotional exercise to be practised intensively one day a week;

---

[22] *The Skipper*, 23, 26, 42, 95.

44

(2)   That the distinction between what was 'good form' and what was 'not done' was equivalent to the distinction between right and wrong;

(3)   That discipline was synonymous with drudgery;

(4)   That school work was merely a method of keeping children quiet, and that complete ineptitude at lessons was a badge of success in after life;

(5)   That one's own ideas were of no value;

(6)   That filial affection was a thing which one did not display in public;

(7)   That bullying was a natural perquisite of seniority;

(8)   That uncomfortable clothing was essential to moral development;

(9)   That children should be seen and not heard; and

(10) That everything which is good for you is unpleasant, and vice versa.

All these things seem to have been regarded as quite natural and proper by one's grandparents, and – to make the subject more depressing – they were commonly coupled with the proposition that one's schooldays were the happiest days of one's life.'[23]

*

The achievement of the Skipper carried on into my time and was spread by his brother Hum (A.E. Lynam) and then Hum's son, Joc (J.H.R. Lynam). From my observation in the 1950s, and research the period, Joc managed to combine some of the best qualities of both his uncle and father. There was the inspired improvisation, and flexibility, dislike of too much bureaucracy, combined with affection for the boys of the Skipper. Yet this was combined with considerable practical efficiency and a complete mastery and quiet control.

These qualities are rather well captured by the science master during my time, Gerd Sommerhoff. 'I do not know whether one should describe Jock [the spelling varies] as good looking. He had an athletic figure. In his student days he had been a hockey blue and he was still a competent and energetic tennis player. He had a humorous face and always wore the expression of a man who was in total control. Very little escaped him. When the day was done he enjoyed his tipple, preferably in the company of leading members of his staff.' We shall encounter some of Joc's views on education throughout later chapters, but for a start Gerd's summary will do. 'One evening, Jock, glass in hand, casually mentioned that he had never read a book on education, but that he had two principles on which he ran this school: if the boys are happy they are likely to learn well and if the staff are happy they are likely to teach well. And he certainly lived up to

---

[23] *The Skipper*, 117.

45

that.'[24]

*

The tendency towards a broad curriculum and not too heavy an emphasis on formal lessons seems to have stemmed from the Skipper's attitude towards children and his high regard for them. As Vyvyen Brendon's account shows, many preparatory schools were largely commercial ventures, often run by sadists or at least by people who feared or loathed children – or both. The Skipper, and as I remember them Hum and Joc, were not like that.

The Skipper was a fan of poetry and used to get all the children to learn poetry each week. It seems likely that the 'Rubaiyat of Omar Khayam' with its famous description of the potter and the pot was at the back of his mind when he made the following remarks to the Annual Conference of Preparatory School Teachers in 1908. 'Our boys are not clay to be shaped as we potters will, all much in the same way and that our way. They are something quite different, and so are we: each one of them is a marvellous complex creature not of our creation, and each one of us is not a god but merely a chance tool; and let us beware lest in our attempts to mould, the chisel may slip, and irretrievably damage the inherent life in what we regard as clay...' Given this view, he believed '...we have failed, unless we have helped the boy to develop his mind and his capacities in his own way, unless we have given him full scope, for all of imagination and originality that is in him...'

The Skipper was aware that teaching in a boarding school for year after year could warp the most idealistic person and engender cynicism or at least staleness. He wondered, therefore, in his 1908 speech 'how can we best try to keep our youth and humanness, though we are schoolmasters and headmasters?' His answer was that 'We should try to retain our humanness in term-time, by refusing to shut ourselves up in our little kingdom, and by seeing as many and various people as we can, at the club, at-homes, as politicians, as members of various societies.'[25] I certainly remember that a number of my teachers seemed to have had serious outside interests, in sport, arts and other things.

*

The Skipper's philosophy lies behind the balanced attitude which the school sustained in relation to academic excellence. On the one hand the Dragon was a famous school for getting scholarships and exhibitions to

---

[24] Gerd Sommerhoff, *In and Out of Consciousness. The Intimate History of A search for Certainties.* (1996), 80_1.

[25] Jaques, *Centenary*, 50.

public schools and in my first year, for example, the school triumphed (exceptionally) in getting the top scholarships to both Eton and Winchester. There was a heavy emphasis on Latin, which was a necessity, and L.A. Wilding who taught the top class wrote one of the two standard text books on the subject. So it might have been thought to be driven towards the obsessive emphasis on rote learning and dry academic work which we find in descriptions of St Cyprian's and other factories for producing Etonians.

Yet from the very start there seems to have been a counter-tendency emanating from the Skipper. At the school Prize-Giving in 1901 he told the parents that 'Our curriculum is more all-round' than that in most other schools of the kind and he expanded on this on a similar occasion in 1903. 'As regards the work of the school I am not sure whether, with a view to getting Public School scholarships, we are quite distinctly classical enough. As far as I can judge we do not give anything like so many hours to classics as others do. We do more mathematics, and considerably more English history and literature. Our top 30 boys get up a whole Shakespeare play very thoroughly every year, besides learning a great deal of poetry; and every boy in the school is taught drawing.'

He reiterated the message in a stronger way to a wider audience five years later in his speech in 1908. He said that it is 'still more grievous if we have tied the intellect of a boy down by the old Jesuit device of vain dialectic, of facile making of Latin verse, etc., instead of exercising his reason and observation; if we have shut up his mind in the past to the exclusion of the present and future; if, when he longs for the bread of knowledge, we feed him with the cold stones of classical paganism without its divine afflatus....'[26]

It certainly seems that though Latin was important there was much else, and we were also encouraged to take an interest in many things such as crafts, music, debating and so on. Perhaps most revealingly, in a way, when there was ice the formal class lessons were abandoned and day after day we would go off skating – far more important than lessons.

The Skipper and his successors seem to have realized that this went against the grain, but it was justified, they felt, by a holistic attitude towards education. Thus in the Prize-Giving speech in 1901 the Skipper told parents. 'We do not have such long hours, and we have more holidays. I give a good many "extra halves" – perhaps too many. Our holidays at Christmas are shorter, in summer longer, than most.'[27]

His view of cramming and formal examinations, completely the opposite of what Orwell reports for St Cyprian's or seems present in many of the top preparatory schools of the time, comes in an article he wrote in

---

[26] Jaques, *Centenary*, 48.
[27] Jaques, *Centenary*, 40.

The Draconian in April 1921. Although he was himself on the Board of the Common Entrance Examinations, 'With this latter institution I am not at all satisfied. Its influence on our Schools seems to me to be disastrous. The papers are stereotyped in form. Thousands of back copies are purchased and used as a standard and as a means of "cramming" boys for the examination. Instead of a boy being judged by his real merit, character, and attainments, he is judged by his mark-getting powers in a very specialized examination, and this seems to me to be destructive of anything like originality or individuality in teaching and training.'[28]

I suspect that his views continued to be an influence until my time and that many of the teachers were aware that too much pressure on children was not a good thing. Thus perhaps the matter of formal class work was also treated with a certain irreverence. In Christmas 1953 Term Notes, it was observed that 'Exam results are posted [in the covered playground], and the urgent injunction to all examinees to study carefully the examiners' comments and reports is dutifully obeyed by those happy few who are reasonably sure of a favourable comment. Of the rest, anyone whose eye is accidentally caught, in passing, by his own name followed by some hostile remark merely murmurs "stale!" and passes on.'

---

[28] *The Skipper*, 39.

7 CULTURE

At the end of each term, as young Dragons, we would come together to sing the School Song. Although somewhat tongue-in-cheek with a hint of irony and playfulness, it is worth indicating a few of the values that we were supposed to be learning from this rousing event.

Long ago there were creatures that ranged
Thro' the forests in hides of tough armour;
But some are extinct and some changed
And the forests are till'd by the farmer:
Yet a weather-cock glistens on high,
And upon it a Dragon is seated,
And the words on that tin mean 'go in and win',
And the Dragon is rarely defeated.

Let us always keep heart in the strife
While our wickets or goals are defended,
For there always is hope while there's life,
And the match isn't lost till its ended!
But whether we win or we lose,
If we fight to the very last minute,
The intent of the game is always the same –
To strive that the Dragon may win it!

There are Dragons in lands far apart,
Where July is as cold as December;
But within they've a warmth at the heart,
And a something that makes them remember!
So they think of the days of their youth,
And they drain to the dregs of the flagon
To the School-house afar, on the banks of the Cher,
And health of the conquering Dragon!

So farewell! For a time we adjourn,
Our health and our spirits retrieving;
And happy be those that return,
And lucky be those that are leaving!
There are visions of mountain and sea,
And of holidays floating before us,

So tonight we forget
Every thought of regret,
And we sing to the Dragon in chorus!

CHORUS (with much spirit, but not too fast.)

Stand up and shout with a ring,
Care to the wind let us fling,
The Dragon above is the Dragon we love,
So to the Dragon we sing!

Here the balance between jingoism and self-mockery is quite delicate and the reference to leaving as a fortunate escape is a particularly nice touch.

*

For many years there used to be an allegorical wall painting in the New Hall at the Dragon. Tom Van Oss painted it in the 1930s and Jacques writes that it was 'prompted by Hum's constant concern to provide Dragons with inspiration and uplift'.[29] A photograph of the painting in the distance is included in the visual essay at the end of the book.

The artist stated that 'The motto of the School being "Arduus ad Solem", the picture represents the Efforts of Man to raise himself from the Darkness of Ignorance to the heights of a Lofty and Enlightened Mind, represented by the Citadel. In the centre the figure of Education – 'mens sana in corpore sano' – spurs on the spectator in strenuous effort. Around him are grouped the elements that go to the building of Character: Study, Athletics, Piety, Lofty Aims, Gentleness, Dreams and Contemplation, and Loyalty...'[30]

The key to the picture went on to explain the significance of every figure and for a while it was a familiar feature of the New Hall until 'a later generation, in the climate of the sixties, began to find its perhaps rather facile idealism not to its taste.' It was possibly painted over, though Harry Machin has suggested that it was painted on canvas and so rolled up and stored away somewhere.

What immediately strikes me about the list of the virtues is that they include, alongside obvious things like study and athletics, gentleness, dreams and contemplation. These are not quite so obvious.

*

---

[29] Jaques, *Centenary*, 50.
[30] Jaques, *Centenary*, 131.

The picture was an exposition of the school motto 'Arduus ad Solem' (which had twenty years earlier been chosen as the motto for the newly founded University of Manchester). 'Arduus' may be translated here as: 'steep, high, lofty, towering, tall, erect, rearing, uphill, arduous, difficult', and 'solem', of course, is the sun.

The phrase is taken from Virgil's Aeneid and describes Pyrrhus attacking the palace of Priam, like a snake striving up to the sunlight after shedding its old skin. The serpent is traditionally associated with wisdom in classical texts, and this may have been one of the reasons for its choice. The name of the school soon became the Dragon and the idea of the serpent clearly fits here. The idea of striving is obviously widespread in mottoes for institutions, as in 'Per Ardua ad Astra', by hard work to the stars, the motto of the Royal Air Force.

In fact a pupil, not a teacher, appropriately enough, invented the idea of the name for a school team. A boy heard that on the governing body there was 'a Mr George, a Fellow of New College. I thought of the gold sovereigns then in currency with the figure of St George and the Dragon on the back. So I suggested, "I believe there is a Mr George who is one of the governors or something. Let's be the Dragons."' This was immediately adopted as the unofficial name, and later the official one.[31]

*

Something of the social system which we were entering can be seen in a unique feature of the Dragon culture, the patterns of what you called people. Many closed institutions use naming to encourage a certain attitude – for example 'Brother' and 'Sister' and 'Father' and 'Mother Superior' in monasteries and nunneries. At the Dragon certain teachers who had a special responsibility to look after one were called 'Pa' and 'Ma', in other words father and mother. I remember this particularly vividly in my first year with my teachers, all of whom in that year were women. For example, in a letter of 11 February 1951, in my second term, my mother wrote to my father. *I enclose Alan's last letter, his writing is improving isn't it? "Miss Cleasby" ... is Jessie who is also a mistress at the Dragon, Ma Cleasby is Alan's usual way of referring to her!* My mother knew Miss Cleasby personally as she was a friend of one of my mother's brothers. So there was 'Ma Owen', 'Ma Mumford' and, as mentioned, 'Ma Cleasby'. I do not personally remember calling anyone 'Pa', but there is evidence that this was sometimes the case.

For example the 'Wikipedia' article on the Dragon notes the calling of

---

[31] *The Skipper*, 9

'female teachers 'Ma' (e.g. 'Ma Jones').' It continues that 'Previously, some male teachers had been called 'Pa' (e.g. Mr. Wyeth-Webb, who was known affectionately as 'Pa Wa-Wa'). This nickname was feminized when male staff members' wives became important figures in their own right (e.g. 'Ma Wa-Wa'). Ultimately, the masculine form fell out of common use, but the female form has remained popular.' It may have been present when Alan was there and certainly Paul Watkins refers to its use in the 1970s. For example his first teacher was Mr Winter; 'We called him Pa Winter.' Perhaps this suggests that teachers had this name if they taught the very young pupils. Yet I certainly don't remember calling my first housemaster 'Pa Plumber'.

As for the use of nicknames between boys, I remember a little of this. Until writing this book I had not thought about, and would not have been able to remember, my own nickname. But John Machin, a Dragon friend, suddenly remembered it as 'Fadge' and this was later confirmed in the page of his friends signatures reproduced at the end of the book. I used this system of nicknames, combined with Christian names (as indicated in my letters) and also the more conventional system described by Brendon who writes that 'In boys' schools the break from home was still emphasized by the widespread use of surnames.'[32] I suspect that in referring to each other amongst boys, or addressing each other, we would use nicknames. But to masters, or strangers, we would refer to other boys by their surnames.

Such naming practices gave you an individuality, even a separateness, which kept you at a distance from others. They made you into semi-adults – 'Macfarlane', not 'boy' or 'Alan'. There are signs that that the impersonal, or special, naming system isolated you from the set of ties of intimacy that would exist if you called someone by their Christian name – as I discovered even when I went to Worcester College in 1960 and was addressed by my teachers as 'Mr Macfarlane'– or one finds in other institutions such as prisons ('Fletcher'), armies and hospitals.

It seems that as widely reported for Eton, and was no doubt the case in many schools, there was also a custom that you kept your distance even from people in other houses. This is suggested by the Skipper in his 1908 address who said that teachers had failed the boys '...if they fall in line with the miserable rules of school etiquette, which, among other silly things, try to prevent two old friends from speaking to one another, because they are not in the same house'.[33]

*

[32] Brendon, *Preparatory School*, 169.
[33] Jaques, *Centenary*, 48

Another Dragon tradition, unique in this school, is central to understanding its culture of semi-equality between staff and boys. It appears that the Skipper may have stumbled on this custom rather accidentally, though it fits with his egalitarian and informal ethos. He explained the reasons in his prize-giving speech to the assembled parents in 1901.

I confess to not attaching much importance to outward politeness. I hate to be called "Sir" every half-minute. I prefer to be called "Skipper". It has been objected that the masters allow the boys to treat them with too little respect. A respect which means subservience and politeness in their presence, with dislike and sneering talk behind their backs, is to my mind most rotten. What I believe to be the true attitude of masters to boys in a Preparatory School is – be an elder brother *out* of school, and a master with the power of at once claiming and getting the closest attention *in* school. I am perfectly satisfied that my staff entirely understand and act upon these principles, and I would not have them change them; and I believe all the better-minded boys appreciate their attitude. The stand-off master out of school is sure to be the greatest fool at keeping discipline in school. Moreover, consideration for others, the true gentlemanly feeling, is to my mind worth yards of outward veneer and polish. The most awkward boy is often the most gentlemanly and considerate.[34]

The result was that masters all had nicknames. 'Wikipedia' mentions 'Inky', 'Guv', 'Smudge', Moocow', Lofty', 'Jumbo', Splash', etc. Of these Inky (Mr Ingram, sometime joint headmaster), 'Guv' (joint headmaster) and Jumbo were all at the Dragon in the early 1950s with these nicknames when we were there. Of the batch noted by Paul Watkins in the 1970s 'Inky, Bleachy, Waa-Waa, Splash, Case, Putty', Inky and Putty were there in the 1950s. Others I recall were 'Oof' (because this is what he said when he opened the classroom windows every morning – Mr Wylie), 'Hum' (the Senior Headmaster A.E. Lynam, because he went around humming). Others were given names based on shortening or lengthening their name. For example, 'Gerd' was just Gerd Sommerhoff's first name, as was the Junior Headmaster 'Joc' Lynam, and 'Bruno' was an obvious name for Mr Brown.

In fact the principles of working out the names were probably similar to the way nicknames were invented for new boys, described by Watkins. 'There was no point having a first name at the Dragon School because nobody used it. Instead they took your last name and said it to themselves a few times, rolling it over on their tongues. They found out if it sounded

---

[34] *The Skipper*, 41–2.

like another word, or an animal or a part of your body. If nothing came up, they'd add an 'o' to the end or 'ers' and see if that worked.'[35] In my case, Jamie has suggested that I was called 'Fadge' because in roll call I would have been read out as 'Macfarlane, A.D.J.', which could be condensed into FADJ.

What effect did this have on us? I do think that, notwithstanding the dissonance noted by the Skipper whereby you could be calling a master as if he was your older brother one minute and being disciplined by him ten minutes later in class, the system probably did add to the relaxed and informal feel of the place. It was egalitarian, chummy, made you part of a club. Later in the army or in some Oxbridge common room you would re-live a world where seniors were half-affectionately referred to as 'Monty' (Lord Montgomery) or with some other diminutive. It somehow creates loyalty, commitment and mitigates a little of the all too prevalent coldness and hierarchy. Snow describes this as 'a clever device which acknowledges and absorbs the pupils' own counterculture'.[36] This was possibly one of the effects, emphasized by the fact that there were many occasions, both in formal and informal games, when masters and boys would rag together. But I am not sure that it was an explicit political move to subvert rebellion.

*

Naming is, of course, only a small part of the linguistic code which any institution will develop to divide insiders from outsiders and express social relationships. All closed institutions develop their own private language, or at least dialect. I suspect that the Dragon slang, which was one of the first things I had to pick up when I arrived, largely overlapped with that in other boarding schools, though there may have been a few special words. Watkins noted that 'Crying was called Blubbing at the Dragon', but this was a word which one can find in many dictionaries and was used well outside preparatory schools.[37] In fact much of the slang was quickly propagated and copied with the emergence, precisely in this period, of a number of humorous books about schools such as 'Down with Skool' and the St. Trinian's sagas and especially in the comics like the Beano and Dandy. It was often a juvenile image of the language which was spread by public schools such as Westminster, Eton and Winchester. Indeed most of the language seems to have been common in schools in southern England at this time.

Yet wherever it came from, it had to be learnt and used properly, and was always changing. A tiny vignette of this is given in a verse of a poem by Roger Wilding published in The Draconian in 1963:

---

[35] Watkins, *Stand*, 7.
[36] Snow, *Oxford*, 167.
[37] Watkins, *Stand*, 10.

'Quis' and 'Ego', 'Bags I'. 'Beef'
'Tich Frater' 'Fleb' and 'Fains'
'Excuse me sir, can we have 'per'
To go and watch the trains?'

The poem proceeded to describe:

'The gravel playground choked with boys,
Hopscotch, marbles, conkers, noise
Rationed nougat, lemonade,
Illicit sweets from North Parade...' [38]

Which suggests that the context was mainly part of social playground activity.

There were also a number of what would now be considered derogatory terms. 'Wikipedia' tells us that 'Temporary teaching assistants (usually in their late teens or early twenties, often natives of former British colonies) are known as "stooges".' As I will discuss below, girls were at certain periods known as 'hags' or 'haggises', but I don't myself remember other derogatory terms such as 'oiks'. 'Wikipedia' also draws attention to other things slightly different – which were almost terms of art, or shorthand, often again used in games. It notes that 'As is the case at most boarding institutions, the Dragon has developed its own unique lexicon besides, incorporating a slang particular to many schools ('pill' meaning ball, 'with you' meaning pass, and so on).

I cannot now remember the slang, but I have combed my letters from school, and my mother's comments on my language, and find traces there. On 29 April 1951 she wrote to my father that I was saying at the end of the holidays, *"fleb" is his favourite expression, meaning everything that is awful, as opposed to "beefy" which is usually applied to himself.* I was still using this expression in my last year at school, when my mother describes in a letter of 27 December my attitude to a party she was arranging for my thirteenth birthday. *Alan had spent the previous two days saying that he didn't want a party and he was going out for the afternoon and what did I want to go and ask a lot of fleb girls for...* I also used to 'lam up' my sisters – which meant 'beat up'.

Another source is the Draconian Term Notes. In Summer 1952 there is mention of a 'wizard' fast bowler, 'absolutely supersonic'. The latter term I remember applying to my favourite cheese, and there are several mentions of 'wizard' in my letters. Another was in my first term when the Christmas 1950 Term Notes mentions that there were few 'bishes' with the production of the 'Mikado'. This was reflected in a letter of my mother's

---

[38] Quoted in Jaques, *Centenary,* 72.

on 3 January 1955 when she wrote to my father *I expect you've been listening to the Test Match most of the time, it is quite encouraging this time if we don't make a bish of it as Alan says.* Another term I think I remember was when, on a visit of the school to Windsor reported in the Term Notes for Summer 1954, 'the guide got in a frightful bate because we didn't know any dates'. From the hints above, it appears that our school slang was not confined to school. It was used in the holidays and in this way would spread to our siblings and even our parents.

*

One of the biggest shocks I remember about going to the Dragon was, in a sense, moving from oriental, or rural, or pre-industrial, pre-bureaucratic time as I had experienced it for the first eight years of my life, to suddenly finding myself in a world ruled by clocks, bells and watches.

Kipling urged us to 'fill the unforgiving minute with sixty seconds' worth of distance run', and this was exactly what we were learning to do. This has had a profound effect on my life, where I follow Kipling's advice daily. And it is something I have seen as one of the central obsessions in schools I have visited in India, China and elsewhere. The easier pace of time in most societies, linked to the agricultural and social calendar, is jolted by lessons starting precisely at a certain time, ending with bells, rushing elsewhere, and then starting again.

Part of the reason for all this is that there always seems too much to do. A school like the Dragon did not want us to be bored and it wanted us to achieve on a wide level. So when it was not formal lessons, then a multitude of other activities meant that we had to work out our time very carefully. In my final year, for example, I had to balance being in Iolanthe, playing rugger, dancing, watching films, skating, doing all sorts of lessons and exams and many other things.

In order to inculcate this attitude to the effective allocation of time, the school ran a highly centralized and integrated time regime. It produced something straight out of 'Alice in Wonderland', with little boys (and often the masters) like the White Rabbit, scurrying from place to place muttering to themselves 'The Duchess, the Duchess', or its equivalent.

The mixture of clocks and bells are touched upon in the Term Notes for Easter 1953 which mentions that when the master clock in the common room and all satellites stopped, 'clock-fed Dragons were soon at sixes and sevens, or to be more accurate, at twenty past nine'. Furthermore, 'Of the various masters responsible for ringing the various bells that morning some knew about the 9.20 idea....'

Public time announced by centrally directed clocks – synchronized time, which collapsed if the master clock stopped – and public bells, gave an atmosphere of something like a medieval village. It is not just a coincidence that the poetic autobiography of an early Dragon, the Poet Laureate John Betjeman, should be titled 'Summoned by Bells'. The situation was a preparation for public school, where it was even worse:

> Doom! Shivering doom! Inexorable bells
> To early school, to chapel, school again: ...
> The dread of beatings! Dread of being late!'

We listened to the bells, watched the clocks, and we also adjusted our lives through our control of private machines for gauging time, the wrist watch rather than the fob watch of Alice's White Rabbit. Here I have only just begun to wonder whether most boys had watches and, if they did, how they were adjusted to school time.

Fortunately I have a partial answer in my own case in two references in my letters. Much of my life has revolved around the hoarding, spending and stretching of time, and I could take some control of this because I knew from minute to minute how time was passing. I seem to have had a watch from at least soon after my eighth birthday, though whether it was a real one I do not know. In a letter of early February 1950 I wrote, *Thank you very much for the lovely watch and letters.* Later, on 30 April 1953, when I was eleven-and-a- quarter, my grandmother wrote to my mother, *I have bought the watch* and in the same letter I wrote to my mother *I have got a new cricket bat to take to sckool and a new watch wich is lovely.* My precise knowledge, as well as an elementary stimulus to mathematics, is shown a few days later on 10 May when I wrote, *My watch is still working very well and it only loses about half a minute everyday.*

Time was measured down to the unforgiving thirty seconds, but it was also measured carefully over the progress of the term. Paul Watkins seems to have been particularly disoriented in his misery, for he writes, 'I never thought much about the passage of time. There was only the black and white of school time and holiday time, class time and free time, and the gradual shift from one dorm to another as I moved up the school.'[39]

This is not my memory or what my letters show. It seems very obvious that I was intensely aware of how many days of each term had passed, and how many were to come. And it is also clear that the passing of the term was marked more generally by customs such as the Gloats which were put up in forms and dormitories about three weeks before the end of term – presumably along the gloating lines 'No more Latin, no more French, no more sitting on the old school bench.'

*

---

[39] Watkins, *Stand*, 73.

Yet while there was a rigid code of time and too much to be packed into the term, the Dragon may have been unusual in also subverting this bureaucratic straightjacket to a certain extent and emphasizing a more chaotic, or creatively charismatic, view of how the world should be ordered. This is something I have only recently rediscovered, mainly through the revealing Term Notes.

This anti-bureaucratic tendency of subversion is closely linked to something else. That is the cult of the resourceful amateur, the person who does not need to stick to rules, who can deal with the unexpected, who is effortlessly flexible and disregards convention.

The rot, as modern management consultants would no doubt describe it, started right at the top with the staff and particularly with the junior headmaster, Joc. The staff meetings seem, as reported in the Term Notes, to have been minimalist and indeed objects of some derision. The most important one was at the start of term, and there are world-weary accounts of them. The Term Notes of Easter 1952 mentioned that 'Last term's intimate details were simply the result of your note-taker's carelessness in forgetting to provide himself, for once, with the crossword.' The following term, 'A Staff Meeting on the first Sunday night, summoned to tie up any loose ends, was soon at grips with the problem of whether boys should write on single, or between double, lines. But when the ladies in the far corner put down their knitting for a moment to point out that down in the 'E' Block they used no lines at all, it broke up in confusion.' In my last summer term the author could not even remember if there was a staff meeting at all.

The tension with other more bureaucratic expectations is shown in the response to the sudden threat that the school was to be inspected. The reaction hints at the conflicts of style in the account written in The Draconian in my last term at the Dragon, Summer 1955. A letter had come from the Ministry of Education pointing out that it was twenty-five years since they had last 'recognized' the Dragon School. An inspection was timed for June 6, 'which gave us less than six weeks in which to get the shop window properly dressed, an undertaking with which little headway was ever actually made since the Dragon shop window is used so seldom that no one even knew where it was, let along what to put in it'.

It is worth noting some of the outcomes of this inspection and the style in which the school responded, as reported in Joc's speech at the end of the term. 'We thought it well to start this off with a Sherry Party, with a view to putting the Inspectors in a good frame of mind; and I think that this was entirely successful. But some of the good was soon undone the next morning when the Chief Inspector sat himself on one of the older chairs in the huts, and tore the seat of his trousers on a nail.... And another Inspector was somewhat shaken on emerging from the Geography Room to be addressed by a small boy as "Spiv": but this was only a case of mistaken identity. In their report at the end of the Inspection, they were rude about the partitioned classrooms, the blackboards, the lighting arrangements, and a good many other structural defects (and quite rightly). But they were very polite about the teaching of the Staff, the confident yet friendly attitude of the boys, and the general atmosphere existing between boys and Staff.'

The whole place seems to have been run with an emphasis on spontaneity and creative chaos by the Junior Headmaster, Joc (his father, the previous Headmaster 'Hum', was now partly a ceremonial figure, though he did comment on all my school reports). The descriptions of Joc by the elderly schoolmaster Jaques, writer of the Term Notes, shows a spirit of friendly teasing which one might not have found in all schools. For example, in the Summer Term 1951 the School Notes mentions that Joc was 'deprived of his favourite sport of posting one programme, announcing another, and carrying through a third...' In Easter 1954, Joc, who was passionate about skating and hockey, tried to maximize both. There was a lot of improvisation to increase the amount of hockey – 'Joc was ready with an assortment of schemes for playing lots of it, and at the oddest times, by converting an afternoon into an evening, Uppers into Lowers, a Monday into a Tuesday, or even lunch into tea.' No doubt many of the other masters, whom we remember as rather quirky, added to this creative sense of spontaneous chaos.

It is appreciatively noted, however, that Joc provided extra skates, bicycles, pens and other luxuries, all of which were known as Joc skates, Joc pens etc., in a way which would again add to the feeling that he was a sort of benevolent uncle. I certainly remember Joc with some affection and he may have been under special pressure when, in Christmas 1954, Jacko notes in The Draconian that the E block 'hitherto a more or less independent body, was incorporated in the main structure, a totalitarian move which accorded so ill with Joc's Liberal principles...' (The E block was the reception year, mainly staffed by women.)

*

The author of the Term Notes lamented that the Summer term 1952 was completely normal without 'that touch of the unexpected which Dragons normally expect'. The general tone of the Notes is one of irony, joking, even mildly carnivalesque. There is a scepticism of rules and government and a commitment not to take anything absolutely seriously. No wonder the masters and the boys revelled in the humour of the Gilbert and Sullivan operas which are precisely about the poking of fun at the establishment – the law, the police, the navy, the House of Lords, the aesthetes. That the school produced a number of people who in one way or another poked fun at authority, whether comedians such as Hugh

Laurie or writers like John Mortimer, is not surprising. We were to remember that the teacher whom we took seriously one minute was also the good sport and 'older brother' whose nickname we could use and who could be teased.

*

It is the absences which tend to be overlooked and so it is worth pausing on the fact that, although the Dragon was a formally Christian school, it was rather laid-back in its emphasis on religion – particularly in comparison to a number of other preparatory schools. Religion was there, of course, and elsewhere we shall examine the sermons which we heard and the Remembrance Day events which moved us. Here it is enough to note that, even as late as 1977, the history of the school notes that 'unlike many other Prep. Schools, they still do not have their own Chapel'. Hugh Sidgwick, writing around the time of the First World War, echoed the 1908 speech by the Skipper in which the latter had warned against 'the falseness of all the gods of society, gold, sham religion, conventionality...'[40] Sidgwick also wrote that, 'In a normal Preparatory School, especially of the more fashionable type, nothing would be more obvious and natural than for a War Memorial to take the form of a Chapel.... But we are not an ordinary school, and our tradition has always been cast in the opposite extreme. Routine, orthodoxy, ritual, unreasoning compliance with *comme il faut* – all these we have deliberately avoided. ... freedom and sincerity and spontaneity and genuineness, and mistrust of the second-rate and the second-hand, are things worth a good deal of risk to obtain.'[41]

---

[40] Jaques, *Centenary,* 84–5.
[41] Jaques, *Centenary,* 48.

8 SOCIETY

One of the techniques used to train us for our future worlds was to arrange life in a series of parallel ladders up which we were encouraged to climb. There were intellectual ladders, the school forms arranged in a dizzying set from Lower Five, where I arrived to Upper 1 (which I never attained). This was based on classics and parallel to it each subject was arranged in sets, from E5 where I started, to A1, which I never attained in any subject. Twice a year there were exams and we were gradually toiling upwards towards a possible distinction of some kind.

Perhaps more significant to us there were the games teams, from fifth game or even lower, up to the First XV or First XI, depending on the sport. From the first, the masters were on the lookout for talent and we were spurred on to try to climb the ladder to win the respect of our peers – and certainly in my case, my sports-loving father. As well as the formal team sports – rugger, football, hockey and cricket – there were others, tennis, swimming, athletics among them, where we gradually moved upwards through teams and sets. These shaded into more informal hierarchies in many of the playground games and hobbies, boys being ranked in marbles, conkers, five-stones and other annual crazes, as well as strength in fighting or facing pain.

Then there were hierarchies in drama, music, art and other activities such as chess. Those who played major roles in the annual Shakespeare or Gilbert and Sullivan events were given considerable status.

There was the equally important placing in hierarchies which were more structured in the sense that this did not depend on personal effort, but placed people in inexorable classes. These structures included school houses, dormitories, 'suppers' and 'tables' (what time and with whom one ate). Special targets were being the captain of a team or, a minor target, a school prefect.

I learnt from all this that life, as the school motto reminded us, was a constant struggle. One might be doing well on one ladder, but slipping on another. Nothing was assured. Only skill, concentration, commitment and effort would move one upwards and gain the esteem of teachers, other boys, one's parents and above all oneself. We were always being watched, judged, examined – formally and informally – and trying to prove ourselves.

This effort, so brilliantly satirized in 'How to be Topp', by Geoffrey

61

Willans and Ronald Searle, is obviously one of the major features of such schools. The ambitious tried to be top in everything, as it is reported of the young Rupert Brooke, the poet, who in an autograph album defined his idea of happiness as being 'at the top of the tree in everything', including his favourite activities cricket, tennis, football, reading and stamp collecting. His diaries describe his excitement as he moves up these ladders.[42]

Of course, this straining upwards could have a considerable cost. In some cases, as with Paul Watkins, one could begin to realize that one was not officer material. 'There were the ranks that had names, like Prefect and Head Boy and Captain of the Rugby Team. I knew almost from the beginning that I wouldn't have a rank like that.'[43] I knew the same – I would never sing a lead part in a Gilbert and Sullivan opera; I would never get into the top class in Latin; I would never be a captain of the team or ace chess player. Yet there were many consolation prizes for those who were not effortlessly brilliant and I was content to strive for these.

There must certainly have been those who felt inadequate and unable to achieve much. Yet I think that the way things were arranged in general meant that even the mediocre, like myself, felt a certain degree of hope, and as we went through the school and automatically moved up in various ways, our self-confidence was boosted. As we will see from an analysis of my school reports, my teachers were constantly writing that I was capable of good things, and often congratulated me on doing well. I was supported and pushed on by what now seems a genuine concern that I succeed as far as my abilities would take me, even if it now seems evident that I was quite clearly classified in formal education, though not in games, as a middling person.

The success of the school in giving people self-confidence through helping them climb the various ladders and in preventing the usual scrabbling of frogs-in-a-well syndrome, found in many schools (where, as in the Indian proverb, the frogs at the bottom of the well would rather drag down any aspiring and escaping frog than let it climb out), only really comes out when we compare it to its opposite, which we can do by mentioning the case of George Orwell.

Here was an obviously brilliant boy – he finally won a scholarship to Eton and Wellington, was second in the national Harrow History Prize (Townsend-Warner) which the Dragon also competed in, was clearly imaginative and sensitive. Yet he writes that he felt damned, 'I had no money, I was weak, I was ugly, I was unpopular, I had a chronic cough, I was cowardly, I smelt.' This had a catastrophic effect on him for many years. 'The conviction that it was *not possible* for me to be a success went deep enough to influence my actions till far into adult life. Until I was

---

[42] Brendon, *Preparatory School*, 57.
[43] Watkins, *Stand*, 74.

about thirty I always planned my life on the assumption not only that any major undertaking was bound to fail, but that I could only expect to live a few years longer.'[44] As I will discuss below I came out of the Dragon with the opposite conclusion: I learnt to believe in myself and what I could do.

*

Part of all this, as Orwell points out, was to do with the system of rules, the breaking of rules and the punishments for such breaches. One of the things which shines out of Orwell's account is that not only were there numerous official petty rules, but that it was impossible not to break them, impossible not to be detected by a severe surveillance system instituted by the teachers, and then impossible to avoid brutal punishments. A similar regime, echoed in Orwell's '1984', can be glimpsed in many of the schools described in Brendon's survey of preparatory schools.

This was to some extent true in the Dragon. We had almost no private space – from the start as boarders we lived communally and everyone could see the shivering, naked little boy in the bath, going to bed or in the changing rooms. The memory of Siegfried Sassoon who 'felt that the only life he could call his own was inside his play-box along with his tin of mixed biscuits' strikes a chord.[45] We were living a life almost completely in public in a very crowded space.

There seems to have been at least some recognition by the school of this difficulty. In the Term Notes for Summer 1954 it was stated that, 'At one end the Junior Changing Room has acquired a new spaciousness most welcome to junior changers, for whom dressing and undressing, probably for the first time in public, possibly for the first time unaided, was quite enough of an ordeal without the additional embarrassment of putting one's leg into your neighbour's shorts.' The baths were at first equally intimidating. Watkins commented that 'We sat two boys in each bath, knees pulled up to our chins.'[46] I certainly remember that at Sedbergh it was sometimes three to a bath.

It was difficult to conceal anything. We did creep off to smoke, or eat illicit foods, in tree huts in summer, or as Jake Mermagen remembers, smoking with home-made pipes. There were conventions amongst the boys themselves which allowed them a tiny bit of personal space. Watkins described how, 'It was always quiet on the first night, and sometimes you could hear boys crying in their beds.' The crying was not brought up the next day, but it had to be as muffled as possible. Watkins himself described how 'For the first days, I cried after the dormitory lights were

---

[44] Orwell, *Essays*, 444, 445.

[45] Brendon, *Preparatory School*, 208.

[46] Watkins, *Stand*, 12.

out. I pressed my face deep into Oscar Bear's foamy yellow stomach because I didn't want anyone to hear me..."[47]

For the most part it was almost like the famous description by Bentham of a model prison based on a 'Panopticon', where the warders were (in theory) watching one all the time. In some ways, the fact that teachers were playing with us, trying to be older brothers and then becoming teachers, made the surveillance deeper. Yet though I remember the shock of the lack of privacy and loss of personal control, I don't on the whole remember a sense of being watched all the time.

*

The absence of bullying as we remember it, may have arisen because at the Dragon, as no doubt at a number of other schools, formal rules were generally kept to a minimum. It was a little like the English system of common law, which is largely based on precedent, on common sense, on the assumption of reasonable behaviour, on only a few and vague absolute rules – thou shalt not kill, attack, steal, etc. A concept of negative liberty prevailed which permitted certain things that were internal, inalienable, rights, but did not, as in continental law, try to stipulate many positive commandments.

The contemporary official Dragon website claims that 'The school has a comparatively informal ethos, relying on common sense and individual responsibility rather than a long set of formal rules.' My own experience suggests that the description is a reasonable one. I do not remember being oppressed by rules and regulations which were difficult to keep, and I suspect that once again this was a long-term influence of the Skipper, who knew as an expert that sailing is best done on the basis of some simple general principles, applied with flexibility and ingenuity to meet the constantly varying circumstances that are impossible to specify in advance. This is exactly how we learnt to play team games – a few negative rules as to what you could not do, and the rest was skill and effort.

*

This can be seen as yet another of the tactics to produce an imperial elite, too arrogant for its own good. My mother implied this on one of her three visits to the Dragon. *'Macbeth' was very well done really... The boys were word-perfect but fearfully pompous and droney ... We went to the service next day and the same lot of little boys got up and droned again, this time they read us Shakespeare's best known sonnet (after explaining carefully what it meant!) and a long excerpt from 'Faust' – can't think why,*

---

[47] Watkins, *Stand,* 11.

but they were all so pleased with themselves.

It is all in line with various mission statements of a number of schools. Brendon quotes some statements which point to the desire to make these schools 'the cradle and crèche of Empire', inculcating the 'virtues of leadership, courage and independence', encouraging 'the sacrifice of selfish interests to the ideal of fellowship and the future of the race'.[48] In other words such schools prepared boys for the loneliness of colonial frontier life, and the legitimacy of hierarchy.

Put in an amusing way, we were being trained to stand on our own feet and to be ready to go out and change the world as a Hobbit might do. Tolkien lived only a couple of streets away from the Dragon and we used to bump in to him on nearby by roads – and indeed Tolkien sent his son to the school. Peter Snow suggests that, 'The hobbit heroes are clearly North Oxford children; they have the bodies of children but the minds of adults; they speak with all the distinctive spry confidence of Dragon School pupils; they are good marksmen; they become extremely distinguished in the outside world: Frodo (Old Dragon, 1929) has done outstandingly well in Mordor...' This is why in 1970 a film unit came to make a film about Professor Tolkien 'who would naturally be perfectly at ease with any sort of Dragon. So fifty of them, including the Professor's grandson, all Hobbits for the evening, milled around a bonfire on the river bank by the Barge, armed with torches...'[49]

To get an idea of this little world which boosted self-confidence and in which the children really ruled their own world to a large extent, one could do worse than study another fantasy classic, the Harry Potter series, which the Old Dragon Pico Iyer felt was closely modelled on the sort of world he had experienced at the Dragon. Part of what makes Harry Potter attractive is that although there are treacherous masters and bullying and some injustice, on the whole the headmaster, not unlike the headmasters of the Lynam family, cares about the boys, believes in them, and supports them. There is a feeling that, in the end, it is a just world where evil will not triumph.

*

It is difficult to keep order in a boarding school with hundreds of very energetic, rumbustious and, at the least, mischievous little boys. There is a temptation, which teachers in many preparatory schools succumbed to, as described by Dahl, Berners, Orwell and others, to do this through fear.[50] At the worst, they could become, as Evelyn Waugh and others described, like

[48] Brendon, *Preparatory School*, 51.
[49] Snow, *Oxford*, 233.
[50] Roald Dahl, *Boy* (1984); Lord Berners, *First Childhood* (1998); George Orwell, 'Such, Such were the Joys' in *Essays* (Penguin reprint, 2000).

prisons, or even more extreme, as Alistair Horne described Ludgrove, 'a Belsen of the spirit'.[51] The boys were regimented, not allowed to make a noise in the corridors or whisper in prep, and constantly checked and slapped down as many of the classic accounts show.

If they disobeyed any of the rules, they were mercilessly beaten or deprived of food or leisure, made to feel both morally sinful and criminally culpable. This is the world which Orwell graphically describes and which, above all, he learnt was unjust, invasive, irrational and cruel.

Orwell, despite his dislike of his father, writes, 'Your home might be far from perfect, but at least it was a place ruled by love rather than by fear, where you did not have to be perpetually on your guard against the people surrounding you. At eight years old you were suddenly taken out of this warm nest and flung into a world of force and fraud and secrecy, like a goldfish into a tank full of pike. Against no matter what degree of bullying you had no redress. You could only have defended yourself by sneaking, which, except in a few rigidly defined circumstances, was the unforgivable sin.'[52]

Thus he seemed to learn the lesson that 'Virtue consisted in winning: it consisted in being bigger, stronger, handsomer, richer, more popular, more elegant, more unscrupulous than other people – in dominating them, bullying them, making them suffer pain, making them look foolish, getting the better of them in every way. Life was hierarchical and whatever happened was right. There were the strong, who deserved to win and always did win, and there were the weak, who deserved to lose and always did lose, everlastingly.'[53]

Orwell was writing about a preparatory school in the First World War and things have moved on very considerably since. It is in the contrast that the change becomes apparent, for this was not my experience at the Dragon. I may have accepted that 'whatever is, is right' as Pope put it. But it also seemed to be a generally benign and quite just world. This even applied, it seems, to punishment.

*

There was a constant debate in boarding schools about the use of sticks and carrots and physical punishment in particular. The Dragon seems to have emphasized carrots, prizes, praise, little marks of distinction and esteem which I remember in school assemblies, note from my school reports, retain in form prizes and in pleased letters from my parents.

Yet there was also the stick, or variants of it such as the slipper, gym shoe, long ruler, bat. Many of the most vivid memories of boys who went

---

[51] Quoted in Brendon, *Preparatory School*, 112.
[52] Orwell, *Essays*, 443.
[53] Orwell, *Essays*, 443.

to preparatory schools, certainly before the Second World War, are of the humiliating and extraordinarily painful beatings they suffered. I have often wondered recently what happened at the Dragon since, unless I have suppressed the memory, I do not remember ever being beaten or even being physically assaulted in other less extreme ways such as having my hair twisted, board-rubbers thrown hard at me, kicked or punched, by members of staff.

Some light is thrown on this by an overview by Jaques who writes that, 'A graph showing the use of this "corrective" on Dragons over their first hundred years would show a steady decline from the "horrors" of the earliest days.' He argues that boys, 'have for the most part accepted a visit to the study as the natural sequel to detection in an individual misdemeanour, and more spontaneous correction with the nearest available implement for any tendency towards dawdling in the changing-room, talking after lights-out, ragging in boot room or passages etc.'[54]

This suggestion of order kept mainly by lesser forms of violence is confirmed by my contemporaries. Philip Steadman told Brendon that, ' 'It is true that there was a certain amount of "knockabout violence" in the classroom, throwing board rubbers, pulling hair or (on one occasion) breaking a pipe over a boy's head.'[55]

Other boys attest to some beating, continuing at least into the 1970s. Watkins describes how Pa Winter had a system: 'Three red marks and he'd give you a chocolate bar... But three black marks and he would beat you.'[56] Brendon notes that 'One father I met compared his children's experiences at boarding school with his own at the Dragon in the 1970s. Even though he enjoyed his schooldays, he could not imagine subjecting his own offspring to the wealth of whackings...'[57]

Two things strike me about the system. One is that the old adage, 'this hurts me more than it hurts you', seems to have lain behind at least some of the punishment.

The Skipper gave his views on the vexed matter of beatings in a speech to parents in 1905. 'I have had a certain amount of correspondence with some parents on the subject of corporal punishment. I believe that boys have been told before they came here that awful horrors awaited them in the study at School House. Well, all I can say is that I set corporal punishment the subject for an essay to the top thirty-six boys in the School, and that they unanimously expressed their approval of it, as far better than "impots", keeping in, or punishment drill. I am afraid that the essays proved that it was hardly as dreadful as it ought to be!'

More curious is the way in which he continues. 'I do not believe in

[54] Jaques, *Centenary*, 43.
[55] Brendon, *Preparatory School*, 200.
[56] Watkins, *Stand*, 10.
[57] Brendon, *Preparatory School*, 200.

corporal punishment a bit for really serious offences. I think that these want treating in a very different way, and that nothing but an appeal to what is good in a boy is of any use under such circumstances – but for faults of forgetfulness, carelessness, and repeated neglect of work, it seems the simplest, least hurtful, and most efficient corrective.'

In fairness to some others, it should be mentioned that beating was not confined to the headmaster. There were several masters who would now have been reported as sadists and who beat several of those who have written to me quite mercilessly, particularly for stubbornness. All I can add is that I cannot ever remember being beaten at the school.

*

The boarding school system was, among other things, meant to teach you how to live the communal life which you would find in an even starker form in public school, and then later in the army or, in a milder form, perhaps, in many of the other clubs of various kinds for which England was famous. Brendon notes that 'commentators have stressed the familiarity such a boy will have with the "mysterious internal workings" of English institutions such as the regiment, the bar, the House of Commons and the gentleman's club. Now, as in the past, these can act as a home from home where a man can "live his school life over again", often encountering men he met as boys in the classroom, dormitory or sports pavilion.' As one Old Dragon, William Buchan, wrote of the RAF in the 1940s, 'I was simply back at boarding school'.[58]

Yet the Dragon may have done this in a distinctive way. As noted, in many schools the boys were suppressed, kept in rigid order, told to be absolutely silent in the passage ways and especially in the classrooms during lessons. It is often noted that Dragon boys (and girls) were permitted to be very noisy and exuberant. I remember this during my time, and it was then that in my last term the Government Inspectors came to the school and the Term Notes state that 'The Inspectors had already commented fairly freely on the amount of noise made by Dragons; they now discovered that they hadn't heard nothing yet.'

Finally, even inside the classroom, although there was not too much noise, there was an unusually open discussion. Jaques suggests that 'from quiet early days the atmosphere in Dragon classrooms was, perhaps, somewhat freer than elsewhere, and the listener at the keyhole might hear the voice of the pupil being raised to make a constructive contribution or put a query, not lowered for a hesitant answer to a peremptory question.'[59]

*

---

[58] Quoted in Brendon, *Preparatory School*, 115.
[59] Jaques, *Centenary*, 44.

68

The Skipper realized that little children taken away from their parents might well be lonely, miserable, lost. He attempted to ameliorate this by various devices. One was to encourage links with home. Rather curiously, in his 1908 speech to assembled headmasters, he said, 'We have failed, if our boys are ashamed to kiss their parents in public', and he defended the long school holidays which would mean that, unlike other schools, parents and children could see more of each other.[60] At the prize-giving in 1901 he told the parents, 'Our boys have more independence, and less supervision: thus certain Headmasters have expressed horror at the way I let my boys go into Oxford, if they ask me; go on the river; go and see their parents in term-time. "Don't you catch all manner of diseases?" they say. Well, we don't, and I don't believe the boys abuse their privileges; I hate the entire severance of family ties by keeping a little boy three months from his home.'[61]

The conscious effort to mitigate the absence from home may partly explain why, while I am sure that Robert Graves is right that we returned home 'with a different vocabulary, a different moral system, even different voices', Royston Lambert's observation that 'boarding life distorted relationships and rendered "a family's holiday-time existence unnatural"', does not fit with my experience.[62] Because I have so much material both on my school life and life at home, I can check this not only from my memory. I saw these worlds as parallel universes. One was not 'natural' and the other 'unnatural'; they both existed, just as we had learnt to operate in many parallel universes through games, literature, films and other imaginative worlds.

There is strong evidence for this, in fact, in the letters from and to my parents which I wrote at this time. These letters kept the connection between the worlds very much alive. A description by Paul Watkins of the letters he received from his parents in America suddenly brings back my feelings about receiving letters.

'The only other contact I had from home was in letters. Some days it seemed that I was living from one delivery of mail to the next. At the end of breakfast, Pa Vicker would walk in with the stack of letters and everyone stopped talking. I scanned the stack for the pale blue of an aerogramme ... I kept all the letters, but I never read them twice. It became a superstitious thing....'[63] As for re-reading them, I think I did re-read them, certainly when it came to answering points made in them. The goings on at home in Dorset or in Assam are constantly referred to and asked after in my letters

[60] Jaques, *Centenary*, 48.
[61] *The Skipper*, 41.
[62] Brendon, *Preparatory School*, 203; Royston Lambert, *The Hot House Society; An exploration of boarding-school life through the boys' and girls' own writings* (1968), 204.
[63] Watkins, *Stand*, 38.

which suggests that I coped with the parallel worlds quite easily.

*

In fact the Skipper founded a tradition, which probably worked particularly well with intellectuals and often interlinked middle-class families in north Oxford, of encouraging the pupils to be particularly considerate with their parents. At the Speech Day in 1898, the Skipper said 'Holidays! Make them pleasant for all around you and then you will enjoy them. Remember the old Commandment, "Honour they father and thy mother that thy days may be long" – I would rather put it that THEIR days may be long!'[64] This seems to have been an exhortation he made at the end of each term according to Canon Mayhew, an early pupil, who remembered that 'He never preached except at the end of each term when he dismissed us with the injunction to be as nice and kind and unselfish to our parents and brothers and sisters as we could.'[65] This ethic was, of course, something most boarding schools were trying to encourage.

On Speech-Day in 1918 the Skipper said, 'The changes have all been to the good, and all the good traditions of the boarders have been maintained ... the almost unique (in Preparatory Schools) encouragement of parents to see as much of their children as possible during term-time and so to keep the home-tie strong – this tradition of our school has been carried on. Hospitality to old boys and parents, another traditional feature, has been maintained as far as and even further than rations will allow!'[66] Often a child's parents were abroad or away, so visits or outings to see guardians, surrogate parents, or other close relatives, such as grandparents, who lived very close to the Dragon in Jamie's case, were also encouraged.

*

It is clear that the Lynam family, and particularly the Skipper, refused to make the normal strong distinction between school and family. This arose out of their own attachment to the school. The Skipper's father was the chief architect of the early buildings and five of his children were associated with the school, including two of the Skipper's younger brothers who were pupils during his time, the medical officer for many years and the Skipper's brother Hum and nephew Joc as subsequent headmasters.

Families have wives and daughters as well as sons, so in line with this the Skipper was very keen that the school should include daughters as well as sons. He sent his own daughter, Kit, to the school in 1896, the first girl at the Dragon, and henceforth, much against the trend of other preparatory schools I suspect, there were always some girls at the Dragon and at the

[64] *The Skipper*, 43.
[65] *The Skipper*, 100.
[66] *The Skipper*, 46.

time I was there were a dozen at the school.

This was a deliberate policy. In 1908 in his address to the preparatory heads the Skipper said, 'And there is one more point. In this assembly I hardly dare to introduce it, but it is this: we see a great deal of boys, but we do not see enough of girls. I believe that the presence of girls in one's school is quite as good for the masters as for boys and for the girls themselves; and I beg of you to consider co-education as a means of making us more human.'

On Speech day in 1914 he noted that, 'For the first time a girl' – Norah Jolliffe – is head boy. I have sometimes been, shall I say, criticized for admitting a few very select girls to the School. Personally I have no doubt whatever of the good effects it has on the boys, nor of the benefit that the girls themselves obtain. It is absurd to say that it makes the boys girlish or the girls boyish ... The prejudice against the presence of girls at a preparatory school is merely a silly conventional attitude.' In the speech the following year he returned to the theme. 'I am more than ever convinced that it is an excellent thing for the School to have about a dozen little girls amongst the boys; and from what those parents say who have their girls here I am equally convinced that it is good for the girls themselves...'[67]

Thus began the tradition of there being some girls, including such distinguished future writers as Naomi Mitchison and Antonia Fraser, or academics such as Caroline Medawar, or international stars such as Emma Watson ('Hermione' in Harry Potter).

The really curious thing to me, though, is that I can hardly remember the girls. I remember some outstanding ones, like the red-haired Tyrell Gatty, (whom Jake Mermagen remembers playing in the rugger team, until opponents asked that she be dropped), and when I see their faces in plays I recognize them. But I seem to have been, as I was with my sisters at home, more or less gender-blind. They were just other pupils whom one liked, respected or shunned. This, of course, was a period when the age of puberty was later and I did not reach sexual maturity until the very end of my time at the Dragon. So apart, as I recount elsewhere, from noting the beauty of chorus girls in 'South Pacific', or asking for pin-ups for the prefects' study, I did not really think much about girls as sexual objects.

My experience seems to have been different from that described twenty years later by Paul Watkins. To start with he says that, 'There weren't many girls at the Dragon, only a couple who were the daughters of teachers.' I am pretty sure that by then there must have been several dozen, and his account, which describes a small army of girls marching through the school announcing his failures, does not fit.[68] When Antonia

---

[67] *The Skipper*, 32–3.
[68] Watkins, *Stand*, 68.

Fraser was there, twenty years before me, she was 'intensely happy' (playing on the wing in the rugby team, among other things) although she was one of only forty girls in a school of some 400.[69] My cousin Anna, who was at the school for three years just before me, says that she had a wonderful time at the Dragon.

I also wonder whether Watkins is right in claiming that 'girls were things that belonged outside the school, to the streets of Oxford and to home and to the holiday. Even if there had been many around, we wouldn't have known where to put them.' I put them where I put everyone else – in the various hierarchies of trust, respect, liking which I assigned to people at the Dragon.

I certainly don't recall the snogging, groping, grabbing at the school dance which he describes.[70] But then I do not remember ever using what we are told was the common nickname for them: Haggis or Hag. Watkins states that 'A girl was called a Haggis at the Dragon School. You had to call them that, even if you didn't want to.' Peter Snow notes that the school is a 'boarding school with some day boys which also takes girl pupils (interestingly known at first to the boys as "hags")'. What he means 'at first' is not clear.

I can't at the moment find anything about the use of the curious word Haggis in relation to a girl. In one of my letters to my mother I described the ladies looking after me when I was sick as Hags and made a joke about their potions being like the three witches in Macbeth. I suppose I may also have been playing on this term, unknown to my mother. Possibly the school banned the use of the word Hag as derogatory, so the boys changed it to Haggis.

*

My life seems to have been rather innocent at this time. In this I seem to be in line with much of what Brendon found. She mentions the consolations of masturbation, but concludes that, 'Generally sex does not loom very large in memoirs of prep school life and still less is it the subject matter of boys' letters home.' Brendon notes that, 'An even more hidden aspect of prep schools is the paedophilia for which they could provide ideal conditions, and refers to Randolph Churchill's 'Twenty-One years' and Evelyn Waugh's 'A Little Learning'. She further writes, 'There can be no doubt that some prep boarding schools have harboured active paedophiles, although it would be wrong to assume that this was common or that large numbers were affected.' She also notes, 'Nor did Royston Lambert's survey find much evidence of "sexual deviation on the part of

---

[69] Brendon, *Preparatory School*, 124.
[70] Watkins, *Stand*, 43, 68.

72

the staff"'. One of the only cases she cites, from another school, is that of my uncle Richard Rhodes James in his autobiography 'The Road from Mandalay'.

One Old Dragon interviewed by Brendon could not imagine subjecting his own children to beatings and to the 'sprinkling ... of dodgy masters', though what their dodginess consisted of is not stated.[71] And Paul Watkins occasionally alludes darkly to dodgy behaviour bordering on abuse. It is only some fifty years later that several people have told me that there was a fairly persistent paedophile in the school. Personally I got on well with this individual and none of his supposed victims, one of whom was one of my closest friends, ever suggested anything about this to me at the time.

We were assumed to be rather innocent of the facts of life, and this is why the 'Official Sex Talk' in our last term, before moving on to the depravities of public school, was considered both necessary and a big event. Paul Watkins remembers this talk, the advance reputation of which was legendary, but which, taken by the female biology teacher in his day, turned out to be a great anti-climax, limp in its contents and even in its graphic depiction of the male member on the blackboard.[72]

*

I had not realized until very recently that there was an official manual of sex instruction for prep schools. According to Richardson it was called 'Healthy Boyhood'. 'It began with the birds and the bees and ended up with this sentence: "And if, when you get to your public school, another boy ever tries to get into your bed, report him instantly to your housemaster."[73] I would have been shocked to read such a book and we were never shown it as far as I recall. I suspect that Joc would have tossed such literature in the bin.

I do, however, remember that the sex talk was given in the Quiet Room or School Library. It was given by the Headmaster, Joc. I vaguely remember that it was quite calm, low-key, matter of fact and vaguely helpful. The strictly biological side was dealt with by Gerd, the biology teacher, who I seem to remember showed us slides of live sperm swimming along (reputedly his own).

My recollection of the fact that the sex talk was by Joc, and also the slightly tense anticipation of the event, is brought home by a vivid memory. Joc was going round the room asking whether we could attend at time A or B. Some of the boys had answered with the pronunciation of the word 'either' in one way – say 'Ayther'. I then answered deliberately 'EETHER'.

---

[71] Brendon, *Preparatory School*, 65, 163, 155, 164, 200.
[72] Watkins, *Stand*, 86.
[73] Maurice Richardson, *Little Victims; Preparatory School School Memories* (1968), 124.

Everyone laughed and relaxed a little and Joc complimented me on my humour. It was one of the first times I realized that humour could deflate embarrassment.

9 CEREMONIAL

The school had built into it a number of safety valves or ways of diminishing pressure of hierarchy or authority. Any anthropologist familiar with intense, bounded and normally strongly stratified societies based on face to face relations would recognize these cathartic outlets of the kind often analysed in relation to carnivalesque inversions of the social order. Carnivals and charivaris reaffirm the social structure by either mirroring it through rituals, or by temporarily inverting it. These are mixed in with special events which give something to look forward to and an atmosphere of excitement, even euphoria.

There seem to have been quite a few of these special events at the Dragon, and although I don't personally remember any of them in detail, I remember in general that they were hugely enjoyable and that I looked forward and participated where I could with gusto. Apart from Guy Fawkes, there is no mention of these events in my letters. Perhaps this is partly because they often took place just before returning home at the end of term, and partly because I was not sure how to describe them to my parents.

*

Towards the end of term, we would begin to celebrate the coming release from school and the excitement of Christmas in our own way. In my first term it was noted that there was 'a widespread outbreak of Christmas decorations in the dormitories...' In the Summer Term of 1953 the Term Notes refer to the fact that 'Only three weeks more now, and in class-rooms and dormitories highly-coloured "Gloats" appear on the walls...' The following Christmas term it again mentions Gloats on classroom and dormitory walls. There was also in Summer 1955 'An outbreak of Form Feasts', though whether this was something new or applied to other terms, I do not yet know.

*

There was a communal Sing Song, which seems to have occurred at the end of other terms as well. I dimly remember this, and that one of the

75

staff particularly captivated me with his rendition of 'Abdul and Ivan'. I now remember that this was 'Jacko', C.H. Jaques, the author of the 'Centennial History of the School' and Term Notes.

A vignette from a more recent leaver, Paul Watkins, describes how, 'On the night before we left, we all crowded into the Old Hall for the Sing Song. The teachers dressed up in their old Army clothes or jammed their butts into a pair of boy's corduroy trousers and made fun of themselves on the stage. They threw sweets out into the audience.'[74] This is real topsy-turvy carnival, though there is no sign that we as boys put on a performance to satirize the school and the authorities, which I remember from my public school end-of-term House Concert.

The former Dragon master Bev MacInnes provides another picture of this event. 'The boys and a few girls started off with a selection of well-known songs; often with words referring to contemporary events at school, "Old MacDonald", "The Drunken Sailor".... The compere worked the audience into a good mood. After half an hour of singing, then the Sing Song went up a gear to the staff acts.'[75] MacInnes gives the text of a spoof with Latin interspersed in it. This 'impressed me because, no matter how senior and awe-inspiring some of the senior staff were to me, and no doubt to any children as well during the School term, they also positively relished the chance for a bit of slapstick at the Sing Song. It showed that there was no place for pomposity or hubris. This is an essential thing to remember if a teacher is to be a success.'

Later, according to Bec McInnes, Jacko appeared as a French Canadian Coureur Bois, with a plaid jacket and fur hat, and with his ukulele, played "Olga Polouski", and "Jean Baptiste and his Doggie". Finally, 'Joc as Headmaster came on to round out the evening. He sang a song about "The School along the Bardwell Road" to his own words and very much reflecting what had happened that term. We then linked hands and sang "Auld Lang Syne" which means long ago, and went off to unwind before bed.'[76]

Another interesting account of the Sing Song in my time is given by Gerd Sommerhoff:

On the last night of the autumn and lent terms,[77] the staff would entertain the boys to a little variety show, called the "Sing Song". It was performed on a rickety stage in the old assembly hall. So that the performers would not have to stand on their dignity (there was not

[74] Watkins, *Stand*, 48–9.
[75] MacInnes, *A Sense of Purpose*, 113.
[76] MacInnes, *A Sense of Purpose*, 115.
[77] Gerd says that this occurred in the Christmas and Easter terms, while Paul Watkins and the Term Notes state that there was also a Sing Song on the day before the end of the Summer Term.

much of that anyhow), no adults were admitted to the audience except other staff. At these occasions I would often play the part of a mad professor all of whose experiments went disastrously wrong.

The Sing Song would be concluded by the Headmaster's Song: a string of ditties sung by Jock, accompanied on the guitar by Chris, a classics teacher. In this song Jock would mention all the naughty things that had happened during the term which he was not supposed to know about: that midnight expedition of dormitory X, or that pint which had been one too many for teacher Y. But, if the crime was mentioned it was also thereby pardoned. One can imagine the boys' suspense before Jock started on his revelations. One can also admire the low cunning of this item. Since the prefects knew that any misdemeanour they might betray to Jock would also be forgiven, they had no qualms about slipping him enough information to give plenty of spice to his song. It was a brilliant way of keeping the Headmaster's finger on the pulse of events![78]

MacInnes comments that, 'The legacy of the Sing Song was that the children and staff laughed together. It was not a case of the children laughing at the staff ... self-parody...' Later, after he had left the school for some years, he reflected that 'I believe that the Sing Song was more important than any of us realised at the time.' This, he felt, was because 'As with the Sing Song, the dancing and the School Dance were a coming together. We were all equals again and it did much to reinforce a feeling for the School and to increase everyone's respect for it as an institution.'[79]

*

The last term of the year was special, partly because for one fifth of the children it was their last term, partly because uproarious events could usually take place outside, and particularly along the river, as well as indoors. One special event was the leavers' picnic, when we took strawberries and fruit drinks on punts up the Cherwell and played games and fooled around. In the summer of 1951, the Term Notes describe how, 'The leaver's picnic up the Cher followed the usual lines, short oblique ones from bank to bank, the only straight one of any length being the one followed by Tubby overland from the point of disembarkation to the Victoria Arms. A feature this year was a game of rounders between the boys and the junior members of the staff...'

Another description is of the picnic I went on in my last term, the Term Notes for 1955 describing how, 'The Cher had a bumper season, the adjective being particularly applicable to the closing stages of the Leavers'

---

[78] Sommerhoff, 83.
[79] MacInnes, 117.

Picnic.

There was also the 'Rag Regatta' which usually features in the Term Notes. That for 1951, for example, is described as follows: 'It is the last afternoon, and a large crowd is assembled at the river, drawn there by the rumour that the Rag Regatta is to finish with yet another show devised, produced, and directed by Gerd Sommerhoff. The show begins; the expected succession of startling apparitions, including an alligator, come round the corner of the Barge, and the spectators are just dropping into their usual 'nothing can surprise me now' frame of mind when round the corner of the Barge comes the Junior Headmaster on a horse – and they find that something still can.'

In 1952 the theme was 'Invasion through the Ages', and included the cooking of a missionary. The 1953's Notes contain the following description: 'The Rag Regatta developed along the usual lines. J.O.U. carried his female impersonation one step further, and, needless to add, one step too far. All the Australians on the Staff hurtled down the bank into the river on one small bicycle. But "the usual lines" hardly applies to the lines on which a simian "Ticks" swung himself across and above the river with the help of a hitherto unsuspected tail.' In my last year the Regatta features the staff in a Bathing Beauty Contest – cross-dressing again.

A central organizer of the event was Gerd Sommerhoff, and his description of several of these carnivalesque events is worth quoting:

> The end of the summer term would be marked by different frolics: a Rag Regatta on the river. The climax was always a set piece enacted by costumed members of the staff, and there was never a lack of volunteers, despite the convention that they would all finish up in the river before the show was over. For most of my years at the school I was put in charge of this event, since I was one of the few teachers who did not at that time have exams to correct or reports to write. It gave full scope to the imagination.
>
> One year, I remember, I decided to stage an invasion of ancient Britain by a contingent of Roman warriors from across the river. The invaders were to be equipped with a powerful ballista, designed to catapult missiles consisting of rotten fruit across the river at the community of ancient Britons whose menfolk were at the time happily engaged roasting a captured missionary in a barrel over a merry fire, while the wives looked on impassively from their spinning wheels. Secretly, however, it was also arranged that half the missiles would overshoot this target and hit the audience sitting on a slope beyond the main scene.[80]

---

[80] Sommerhoff, *Consciousness*, 84.

The account describes how, through a miscalculation, the missionary's feet were actually boiled and his screams were all too real!

Another year the theme was 'the conquest of the West, with Jock, dressed as an Indian chief, another was the Belles of St Trinians (all played by male members of the staff)' and 'a mock Royal Tournament at which the Royal Box consisted of two decorated chairs placed on top of the high diving board!'[81]

The Regatta was just the start of the day, for there was then a formal concert, a feast and afterwards a Sing Song. According to the Term Notes for Summer 1953, for example, 'The concert in the evening was so popular that it finished an hour late. The time-lag increased with the House Supper; and after a two hours sing-song it was hardly worth going to bed.'

Finally, 'By tradition, every five years Trial by Jury was produced, with the Headmaster as the judge, members of the staff as the learned counsel and drunken jurors (performed with amazing realism!), and the boys as the bridesmaids.'[82] This occurred during my time in Easter 1952, and the photographs, particularly of Joc looking slightly amused in an imposing wig, bring back dim memories of the event.

As we left the school, there might be some final last act of defiance and subversion. I don't remember any myself, but the Term Notes for summer 1954 mention that, 'In the last few days one expects some piece of somewhat eccentric behaviour on the part of those who are just about to become O.D.s, and this term was no exception.' This took the form of some pyjama-trousers on the School flagstaff.

*

Yet, in a way, Old Dragons never left, especially if they died in an heroic way. It is worth briefly considering one final unifying part of the ceremonial cycle, the Remembrance Day service at the memorial cross on the playing fields. These services in memory of the deaths of distinguished Dragons, several Victoria Crosses amongst them, were largely occasions of sadness rather than the extolling of military valour. The attitude and feelings are caught in the poetry of two Old Dragons of an earlier period. John Betjeman wrote in 'Summoned by Bells':

Before the hymn the Skipper would announce
The latest names of those who'd lost their lives
For King and Country and the Dragon School.
Sometimes his gruff voice was full of tears
When a particular favourite had been killed.

---

[81] Sommerhoff, *Consciousness*, 83.
[82] Sommerhoff, *Consciousness*, 82.

Then we would hear the nickname of the boy,
"Pongo" or "Podge", and how he'd played 3Q
For Oxford and, if only he had lived,
He might have played for England – which he did,
But in a grimmer game against the Hun,
And then we'd all look solemn, knowing well
There'd be no extra holiday today,
And we were told we each must do our bit,
And so we knitted shapeless gloves from string
For men in mine-sweepers, and on the map
We stuck the Allied flags along the Somme;
Visited wounded soldiers, learned by heart
Those patriotic lines of Oxenham
    What can a little chap do
    For his country and for you –
"He can boil his head in the stew",
We added, for the trenches and the guns
Meant less to us than bicycles and gangs
And marzipan and what there was for prep.[83]

The emphasis was on sacrifice – on repaying the sacrifices of those who had died in two world wars that we might live. Each Memorial Day when we were at the Dragon, one or two boys would read 'The Trust' by C.A. Alington. I do not remember this reading, but it was clearly important at the time.

THEY trusted God — Unslumbering and unsleeping.
He sees and sorrows for a world at war,
His ancient covenant securely keeping,
And these had seen His promise from afar,
That through the pain, the sorrow, and the sinning,
That righteous Judge the issue should decide
Who ruleth over all from the beginning —
And in that faith they died.
They trusted England — Scarce the prayer was spoken
Ere they beheld what they had hungered for,
A mighty country with its ranks unbroken,
A city built in unity once more;
Freedom's best champion, girt for yet another
And mightier enterprise for Right defied,

A land whose children live to serve their Mother

---

[83] From Betjeman, *Summoned By Bells*, 44.

And in that faith they died.
And us they trusted ; we the task inherit,
The unfinished task for which their lives were spent;
But leaving us a portion of their spirit
They gave their witness and they died content.

Full well they knew they could not build without us
That better country, faint and far descried,
God's own true England; but they did not doubt us —
And in that faith they died.[84]

The reading of this poem helped create the mood celebrated in
another Dragon poet's lines about the Remembrance Day service, in 'No
Ordinary Sunday' by Jon Stallworthy.[85] The second and third verses are as
follows.

A granite cross, the school field underfoot,
Inaudible prayers, hymn-sheets that stirred
Too loudly in the hand. When hymns rang out,
Silence, like silt, lay round so wide and deep
It seemed that winter held its breath. We hear
Only the river talking in its sleep:
Until the bugler flexed his lips, and sound
Cutting the fog cleanly like a bird,
Circled and sang out over the bandaged ground.

Then, low-voiced, the headmaster called the roll
Of those who could not answer every name
Suffixed with honour – 'double first', 'kept goal
For Cambridge' – and a death – in spitfires, tanks,
And ships torpedoed. At his call there came
Through the mist blond heroes in broad ranks
With rainbows struggling on their chests. Ahead
Of us, in strict step, as we idled home
Marched the formations of the towering dead.

I did mention the Remembrance Service in my letters, for instance, on
2 November 1954 writing to my mother that, *There is a service on the field
in commemoration of the two world wars and it was poppy day the day
before yesterday, and Guy Fawkes day was yesterday.* I also noticed the
tears in the voice of the Skipper's nephew, Joc, at another moving

---

[84] From *Valour and Vision: Poems of the War*, ed. Jacqueline Trotter, (1920), 120.
[85] Reprinted in Desmond Devitt (ed.), *A Diversity of Dragons* (2003)

81

occasion, namely the death of the King. On 11 February 1952 I wrote home that *Jock made a very good speech on the day the king died and he was nearly crying and he was faltering. And lots of people were crying.*

PASSING THROUGH

School House, to which we moved after a couple of years. The tennis lawn in the foreground was the scene of winter skating. The boys' locker room where we sang in the evenings is on the ground floor, left.

10 EARLY YEARS

I do not recollect my departure from Broadstone for the Dragon in September 1950, though the moment was caught in a photograph which shows me in my Dragon uniform, with my suitcase, and accompanied by my grandmother. We are standing in the drive of our house in Dorset, presumably in later September, from where I would proceed to Broadstone railway station, then to Paddington, and on to Oxford. I am wearing the dark blue uniform, a tie, long socks and lace-up shoes and a rather apprehensive smile.

The next three months are a blur. I do not remember the details of the reception I received or the misery, except for some mild hazing or initiation rituals involving being made to jump off chairs blindfold and so on. The only external account of myself is that by my mother, who had arrived back from India in October 1950. She came to visit me towards the end of my first term. In a somewhat damaged and incomplete letter to my father she described the encounter with the little boy whom she had left two years earlier when he was aged six-and-three-quarters.

December, Linton Lodge, Oxford

As you see I have given in and come to see Alan – chiefly because it'll be difficult to get away at the end of term as Fiona's dancing class are having their 'ballet' then – so he'll be coming back on his own and I couldn't wait until the holidays could I?! Anyway here I am holed up in a very comfortable, warm room and feeling confused and a little sad but mostly relieved. I arrived after lunch and after an uneventful journey and was feeling pretty scared when I walked up to the front door of 6, Bardwell Road as you can imagine. Alan finally emerged from a room on my left and greeted me with a scared glance and a mumble that he had lost his shoe and disappeared into a pile of mackintoshes. I had been steeling myself for something of the sort and anyway hadn't time to burst into tears as matrons and housemasters wives appeared on all sides and had to be coped with. We got away in a few minutes. My heart sank rather at the completely silent little boy at my side – he has changed even more than Fiona and is no longer the 'heart throb' of the family. Actually I didn't think he was looking very well, his face is much thinner and he has deep black lines under his eyes again and frowned a lot, however I hasten to add that he seems very happy at school and I expect after this first term (which is bound to be a strain) will probably lose that anxious expression. It must have been an ordeal meeting me again and he told me later he didn't recognise me.

We had lunch here and he thawed a lot, and afterwards he taught me 'knock-out Whist' a whizzo game that is the rage at school now. I had to be careful not to win too much and after we had evened the score satisfactorily we set off for the shops, where he was to choose himself a present. Oxford seems fuller than ever, we had to let several buses go and were finally disgorged into a seething mass of humanity that became perfectly impenetrable outside 'Marks and Spencers' – Alan finally had the bright idea of following the queue in at one side of the door and then skipping across the shop and following the outgoing queue into the street again. If we hadn't done this I think we'd have been wedged there yet! We tramped round for a solid hour trying to find that chemist's shop with toys downstairs that we used to go to, but couldn't track it down. However found a shop with 'FROG' model aeroplanes and bought one of those. Then we had a nice tea and caught a bus back quite easily and had a couple more games of cards before it was time to take him home. His house is a most friendly place, and a small girl in a dressing gown was sliding down the banisters when we got in, the housemasters daughter, announcing that she was going to.... [the rest is missing]

*

Here I will stick to the objective, outside, world of formal of classwork and reports.

The Dragon was a very large school, with over 400 pupils, and consequently broken into many classes and sets. The structure of these needs to be explained briefly. The pupils were allocated to the classes on the basis of their proficiency in the core subject of Latin. They were allocated to sets independently of this, again on ability. So someone could be in a high class in Latin, a low set in French, high set in mathematics etc.

There were six classes in the Lower school (Lower 1-6) seven in the Middle (Middle 1-7) , and ten in the Upper School, (Upper 1, 2A,2B,3A,3B,3C, 4A,4B, 5, 6, 7). The subject sets ran from A through to D, each letter having five sets (A1, A2, A3, A4, A5, for example). Only in the bottom three classes, Lower 4, 5 and Lower 6 were the classes and the sets the same – thus all pupils in Lower 4 were in sets Lower 4 for everything.

I seem to have gone in at the second to bottom, Lower 5, and hence at the start my subject sets were the same as my class. I was taught by Mrs

A.T. Owen (Ma Owen), whom I remember as a rather kindly figure and who first presented to me the shocking complexities not only of a foreign language, but one with so much grammar. We were, I believe, taught out of Kennedy's 'Shorter Latin Primer' (which we modified to 'Eating Grammar'), though it may also, or instead, have been from L.A. Wilding's 'Latin Course for Schools', Wilding being the senior Latin master at the Dragon. I vaguely remember the puzzlement of having to decline and conjugate verbs, the effort of learning 'amo, amas, amat, amamus,...', the rest escapes me. Yet the first report I have, the fortnightly one written on October 7 by Mrs Owen, states that in a form of 16 I was equal 10 and had made 'A satisfactory start'.

In all other topics we were in sets, numbered from A to E, and with five divisions 1 to 5 in each. I was in E3 for English, and was equal fifth. My report from Mrs Owen reports that for English: 'Good, intelligent work'. In French I was in the same Lower 5 class and there was no placing. The comment by BD was 'Satisfactory'. My best subject was mathematics where, although I was in E5, the lowest class, MPS noted 'Good work', and I was equal first out of thirteen.

I have preserved no more fortnightly reports for this term, but do have the termly report in December 1950 when I was aged 8.11. I was never absent, so my health seems to have been all right. In Classics, a month above the average age, I was tenth out of sixteen in term marks and fifth in the exams – amazing that we were already doing exams! Mrs Owen commented here that I was, 'A quiet little person, who promises well – he is an excellent examinee.' In English I was again a month over the average age and was seventh out of sixteen and second in exams. Mrs Owen noted – 'Good – v. keen and interested in all he does'.

In Geography there is as yet no set given but I was fifth and it was 'A good term's work' according to J.W. In French, however, I was 15 out 16 in both marks and exams, and it was commented (and emphasized in the headmaster's red ink) 'Slow progress: more effort please'. In Divinity I was 'keen and accurate', again according to Mrs Owen, and in Biology there was 'Very neat and accurate work' according to EAB. Mathematics was my best subject. In Set E4, out of fifteen, I was equal third in marks but only equal sixth in the exams. RCM (whom I recall as Mrs Mumford) wrote, 'A very good term's work with a disappointing drop in the exams.' My housemaster, L.C. Plummer, wrote he 'Has settled down very well' and the Junior headmaster, Joc Lynam wrote 'Mostly good work.'

It is worth noting in this most important of terms, with its negative portrayal by my mother, that my art and handicrafts were reported on encouragingly and that I played rugger 'with incredible dash'. It does not seem to have been as gloomy as I dimly remember. Indeed, apart from a continuing frown of concentration and a serious demeanour, remembered to this day by some of my friends, I seem to have been moderately happy right from the start.

*

I have one fortnightly report on 1 March 1951 for this spring term. I was first out of 14 in Latin, and Plummer commented 'Well done!' I was ninth out of fifteen in English, which was 'very fair'. My Mathematics was 'Satisfactory work' and I was 9 out of 16, and 8 out of 16 in French exams, with 'Satisfactory progress'. The headmaster commented 'Good'.

At the end of my second term, in March 1951 when I was nine years three months, the termly report showed that I had been quite ill, absent for 13 days, by far the largest number of any term at the Dragon. I had caught both flu and chicken pox.

The report in general was a considerable improvement on the previous one, and my mother's return from India and the Christmas holiday, the first together for three years, may have helped.

I was up one class in Classics, in Lower 4, and my age was just one month less than the class average. There was no exam this term, but I was equal tenth out of 15. Mrs Mumford wrote, 'He has at last realised that there is real satisfaction to be gained from work well done. Some pleasing progress latterly.' She also taught me English/History (the reports always came together for these subjects) where I was up a set in E2 and was equal eighth out of 15 and in English my 'Written work shows marked improvement' and 'Some good History results'. She also taught me Mathematics in the same set as before, E4, where I was now equal first out of 16 with 'A term of very good progress'. I had 'worked well' in Geography and in French was up a set in E2 where I was 9 out of 15 and there is the comment that, 'He has gained self confidence and made good progress'. Mrs Mumford also taught divinity where I was 'Good' and in Biology it was 'Very good work'. The housemaster commented 'A good term. He is coming on well', and the headmaster wrote 'Alan has come on admirably all round.' The fact that it was the soccer term, where I was 'keen and skilful' may also have helped.

Then came the school holidays. At the end, on 24 April my mother wrote *This week I've got to get Alan cleaned and mended up for school and his trunk off in advance quite when I don't know!* Five days later she wrote of my imminent departure: *it was all great fun but tiring and I'm quite glad the holidays are drawing to their close! ...I shall miss him so much, he is more of a companion to me than the girls are yet. And is a very affectionate little boy, although terribly irritating at times!*

On 1 May my grandfather noted in his diary 'Saw Alan off to school'. On 6 May my mother wrote a revealing piece about the tension between holidays and school and some of my character at this point.

Alan went off on Tuesday, very cheerfully I was glad to see. I think he was quite looking forward to being among the 'chaps' again... Anne and I took him by train to Bournemouth station and he didn't seem at all worried at the thought of the 3 and a half hour train journey. He was well supplied with comics and would have lunch to break the monotony. He was looking so well when he left, fat rosy cheeks and his hair bright and curly. When I take him out from school he has dark lines under his eyes and the little hair they leave him is plastered to his head and he looks awful.

On 23 May my mother wrote: *I must write to Alan now. I enclose his first report, thank goodness he has your ability to do sums. His letters have been a couple of scrawls saying when is half term and the end of term and could I send him a tennis ball and some lemonade powder!* On 6 June my mother wrote *I heard from Alan yesterday, six riddles and the startling news that they were wearing Aertex vests! He seems happy though.*

There are four fortnightly reports for the summer term which I shall give in a little more detail as my copy of the termly report for the summer term is missing, though I do have The Draconian summary of the term. In Latin I was in the same class of 16 and was 8, equal 8 (twice) and 9. I note that a number of the boys in this class later went on to win scholarships to top public schools and I was above a number in lower classes who later overtook me. In English/History I had moved up to set E1 and was around the middle of the class. The comments were, 'Some improved written work. Come on well.' 'Most satisfactory', 'A very good essay. History less good.', and 'An all round improvement. A big effort in the exams please.' Both subjects were still taught by Miss Mumford. In French there was no placing in the fortnightly reports but I ended up equal 15 by the end of term. I made 'a fair start', was 'V. fair', 'improving' and 'V. fair'.

Mathematics was again my best subject. In the first report by **MHB** I was up two sets into E2 and was equal first out of 17 with the comment, 'Very good'. The next week I was back with Mrs Owen but up one set to E1 where I was equal eighth out of 17 and 'Quite promising'. I ended up the term as equal eighth. The headmaster's comments were 'doing well' and 'good' three times. It is worth noting that the amount of care taken to report back with these fortnightly reports sent to our parents with our letters is rather impressive.

There was no housemaster's report on the fortnightly reports, but my headmaster commented that I was 'doing well' and then 'good' in the next three reports.

I was clearly aware of the high standards of the school, noting in an undated letter in the summer term, *We had no prep on Monday because ther was seven scholarships 1st 9th 14th at Winchester 1st at eaten 4th at charter house and a few other ones.* The first scholarships at Eton and

Winchester were special and were noted in the Term Notes as leading to 'unconditional no-prep' and described in the Century History of the school as follows. '1951 will always be remembered as The Year of the Double Top, when the first place on the Winchester Roll was won by John Dunbabin and on the Eton Roll by Luke Hodgkin.'[86]

*

My father took me back to school for my second year on 24 September 1951, according to my grandfather's diary. This was the only time he took me to school in my time there. I wrote a couple of weeks later from 6 Bardwell Road, on 17 October: *Dear mommy, I hope you are very well. Actually there are 6 new people in our house and one of them are in our dorm....* That term there are a couple of letters from me and several from my mother who spent some time in hospital being tested for tropical diseases.

There are two fortnightly reports which talk of 'a very fair start', 'some good work', 'good progress', and so on. I had now moved up to M7, that is middle seven. My form teacher was also my housemaster, Mr Plummer. I was clearly fit as I missed no days during the first term. In Classics I scraped along. Plummer wrote, 'Very fair. He could have done much better with a little more effort.' Likewise in French it stated 'Takes things much too easily. Is capable of good work when he really tries.' In English and history, 'Has come on well in history'. Likewise in geography, 'Good steady work'. I was also taught by Plummer in mathematics – I had made 'Good progress'. Both my divinity and science were satisfactory and my housemaster's report was 'A good term', and the headmaster wrote 'Much good work. Some improvement will be hoped for in certain subjects.'

At this time my parents were still both at home and I was looking forward to my first family Christmas since India, but no doubt also aware that they would both be leaving again at the end of the winter holidays.

After Christmas my parents left shortly after I went off to school. On 18 January I wrote to my grandmother

Dear Granny, Please could you tell me what the Adress is of mummy. I hope this letter gets to you in time. And will you tell mummy that I have got one of her yellow gloves lots of love to mummy the girls daddy. And lots of love to you and Grandpa Love Alan. And pleas when you right tell me wether Ordanary envelopes are allright.

A few days later I wrote again, *Dear Granny, I hope you and Grandpa*

[86] Jaques, *Centenary*, 192.

are well I should think this letter will be After mommy has gone off. I am enjoying school Already and the days are much quicker now. A couple of days after this on 22 January my grandfather noted in his diary, 'V sees Iris and Mac off in Billy's Car'.

*

In the school reports for the next term-and-a-half there are signs of a diminution in my effort and energy. It is true that I was ill for seven days in the term, and one of my mother's letters refers to this. On 3 March 1952 she wrote *Thank you for your letter this week, but we were sorry to hear you'd been in bed a week, was it your cold or something else? I hope you're quite alright now.* But this may not have been the root problem.

I was still in Middle 7, but had moved up in sets in all other subjects and may have been pushed beyond my level. In classics I did 'Variable work. When he really tries hard he does quite well.' In English, 'Rather colourless work and lacking in drive'. In French, 'Has done some satisfactory work – but more effort and perseverance are still necessary'. In mathematics, 'His work is good, but he is held back at present by being so slow in his written work.' All this suggests a loss of impetus and even in art I was, 'still using weak colour'. Games were fine as was science and geography, but even divinity was only 'very fair'. On the other hand the housemaster was enthusiastic, 'A very good term', though the headmaster noted 'Moderate results. Alan must <u>go hard.</u>'

On 30 April, after an Easter holiday with neither my parents nor sisters in England, I wrote to Assam, *I am writing this Just before going to school robert is taking me to Watrloo and he will put me into the Oxford train at paddington.*

The summer term started well with a fortnightly report on May 17 where I came second in Latin which was, 'A most encouraging start'. Other subjects were satisfactory and 'mostly good'. I did not miss any school this term. The results and reports suggest a slight improvement.

My uncle Richard took me out once this term, my grandfather noting on 2 May, 'Richard takes Alan out at Oxford', and again by my grandmother on 28 June, 'V goes to Oxford to see Alan'. I do not recall these visits, nor the journey home at the end of term, when I arrived finally at Broadstone where on 24 July, 'V fetches Alan from Broadstone'.

There is a little evidence that, perhaps because the effects of my parents leaving home began to be offset with the plans being discussed for my visit by air to them in December, I began to pick up. In French there was, 'A considerable improvement during the latter half of the term – reflected in a good exam result'. The housemaster thought I had had, 'A very good term', but the headmaster wrote 'Results at present moderate. We hope for a "big push" next term.'

90

On 22 September 1952 my grandfather noted, 'Alan leaves for school'. My first fortnightly report for the Christmas term on 4 October showed that I had moved up from Middle 7 to Middle 3. This was a class run by J.D. Briton, whom I vaguely remember as a pleasant teacher. He noted, 'A satisfactory start'. In mathematics, I had only moved up two sets from C4 to C2 and was next to bottom at number 17 – which was only 'Fair'. In French I was only up one set to C4 and was equal ninth out of 17, 'very fair for a start'. In all, the headmaster thought this 'Moderate'.

The end of term report, when I was 10 years 11 months, shows that I had missed no days through illness. I was three or four months over the average age in Latin class and in all my sets. My classics report was again weak. 'With more effort, he would make the progress, of which at intervals he shows himself capable.' In mathematics 'He is rather slow and appears to find the work difficult.' In French I was 'Quite good – and with even more care over his written work he will become much better.' My geography and divinity were 'Satisfactory' and my Science, with Gerd Sommerhoff for the first time, was 'Good'. My only real improvement was in English. Joc Lynam as housemaster commented, 'Coming along well', and the senior headmaster A.E. Lynam, 'Moderate success in school work'.

Even before I left for school I was anticipating with excitement the trip by air to Assam which I would take after the end of term. On 19 September I wrote to my parents. *I am getting excited about my trip to India. How nice it will be to see you all again. Best love to you all Alan.* On 12 October I wrote, *We have had thick frost here and I expect we will be having snow quite soon it is only about another 6 weeks till the end of the term, and it goes quite quickly.* A week later I wrote, *Dear mummy and daddy it is only a very little time till I will be seeing you again.* And then, just before the end of term, I wrote on 7 December, *There are only 9 days untill the end of term so I will probably arrive about a week after this.* It looks as if I went straight to London from school, for on 16 December my grandfather notes, 'Violet leaves for London' and the next day 'Alan flies to India'. Sadly I have no real memory of India or being with my family again.

I arrived back by Comet, on 15 January 1953 and was met by my grandmother. I probably went straight to the Dragon as my grandfather notes on 22 January, *parcel of Alan's clothes to matron*, presumably because they could not go in my school trunk. Certainly by the 18, three days after I arrived back, I wrote from the Dragon *I am in the same form and dorm but I have moved up to 4 from 6 in soccer.*

I was clearly looking forward to the end of term, writing on 1 March *Dear Mummy and Daddy, there is only about four more weeks until the end of the term.* Two weeks later on the 15 I was more explicit. *There is only about 13 more days until the end of term and I am getting very exited.* But it seems not to have been too bad a term, unless I was keeping up a brave front, since I wrote on 25 March to my parents from home that, *It was nice getting back to By-the-way after a very pleasant term.*

There are no surviving fortnightly reports for this term, but that of March shows that I was doing well in all subjects except the crucial one of Latin. Even the housemaster, Joc, commented that though I was 'Coming on well', 'He must go very hard at his Latin.'

Most interesting is the report on English, where the effect of going to Assam might be behind part of the change. Although I was only 11 out of 17, the report was, 'Very satisfactory. Lately I have been much delighted by the vividness of his essays.'

There was then an Easter holiday and my mother, remembering her own school days, wrote towards the end of them in commiseration on 24 April. *Darling Alan, No letter from you this week, perhaps you've been too busy! I suppose you're beginning to think of the end of the hols now, depressing thought, but the summer term is the best really isn't it?* I wrote six days later, on 30 quite cheerfully. *This is the last day of my holls... I have got a new cricket bat to take to sckool and a new watch wich is lovely...* My grandmother's comment, appended to my letter, is revealing. *He comes back from school so mute and quiet but returns to his own cheery – even cheeky – self and he <u>does</u> look grand.*

On 3 May I wrote with a picture of my new dormitory and the placing of my bed in it, as follows: *I have been at school for 2 and a half days so far. I am in a dorm called Pheonix wich is a big dorm and I am having jolly good fun.* I suffered an accident shortly afterwards as I wrote on 18 May that, *I have been off games for a week because I was hit on the eye by a cricket ball.* But since I missed no days of school this term, it was clearly not too bad.

*

The big event of the term was the coronation of Queen Elizabeth on 2 June. I remember this as traumatic for a strange reason. I had a box brownie camera and lent it to a bigger boy who said he would take some photographs of the procession to which he was going. When I received the prints they were totally hopeless – I have one or two still which show just a few heads. He kept asking me how they were and I was too ashamed to admit they were terrible – a farce that went on for some weeks as I tried to avoid meeting him in the playground. This has remained indelibly with me

92

– along with the dispiriting photos.

As for the lavish events of the day put on by the school, I can't remember anything. They are described, however, in the Term Notes for Summer 1953 as follows. 'The day began, decently late, with bacon and eggs and a Coronation pencil all round. And for the rest of the morning the television screen in the New Hall was the focus of attention, and in excellent focus too. And a good many of us were soon feeling a little uncomfortable about the lukewarm, or even hostile, reception given to television on its arrival last term.' Further excitements included an Emmett train, and, 'an evening party in the New Hall, including musical chairs – an elongated fiery Dragon along the river bank and fireworks – finally a hot sausage on a stick on the way to bed, and the unusual experience of saying 'Good morning instead of Goodnight...' It is strange to me that I do not even remember the special hot sausage. Nor do I remember the events, fun fair, fete, bicycle games and other excitements described in meticulous detail in a number of articles in the same issue of The Draconian, and illustrated with a series of photographs.

My mother wrote about this event on 5 June.

Darling Alan, So the excitement is over, and everything back to normal again I suppose – here we haven't felt it the same way but we managed to get all the commentaries on the wireless, not the same as Television which must have been wonderful... That seems about the lot darling, no letter from you this week, hope all is well, I expect there was too much going on. Send us the pictures of the Coronation if they come out.

Lots and lots of love, Mummy x x x x

I am glad that she added 'if they come out'.

None of my letters for this June have survived, but on 2 July there is the first reference to school exams. I wrote, *There are only eight more days untill we go home. We have done the science exam and the Geography exam.* I also have my first school prize beside me, for 'Middle 3 for Recitation', signed by Hum.

*

I arrived home on 21 July, and my school report arrived either with me or slightly later. It is worth noting a real delight on the part of my mother that, at last, I seemed to be picking up. On 13 August she wrote, *No letter from you yet these hols, but I know you've been very busy one way and another! We got your report last week, very good, Daddy and I were thrilled and Daddy promises me he is going to write to you about it to-morrow. Jolly good show.*

The final term report when I was aged eleven years six months showed that I was not away ill. In classics, 'He has not found the work easy, but has made splendid efforts'. In English and history I was, 'Very good. One of the most enthusiastic and improved members of a goodish set.' In mathematics I was first in both term and exam marks and the report was, 'Good, steady work. Well done!' In my letter on 6 July I had noted, *We had the Ned Bathew wich is a maths paper and I got 77/100 I was =35 out of three hundred.*

In French, likewise, I was first in both term and exam marks and was 'Excellent!' Only in science was I now only 'Quite good' and even 'Weak' in geography. The housemaster wrote 'Does well in his quiet way', and Hum wrote, 'Admirable work and progress'.

This was indeed by far the best report I had received so far at the school and the first time that I was coming top in one or two subjects. After a real struggle with both French and Latin I was increasingly able to master language and grammar. I really seem to have pulled up. I suspect that at this time the school still had hopes, after three years, that I might be in the upper stream.

11 PARADISE

I returned for the start of my fourth year and wrote to my parents on 27 September, *Dear Mummy and Daddy, I hope all is well out there. I am back at scool now. I have moved up two forms And I have moved up 5 sets in maths, English, French. I am in 3 game.*

I wrote several letters home in the first term, but hardly noted anything more about formal instruction except that on 30 November I wrote, *We had the Geography Exam on Thursday.* I also noted that, *There is only about another 2 and a half weeks left until the end of term and exactly 3 weeks untill my birthday.* The term obviously ended in mid-December and I either went from school, or immediately from Dorset, to Scotland, for on 15 December, as my grandfather noted in his diary, 'V. goes to London to send Alan off to Scotland.'

The termly report shows that I missed no days at school. In Classics it was 'Steady work and progress'. There was, 'Very good progress in both English and History'. In maths, 'Much good work. He has made steady progress'. In French 'Quite keen work. Grammar good.' Other subjects were 'good' and the housemaster Joc noted 'Continues to do well', Hum the headmaster commented 'Alan has come on well'.

In all subjects I did better in exams than in the term marks, so there was hope. But I was still in a rather middling level of class and stream and not moving into being a high flyer, the sort the school spotted as potential scholarship boys for Eton and Winchester, though they may already have realized that my parents were unlikely to enter me for such expensive places.

*

After spending the Christmas holidays with my godmother and aunt in Scotland, I returned south.

I wrote to my parents on 17 January that, *I have been back at school two days and so I have not much to say I am in 1st game and with considarable luck I might get into the first 11... We have had lovely weather at school already but I don't doubt there will be bad weather and diseases ahead Well thats all for now Lots of love Alan.* In fact, if there were diseases, I do not seem to have been affected by them since I missed no days at school.

A letter home describes the bitter weather with a good deal of skating, and I was obviously cold, but seem cheerful. On 2 February I wrote: *we have had freezing weather. And I have not played any games (except ice hockey). We have had a wizard time except for the cold as I have lost my gloves.* Two weeks later I mention that, *The end of term is on the 26th of March,* and sure enough my grandfather in his diary mentions on that date 'Alan arrives back'.

The term report was encouraging and I also appear, significantly, to be enjoying myself. In classics there is 'Good, steady work and progress – and there have been more smiles than last term!' In English it is 'Quite good all round'. In mathematics 'Very good work and progress this term'. Even in Geography I am 'Keen and interested'. My divinity is still a tick and now my Science is 'Very good'. Not only did Mr Wilkinson note my smile, but also Joc my housemaster noted, 'Doing well and smiling more.' The headmaster Hum wrote 'Most satisfactory work and progress'.

The frequent references to smiling reminds me that sometime in my third year I was offered two shillings and sixpence by the matron in the School House if she ever saw me smiling – and I don't recall her ever having to pay me. My mother also talks about my anxious look. Others have commented that I was very quiet and subdued. I was clearly quite a repressed little boy, small for my age and filled with a certain sadness, or at least anxiety – though whether this was mainly the effect of my mother leaving me, or the boarding atmosphere (my grandmother's comments on how I revived with good food and freedom in the holidays is indicative here) it is difficult to say.

*

My increasing smiles may have been linked to my knowledge that my mother would be returning within a few months. After the Easter holidays I wrote on 6 June to my father, *Dear Daddy, I hope you are not feeling too lonely without Mummy there.* My grandfather notes in his diary on 12 June, 'Iris arrives in England [Iris here, flight no. BA919]' and the next day, 'Meet Iris'.

My mother soon decided to visit me at school, writing to my father on 21 June *We're going to Oxford this week-end to see Alan. I hope it won't be too ruinous, but will be our last big expense...* My grandfather notes that she left for Oxford on 26 June and returned on the 28.

My memory of this, or perhaps another, re-union is painful. I awaited the precious mother I had not seen for eighteen months, having said I would be by the pillar box on the corner of Bardwell Road and Charlbury Road. Finally a figure emerged from a taxi. Instead of the beautiful lady I thought I remembered, a small, limping, woman emerged. I had somehow not noted before that polio had given her a limp. I was so ashamed that when we walked off I walked a good few feet behind (or in front) of her so that my friends would not realize that this was my mother. It seems that she also had my two sisters with her, but I cannot recall that part.

Since there are only a few accounts of my mother's visits to take me out, which give some insights into how she perceived the school and how she found me, I shall quote a lengthy letter she wrote the day after she returned from the Oxford visit which continued with a trip to the zoo in London.

She wrote to my father on 29 June as follows.

My dearest, I took my paper with me to Oxford, but didn't find a minute to write so I'm afraid this will be overdue... we got back at 10 p.m last night and I'm still aching all over from the almost non-stop catching of trains and buses which the week-end involved. It was most exhausting and expensive but of course lovely to see Alan again, just the same, he doesn't appear to have grown much but was looking very well and was full of chat. We left Bournemouth soon after nine and got to Oxford a bit late, about 1.20, then had to queue for a taxi so arrived panting at the school to be met by the matron with the vague information that Alan "might be anywhere"! There were thousands of small boys swarming everywhere and I thought I'd never find him, was getting hysterical and the taxi driver nasty, when he eventually appeared and we raced to Linton Lodge arriving as they were clearing away lunch! However we got some (at vast expense) and then carted ourselves and luggage back to our hotel in the Cornmarket. It was a gloomy place run by two old ladies and only served meals on Sundays, so we had to trail out to look for tea, back to the Dragon for "Macbeth", back again to look for supper and finally to bed at 11 p.m. frozen cold as I'd forgotten my bottle! "Macbeth" was very well done really, but as usual one could see nothing except the hats in front, the girls were thrilled however and Anne kept up a running commentary which my neighbours said "made the show" for them. Ann, when Lady M. appeared in her nightie – "Ah, here comes an angel"! and after the murder when she appeared surprised – "She knows perfectly well whats happened" in an indignant voice! The boys were word-perfect but fearfully pompous and droney, I was struggling not to giggle half the time and when Lady M. slapped her bony chest and shouted "I have given suck and know how sweet to love the babe that milks me" I nearly collapsed on the spot. Everyone else was frightfully impressed so I fear I must be flippant. We went to the service next day and the same lot of little boys got up and droned again, this time they read us Shakespeare's best known sonnet (after explaining carefully what it meant!) and a long excerpt from "Faust" – can't think why, but they were all so pleased with themselves. It was very hot in the hall and several boys were sick so I was glad when the service was over. As usual I spoke to nobody and no-one to me and was quite glad to get away from the place – not a satisfactory school from my point of view. Robert joined us for lunch, very smooth and undergraddish, off to Goodwood one week-end and Henly the next ("Going in a party, care to join us old chum"?!). He suggested we took a bus to Cumnor and walked to Bablock Hythe which was only about 5 minutes – we actually walked for 40 minutes, and after a row on the river and a long tea we looked for the buses back and found the next was 9.30 p.m! It was then 6 but Robert said we could easily thumb a lift so he and Alan went on ahead and sailed off in a car almost at once, we walked and thumbed without success and finally got the 9.15 bus – I'll leave you to guess what the 3 and a half hours were like! It even rained! On Monday, yesterday, I took them all up to London to the zoo – not as crazy or extravagant as it sounds – the trains from Oxford here are so bad I would have to stay another night there and fed and amused them all day so it wouldn't have worked out any cheaper and I didn't know what to do with them in Oxford anyway.

*

The term continued and towards the end my mother wrote to my father on 19 July, three days before her birthday, *Alan is coming back on Thursday (a nice birthday present) and Robert is coming with him so the fun starts.* I arrived on her birthday, as my grandfather noted in his diary: 'Robert and Alan arrive'. My mother reports on me three days later in a letter on 25 July to my father.

Quite an eventful week and the house is bulging at the seams with Robert and Alan back, its great fun to be held up by masked gunmen behind every door and the stutter of machine gun fire echoes down Corfe Lodge Road to the discomfort of the few of them who aren't stone deaf. Alan looks very fit but is slightly husky, he was very pleased as he got his cricket tie before leaving ("by some fluke") and has brought back a picture of himself in his team which I'll send onto you – he looks terribly tough but rather sweet! He and the girls get on very well at the moment.

The termly report when I was aged twelve-and-a-half shows that I was not absent at all. I was till in the same classes and sets. In classics I had, 'Worked hard and has made definite progress.' In English C.H. Jacques or 'Jacko' wrote 'A good Term. Quite a flair for writing; and knows some History.' In mathematics I was 'coming on well'. In French also I was,

98

'Coming on well: he has ability and with real hard work he should make this a strong subject'. In geography I was 'much improved: a better understanding of the subject'. My divinity was good and my science very good. Joc my housemaster thought it 'A very good term' and Hum wrote that, 'Alan has done well – rather older than the form age average.'

So, by the end of my fourth year I was still in the Middle Stream, and in the final year had to move as far up the ten classes in the Upper stream (1a, 1b, 2a, 2b, 3a, 3b etc.) as possible. It was a big challenge.

*

My grandfather noted in his diary on 21 September, 'Alan goes to school'. Two days later my mother wrote to my father that, *Alan went off very cheerfully, I haven't heard if he arrived, he was to spend the day with my godmother in London and catch the train to Oxford in the evening.* I was travelling from the Lake District on my own, after the family had moved from Dorset to the north.

My mother was clearly worried about my academic progress and, particularly, having already been accepted in principle by Sedbergh School, whether I would pass the essential Common Entrance exam. On 30 September she wrote to my father, *Alan writes to say he is in 1st game at rugger – don't know if that is the 1st XV – and has gone up in form. I must find out if he's going to pass his common entrance. He says he took the exam last term and passed so there's no reason why he shouldn't next year.* Shortly after, on 10 October, she wrote proudly of some of my achievements; *Alan is in 1st game at Rugger so may be in the team. I've found the picture of him in his cricket team and will send it separately. I wish I could see him playing in a match, perhaps we will next summer.*

I hardly wrote about my intellectual pursuits except on 2 November when I wrote to my father about one of my favourite subjects, science. *I am in the science club and at the moment I am making a one valve wireless set.*

*

There is a revealing and detailed account of a further visit paid by my mother to the school. The two main aims were to watch me in the opera Iolanthe and to talk to the headmaster Joc Lynam about how I was getting on and, in particular, whether I would pass my exams. She wrote to my father on 14 November.

I'm just back from a Sunday taking Alan out, and am sitting in my cheerless hotel room feeling very tired and a bit sad as I always do after leaving him, wish you were here to take me out and give me a brandy! But I was very pleased with Alan who looks very well and was most cheerful and full of chat.... I went to the evening performance of

"Iolanthe", meeting Robert at the door, and being related to a performer we had good seats and it was really very well done. Alan was nearly invisible under an enormous coronet and being second row chorus was hidden a lot of the time but didn't disgrace me by dropping anything or singing out of turn. After the show parents of performers were invited to a fork supper by Joc, and Robert and I ate ourselves to a standstill and drank a lot of cider but of course nobody spoke to us and when we were full we quietly left! I went to chapel service this morning and afterwards had my interview with Joc. He was very charming, gave me a sherry, and said Alan would definitely get through his Common Entrance but didn't think there was much hope of a scholarship but he would discuss this with his masters at more length. He said Alan was very popular with the other boys and with the staff which pleased me as Alan never introduces me to his friends or in fact mentions them! He also praised his rugger, especially his tackling which was marvellous he said, poor Alan, he told me he never enjoyed a game of rugger till it was over! Joc said there was terrific excitement over his Colours, much more than over the average boys, all of which pleased me a lot and will you too I'm sure, apparently he isn't the problem we have always imagined him to be! Robert joined us for lunch and we spent the afternoon in the usual way playing ping pong etc then ate a large tea and watched children's TV, which was a pirate play but the large meals and over-heated hotel were beginning to tell on me and I dozed through most of it. After that there was nothing to do but read for an hour and then I took him back and caught the bus back here and here I am! I have a front room and the traffic kept me awake most of last night, hence my more than usual weariness, also have a sore throat so am in for a cold I expect.

*

Strangely, though I had gone home a few days early because of flu, the Termly Report noted me as not missing any days – perhaps taking a child away on the suggestion of the school did not count as absence. In classics it was, 'A good term's work: he works neatly and sensibly and should do well.' In English it was, 'A very good term's work'. In mathematics I was just younger than average in the second to top set, and came equal tenth out of fifteen in term marks and eight in exams. This was, 'A fair terms work – he tries hard and has made good progress in recent weeks.' In French there was, 'Much good work. He is coming on well.' My other subjects were mainly satisfactory. The housemaster Joc again noted that I was getting ever more cheerful. 'A thoroughly good term all round – with the smile emerging most satisfactorily!' Hum wrote 'Good work and progress'. Clearly I was now climbing fairly steeply.

*

My grandfather notes in his diary on 14 January 1955, 'Alan goes back to school'. My mother commented on other aspects on 17 January. *I shan't go down to Oxford this term, Alan doesn't seem to mind whether I do or not! He has had a very good Rugger write-up in the magazine, his play would have warmed the hearts of Old Dragonians! I'll send it out to you to frame... Also a note from Alan to say he is a prefect this term – very fed up because it's thawing there.* This was supplemented by further news from me in a letter of February 1 to my father who was still in India, but due to return in April.

> *Dear Daddy, I am back at school now and we have had two week(s). There are lots of things to write about for a change so I will start from when I came back. I had an uneventful journey back but when I got to Oxford I had to wait for over an hour for a taxi when I got to school (I forgot to pay the taxi driver) I found out when I got to school that I had moved up in dorms to 'Leviathen' the top one also I am a prefect (Which means I have to be a saint and I have a few privelages) I have also moved up in French.*

In relation to the status of prefects, the Term Notes for Summer 1955 mention that there were three heads of house and twenty-one prefects at that time, of which I was one. Since there must have been about eighty boys or so a year moving through the school, I was in the top 25 per cent or so in terms of perceived leadership qualities. My feeling that it was mostly duty and little privilege probably reflects a tendency at the Dragon to play down authority – whether of the teachers or senior boys. As early as 1901 the founding Head Master, the Skipper, had set the direction when he outlined as part of his philosophy that 'I don't believe much in a *prefect* system among *little* boys. I trust in a general way to the bigger boys keeping things straight and keeping up a good tone, rather by example, than by being given authority over the kids. I think such authority often makes boys prigs, and sometimes bullies. Of course I am not speaking of boys at the top of Public Schools. That is quite different.'[87] Unlike the customs at a number of other preparatory schools, it seems that Dragon prefects were never allowed to beat younger boys.

*

My promotion to being a prefect for the last two terms may not have

---

[87] *The Skipper*, 41.

meant much in the un-authoritarian atmosphere of the Dragon, but is a curious insight into the approach of puberty, the relaxed school rules, the degree of my saintliness, and one privilege I did have is shown in a couple of letters at this point.

On about 18 February I wrote to my mother:

By the way if you have not sent the tuck you could cut the front Pictures of the 'Picture Post' and the big double page ones inside of film stars and send them along some time next week because we stick them up on the walls of the Dark-room (the special room of the prefects) Lots of love Alan
   P.S. don't forget the tuck?
   P.S.S. Don't forget the pin ups?
   P.S.S.S Don't forget either?

My mother wrote on the same day to my father in amusement. *Alan has got his football colours as you probably know, his ambition is to get them all but he is a little doubtful about hockey. He wrote asking me for Pin-Ups to put on the wall of the prefects study. I ask you! I sent a pile of women in bathing dresses which will probably be rapidly confiscated.*

The only piece of academic news was slipped in casually in a letter on 13 March to my father that *Common Entrance is over and no one has failed.* Thus my smooth transition to Sedbergh School was safe. Then on 25 March my grandfather noted in his diary, 'Alan returns from School'. On 2 April my grandfather noted in his diary, 'Alan's term report came. 1st in form in classics'. I was clearly very small, my mother noting the next day, *Fiona now weighs 5 st 12 lbs and Anne not much less. Alan doesn't seem to alter at all!* But I was ready for the big event which was the arrival of my father back from India, arriving in England on 21 April, the first time I had seen him since Christmas 1952.

I went back to school on 27 April and on 10 May I had my first ever joint visit from my mother and father, as noted by my grandfather in his diary when he wrote, 'Iris and Mac go to Oxford to see Alan'. I can't really remember this visit, but suspect that if they had a car it was less hectic than my mother's visits.

Nor do I make any note of the General Election which took place that term. I do vaguely remember that people were going round canvassing for something, but it may have been for our own mock elections. It seems that on the whole the boys were not encouraged by the school to take too much interest in national politics. In the election of Christmas 1951, the Term Notes mention that, 'There was little election excitement, and any incipient reactions of an unseemly or unbridled nature were cut short by a reminder that the citizens of to-morrow are not expected to meddle with the elections of to-day. So Dragons adjourned to the New Hall and held their own election, rather well.' And in the one in my last term the Term Notes comment, 'Meanwhile a General Election had come and gone, without noticeably disturbing the equilibrium of somewhat pre-occupied Dragons. Perhaps a slight swing to the Left could be detected? If so, it was probably not unconnected with the Labour Party's decision to abolish the 'eleven-plus'. After the election, the same source reveals, there were five Old Dragons in Parliament.'

*

I seem to have taken a further examination, for on 11 July my grandfather noted that 'Alan has passed his school cert exam'. How this school cert differed from Common Entrance (and indeed it may well be the same) I am not sure, but in a letter of about 10 July I gave my results to my parents. *Dear Mummy and Daddy, I am so sorry as this letter will probably not reach very soon but I think I might as well wait until my results come and I have my papers back.'* At the bottom I wrote in the results:

	'A' papers	'B' Papers
Latin	*76%*	*50%*
French	*60%*	*average of both*
English	*60%*	*average of both*
History	*60%*	*" "*
Geometry, Arithmetic, Algebra	*80%*	*average of all*
Scripture	*60%*	*average of both*
Geography	*60%*	*average of both*
Average	*69%*	
Result	*Pass*	

Here are my C.E.E. results (I don't know them yet)

I seem to be referring here to the Common Entrance Examination and be giving my parents my marks to an exam I had stated no-one failed. How a mark of 80% in mathematics and the 60% in many others compared to the general standard either in this school, or more widely, I have yet to discover.

*

My grandfather on 21 July noted, 'Alan arrives today' and again noted in his diary on 23rd 'Mac showed me Alan's prize for Latin French and Divinity and certificates for other things.' I still have the prize book itself. It has stuck in the front a label stating 'July 1955 Dragon School, Oxford, Upper 2b Prize for Latin, French and Divinity, awarded to A. Macfarlane,

103

signed by A.E. Lynam and J.H.R. Lynam'. The prize, chosen by me, was a copy of 'Fishing' by George Clifford (1948). I also received a prize for Rugger for year 1955. A Prize for cricket (batting and fielding), an 'extra' prize for soccer 1955, and a Prize for the General Paper 1955. These prizes were a few among the more than two hundred prize books and cards awarded that term, according to the Term Notes.

I also received as I left the Order of the Dragon, July 1955, 'Arduus Ad Solem', 'Others before self – God before all', signed by A.E. Lynam and Joc Lynam. God had not made an unduly strenuous appearance at a school which did not even have a chapel. But in that moment I turned from Dragon to Old Dragon.

There are two fortnightly reports for the term. They show that I had moved up in form from Upper 4A to 2B, which was the third form from the top. I was being taught Latin by the future headmaster M.W.A.G, Mike Gover or 'Guv' whom I remember I liked, and though I came only thirteenth out of seventeen that fortnight, had made, 'Really excellent progress. Translation really good.' I was in the same sets for other subjects and though mathematics and French were good, my English was not – 'Some rather poor work'. But my last fortnightly report is interesting. It was written on 10 July, just after our Common Entrance Exam results were known. Out of a class of seventeen I was equal thirteenth and Mike Gover noted 'Good results in C.E.Exam'. In English I was equal eighth out of seventeen; 'Well done in C.E.E.' In mathematics I was equal first out of eighteen, 'Well done'. And in French, equal second out of 15 'v.g.'.

At the end of all this, my final termly report in July 1955 was very satisfactory. I had missed one day in the term, and was a few months older than the average in most classes, but was now doing well. In classics in Upper 2B I was placed thirteenth in term marks and eleventh in a class of seventeen. 'He has made v. good progress with v. good exams to finish up. Best wishes.' In English and history, in a class of seventeen I was equal eighth, and in the exams equal ninth in English and equal sixth in history. 'A very good term's work. Don't stop using your imagination in English. Well done.' In mathematics, which was my best subject, in the second to top set I was equal first in the term's marks out of eighteen and fourth in exams, 'A thoroughly good term's work: well done!' Even geography, which had long been my weakest subject, was satisfactory. I was equal tenth out of thirty-four in term's marks and twelfth in exams and this was 'Very good'. My divinity was 'v.g'. and my science 'Very satisfactory'. Joc the housemaster wrote 'Alan has done very well all round, and the smile has nearly ousted the frown! Best of luck to him at Sedbergh.' Hum the headmaster wrote, 'Highly satisfactory – We all wish him a happy and useful career'.

So my Dragon days ended, with even the weather smiling on me as I left. The Term Notes for this last Summer term mentions that 'the thermometer moved purposefully upward towards the eighties and stayed there or thereabouts for the rest of the Term, providing a finish such as we had not experienced for three years. But blue skies and hot sunshine for the final fortnight...' Dragons, we are told, 'went home for their summer holidays well and truly sunburnt'. My grandfather noted in his diary at the end of this month 'Record month for fine weather. No rain for 29 days.'

CLASSWORK

The quiet room and library in School House where we borrowed
books and learnt to appreciate music.

12 LEARNING

Several impressions are worth noting. First, a lot of people other than the school matron were aware of how I went around frowning and looking anxious and hoped I would cheer up – which I did towards the end. So my long-held view that I moved from Inferno, through Purgatorio to Paradiso, seems to have some substance. By the end I really did not want to leave and loved my last year with Iolanthe, school colours, being a prefect, etc.

Secondly, my effort and attention took a definite dip in about my second to third year, after my mother had gone back to India, and then began to pick up again after she returned in 1954. In particular, after my own trip to India my writing in English seems to have improved.

Thirdly, my best subject seems to have been mathematics. As more or less top of A2, I was in the top tenth of the final year. My Latin was not as bad as I remember and I even got a prize. I was warmly praised for it, and on 3 April my mother wrote to my father, *His school report has come and is very good, 1 in Classics! This, he says isn't really up to much as its an unbrainy set, but he seems to be doing well all round.* Likewise my French improved, and I got a prize in this subject too. The prize for the General Paper was a great surprise, and also the fact that I apparently did very well in the Common Entrance exams.

On the whole I am quite impressed by the reports, but not by my own achievements, which were about middling. I was not 'brainy' as Jake Mermagen remembers, and hence my later career as an academic was not predicted, but rather the product of the care which the teachers took. The fortnightly reports were thorough and the comments in termly reports both encouraging and often perceptive. We had exams twice a year and there was quite a broad range of subjects taken. It gives the impression that this was an academically minded school, and the results of the debates, reported elsewhere, suggest that achievement in formal learning was valued as highly as sporting abilities.

Other things I don't remember were how much prep we did and when, yet I don't remember it being a particular burden. Nor did we take a mountain of work home in the holidays. The voluntary diaries and paintings and other things boys were encouraged to do in their holidays are all I remember. We were given frequent extra holidays for skating or for when boys won scholarships, and work was put in its place alongside music, plays, films, games and other things. It seems to have been a balanced school.

I do not personally remember being driven on by fear of punishment. There is no mention anywhere at all of the stripes which led to canings for Roald Dahl and his friends. I do not remember bad marks – but neither do I remember an elaborate system of stars or good marks.

We seem to have been encouraged along by a string of often really first-class teachers who tried their hardest. I do not remember, as Julian Hunt does, flying board rubbers or any physical punishments, whether a cuff round the ear or anything else. For me, there were real attempts to inculcate a sense of intellectual excitement as an end in itself.

I won a prize in my third year for 'Recitation'. I suspect that my love of poetry started at the Dragon. I was taught by the editor of 'The Dragon Book of Verse', which I still possess, and I learnt to love a number of the poems there – Chesterton and Pope among them. I don't think we saw the jokes in the book, including the strange Freudian inclusion of a weak poem starting 'My ball is in a bunch of fern, a jolly place to be' and then referring to an elderly male who was 'waving his stick at me'. Hardly very subtle.

It is worth noting the undoubted influence of the 'Dragon Book of Verse' on many Dragons, a symbol of the affection which the Skipper and other masters had for poetry. It is well put by the Old Dragon poet Jon Stallworthy in his autobiography. He analyses the content of the book and shows certain biases in the work, compiled by teachers at the school for use of the pupils, but concludes as follows. 'It is easy to deplore the male and martial bias of 'The Dragon Book of Verse', but it needs to be seen in its historical context, and what other school ever cared enough for poetry to commission its own anthology? No book I have ever owned has given me more pleasure or, I believe, more profit.'[88]

So, on the whole, I could not have had a better and more rounded kind of education. Small classes, excellent teachers, an esteem for academic things, but also a realization of how they should be part of a broader liberal education. It was a very suitable start for a process which would lead on smoothly to a boarding school and then, hopefully, to university and a successful career in the middle class as a doctor, lawyer, academic, civil servant, or even city type.

*

One particular skill or ability which seems, like music, to be a gift one either has or does not have, is mathematical ability. Here my assessment of

---

[88] Jon Stallworthy, *Singing School; the Making of a Poet* (1998), 44.

myself is confused. I think my father was a good mathematician – certainly as an engineer and in my mother's letters he is represented thus, especially in comparison to herself – (she represented herself as absolutely hopeless). However, I think my mother's feelings of inability and the accentuation of the arts and humanities against the sciences through her and my other relatives (my uncles Richard and Robert studying history at Oxford), meant that I never thought seriously about the sciences.

I must have done a little science, and see that I was even mentioned in The Draconian as distinguishing myself in some way in Gerd Sommerhoff's class, and my school reports speak highly of my science. But on the whole very early on I seem to have been streamed into arts and certainly never did any science at all after the Dragon. I continued to do maths up to O level, thus from six to sixteen. The reports on my ability surprise me since at times I was pronounced to possess some gift in the subject. I do not remember ever enjoying or feeling an aptitude for arithmetic, algebra or geometry. From memory it all seemed dead and artificial. Yet it appears that this is a later impression and there were times when I came top of the class in this subject.

Another surprise is in relation to languages and especially Latin. In my memory, I struggled inadequately with French and even more so with Latin, and was always hopeless at both. I recall the strain of Latin in particular and can still remember the lightning flash of my first Latin lesson with Miss Mumford, in the ground floor on the right in the new hall. I found it tedious, and despite being in a school famed for its Latin with many top scholarships requiring Latin, I progressed dismally, though scraping through the Common Entrance. Later I failed Latin at O level, (with foreign texts) at A level, and on my first attempt at university. So I think of myself as having a little Latin and less French.

It was only on my first trip to France at age seventeen that I saw some point in learning a foreign language. As with much of my learning, unless I could see the knowledge as a means to something, I found it dry. So my general image is that I was hopeless at languages until, with a reasonable ear and seeing a point to it, I learnt some of a Tibeto-Burman tonal language when I was doing anthropological fieldwork in Nepal. This drove out almost all remnants of French from my mind, and I've often thought my brain has only a tiny area where I can store only one language.

I think the moral of both maths and languages is that natural aptitude or ability is pretty evenly distributed. If my imagination had been gripped; if, as a rather practical child, I had seen what one could do with these hard-won skills, then I would have, and could have, become quite proficient.

I could see easily enough the value of learning to read – although it took a little effort to get me over the first barrier – for how else could I enjoy Biggles or Robin Hood? Reading was worth the effort and so the subjects around it – English and history – are the ones which I developed, particularly at Sedbergh. But again perhaps I have extrapolated backwards to the Dragon, for the reports on my progress in these subjects there are not particularly good and it may be that at that stage I was not at all tending in this direction.

Writing was clearly important and, among other things, the weekly letter to my parents pushed me to improve my skills, though my spelling level and content remained pretty backward throughout my time at the Dragon. Only very much later, really from my later thirties, did I experience the real pleasures of writing freely, when one suddenly finds one's mind taking over and the pen skimming across the pages, making new discoveries and enjoying the occasional delightful expression. But writing was the way I communicated with the most important person in my life at that time, my mother, and her excellent style and vivid descriptions were a constant inspiration.

*

The influence of my mother on my reading and writing is worth stressing. She had wanted to be a writer from her teens and it is clear from her published books and her more extensive unpublished material that she was, indeed, a remarkably good writer. She was observant, had a subtle sense of humour, a very good control of language and the gift of rhythm, as well as a mystical streak that led her into challenging areas. She had a first-rate mind and throughout her life was frustrated that she could not take up an offer of a scholarship at Oxford.

Anyway, the important thing is that almost every week, from the time I went to the Dragon aged eight, I received letters from my mother. She put her life into these. In her letters, my mother was putting before me a caustic, intriguing and richly imaginative view of life, in tension with parts of my value system at the Dragon and the upper class and imperial messages I was receiving there. Each week she was providing me with a vividly described world of Assam which was real to me and written by someone I knew and loved, a place of which I still had some memories.

I don't think I ever consciously tried to copy or emulate my mother's style or contents, but by treating me as an intelligent and mature reader, interested in a wider world, someone to share her amusement (and pain) about life, she helped me to grow up and to appreciate the fact that words are more than squiggles on paper.

*

We also received regular instruction in divinity. My memory of divinity lessons is slight and before I looked at my reports I was not sure whether we did the subject. But the reports show we did and that I was quite keen

110

and even won a prize, I think, for the subject. What strikes me as somewhat strange now is the rather ambivalent attitude towards religion in the Dragon. Of course there were morning prayers, with our own special 'Dragon Hymn Book' passed out each morning. And we went to weekly services somewhere in the school, with sermons which are sometimes printed in The Draconian. The content of some of these sermons is examined in a later chapter. There were also some special visits to Oxford churches which I shall mention.

*

In relation to what we were actually taught and the level of the expectations of the school, we can only approach this indirectly. Unfortunately I have not as yet been able to find any lists of the set books from which we were taught, any syllabi, or other evidence of the approach to our education. The one piece of evidence, which brings back a few fragments of memory, is an account of how we were taught science by Gerd Sommerhoff, which he briefly describes in his book 'In and Out of Consciousness'. Gerd's description here has more than a local interest, since it was on the basis of what he pioneered at the Dragon that the vastly influential Nuffield Foundation Science Teaching Project was later constructed.

When he was a Fellow of Trinity College, Cambridge, Gerd looked back on this period at the Dragon as follows: 'I can best describe the morning periods as a miniature edition of the popular Christmas lectures at the Royal Institution, whereas the afternoon sessions with the Science Club might be described as scouting in the world of science and technology.' He describes the teaching in some detail, especially in biology, for instance, something which I still remember. 'Thus the first piece of equipment I had built was a micro-projector capable of projecting live specimen.'[89] I still remember the tiny creatures coming up wriggling on the screen.

Equally important, in Gerd's view, were:

the daily meetings of the Science Club [where] everything was strictly organised and the boys did all the work themselves. Here they were offered about a dozen courses of self-instruction, each consisting of 15-20 graded experiments which were described on index cards. If the explanation could not be given on the card, a reference would be given to the appropriate textbook. You could not pass to the next experiment until you had successfully completed the last and showed that you had understood it. These courses covered (often in more than one part)

---

[89] Sommerhoff, *Consciousness*, 84-5

111

such topics as mechanics, chemistry, optics, electricity, magnetism, and engine types... Alongside these structured activities the boys also built model aircraft and the odd model boat.[90]

I was a member of this club, whose activities were described in detail each term, though I only distinguished myself once in my last Christmas term (1954). During this term 'thirty-three stars were earned by boys for completing successfully either a set schedule of experiments, a working model aeroplane, or a (valve) wireless set'. I was one of the winners of a star and report in a letter to my father on 2 November, *I am in the science club and at the moment I am making a one valve wireless set.*

Another way to try to recapture a little of what we were being taught in class is to examine some of the sample exam papers which were printed from time to time in the summer editions of The Draconian. I will give just one example of each subject, starting with the core subject of Latin. All the papers are from the period 1950–5 when I was at the Dragon.

The school, like other preparatory schools, taught Latin from Day One and there were two prizes for outstanding work in this field: A.E.L's Latin Prose Prize, and Prize for Latin Prose. The classes were arranged around proficiency in Latin, with Upper 1, IIA, IIB, IIIA, IIIB, IVA, IVB, V, VI, VII in the Upper School. There were seven classes in the Middle School and six classes in the Junior School.

The one Latin paper I still have from my time at school is for Upper 5, the eighth class from the top of the school. I skipped this class during my last year, moving into Upper IVA and then quickly up into Upper IIB. So presumably I would have found this paper relatively easy at that time, especially as I won a prize for Latin in my last year. Here is the paper.

Section A: Translate into Latin:
1. Haven't you already sent three messengers to Rome?
2. The journey was so long and difficult that the soldiers all died.
3. A brave soldier says that he does not fear the enemy.
4. I have often asked the boys to be silent.
5. I told my friends why I had not come.
6. The Romans captured the city and remained there.
7. A certain schoolmaster decided to go into the country with six boys. When they had finished (conficio) their work, they set out at the seventh hour. They carried food with them, but they hoped to find water in a little spring (fons). The wise master told them not to wander far from the road, but suddenly a cry was heard. One of the boys, who had not obeyed him, had fallen. His foot was severely hurt (use vulnero), but the others were able to carry him home.

---

[90] Sommerhoff, *Consciousness*, 86.

Section B. Translate into English:
Scaena – In Ludo (Discipuli in sellis non sedent: inrat magister.)

> *Discipuli*: Salve, magister!
>
> *Magister*: Salvete, discipuli! Adestine omnes?
>
> *Robertus*: Johannis abest. E. collo inflato laborat.
>
> *Magister*: O puerum miserrimum! Ille non saepe abest. Is quis saepe abest nihil potest discere. Nunc animam attendite omnes et libros aperite! (Caballus per fenestram spectat.) Quis vult recitare?
>
> *Christopherus*: Licetne mihi, magister?
>
> *Robertus (interpellans):* Tu heri recitavisti. Hodie me opportet recitare.
>
> *Magister*: Nolli ingerpellare, Caballe. (*Caballus iterum per fenestram spectat.*)
>
> *Paulus (e libro recitans):* Olim homo quidam in horto suo sedebat...
>
> *Caballus (interpellans):* In horto tuo...
>
> *Magister*: Tace, Caballe! Non est 'in horto tuo.' Specta librum! Est 'in horto suo'.
>
> *Paulus (pergens):* ... qui vinum bibebat, cibumque edebat...
>
> *Caballus (interpellans):* Nunc est...
>
> *Magister*: Non 'nunc est', sed 'olim edebat'. Tu animum non attendis sed per fenestram spectas. Librum specat et noli itgerum interpellare. Si iterum interpellabis, te virgis caedam. Perge recitare, Paule!

Here, having given about half of the Latin part to be translated, we will leave this exam since many readers will not be Latin scholars. But I have to say that nearly sixty years later, though I get the drift and can translate bits, much of it is lost to me. I tremble to think what a Latin paper for Upper 1 would look like; they were taught by L.A.Wilding, author of one of the standard Latin textbooks for schools – and all of them were hoping for scholarships to the best public schools such as Eton and Winchester.

The modern foreign language we were all taught was French, which was also on the curriculum from the first term. Let us here move into the top two sets, A1 and A2 (there being approximately six sets in each of the A-E grades). I personally ended up as equal third in set A4, and though again I was awarded a prize for my work in French, nevertheless this paper would be a bit above my level in the last year.

Qn. 1 Lisez, puis répondez aux question qui suivent:
Shelley à Eton
    La chasse à Shelley, en meute (packs) organisée, devint un des grand

jeux d'Eton. Quelques chasseurs découvraient l'être singulier lisant un poète au bord de la rivière et donnaient ausitôt de la voix. Les cheveux au vent, à travers, les prairies, les rues de la ville les cloîtres du college, Shelley prenait la fuite. Enfin cerné contre un mur, pressé comme un sanglier aux abois, il poussiat un cri percant. A' coups de balles trempée dans la boue, le people d'élèves le clouiat au mur. Une voix criait: 'Shelley!' – 'Shelley!' reprenait une autre voix.

(1) Qui était Shelley? Nommez un de ses oeuvres.
(2) Qui était les chasseurs?
(3) Comment Shelley était-il 'singulier'?
(4) Que pensez-vous de lui?
(5) De quelle rivière parle-t-on?
(6) Quand les chiens de chasse donnent-ils de la voix?
(7) Comment étaient les cheveux du jeuene poète?
(8) Que'st-ce qu'un sanglier? Les chasse-t-on en Angleterre?
(9) Qu'est qu'on jetait au jeune misérable?
(10) Quel chapeau porte un Etonian?

Qn. 2. Donnez des synonymes pour:
Un étre, au bord de, une rivière, la rue. Donner de la voix, Une prairie, découvrir, prendre la fuite, Pousser un cri, aussitôt.

Qn. 3. Au féminin: un chasseur (deux formes).
Le contraire de: singulier (deux sens). A travers les prairies. Un autre voix. Enfin.

Qn. 4. Ecrivez les cinq temps primitifs des verbes: étre, devenir, découvrir, prendre.

Qn. 5. Traduisez les deux phrases commencant: Enfin cerné.... Et, A' coupes de balles...'

Qn. 6. Completez:
Une balle trempée dans la boue devient bou ----
On cloue deux morceaux de bois avec un --- et des ---.
Une poète écrit des --- ou de la ---.
Les cheveux au vent veut dire 'tête ... ou ... - tête'.

Qn 7. Mettez aux temps convenables:
Il (entrer) pendant que je (travailler). (Vouloir) vous asseoir.
Il faut que je l'(apprendre). (Vouloir) - vous vous lever?
Il le (faire) s'il le (pouvoir). Croyes-vous qu'il (pleuvoir).
J'espère qu'il ne (pleuvoir) cet après-midi. Qui'il (faire) beau!

114

Qn. 8. Devinette (Riddle)

Cinq voyelles, une consonne,
Voilà ce qui forme mon nom.
Et je porte sur ma personne
De quoi l'écrire sans crayon.

Qu'est-ce que je suis? Qu'est-ce que je porte sur ma personne?

Qn 9. Ecrivez le metier correct après le nom:
Noms: Marie Antoinette, Alexandre Dumas, Pétain, Rodin, Richelieu, Watteau, Joséphine, Pasteur, Napoléon, de Gaulle.
Métiers: Auteur, Maréchal, Peintre, Empereur, Impératrice, General, Chimiste, Sculpteur, Cardinal, Reine.

What strikes me reading this paper is that, apart from linguistic competence required, it also required other things – a knowledge of the life of Shelley, the customs of Eton, the history of France and some ability with riddles. It overlapped quite considerably with the General Paper and other subjects.

*

Another core subject was mathematics. This was my best subject and during my last year I was in the second to top set, A2, ending up as the top of the set. In theory, therefore, my mathematics was up to the standard of the paper for A1 below.

A1

1. Find the value of the following as shortly as possible:
    (1) 201 x 57–57 –201 x 17+17.
    (2) Cost of 99 things at 13/4½ each.
    (3) Difference between 6¼% of 16 guineas and 6¼% of £16.
    (4) Express 1,056 yards per 1½ minutes in m.p.h.
    (5) $2\frac{2}{3}$ x $\left(\frac{1}{5} - \frac{0.9}{7.2}\right)$.
2. Factors of: (1)
    $2x^2 - 6x - 20$. (2)$a^2 + b^2 - 2ab - 4c^2$. (3)$12x^2 - 25xy + 12y^2$. (4) x^4– 1 – 4(x – 1). (5) x^2 – 24.
3. A beginner expands the brackets (x + 4) (x + 5) and makes the answer x + 4x + 15. Is there any value of x for which this could be true?

4. The weight of the weekly meat ration is increased by 5% and the price per lb. is increased by 10%; by how much per cent is the weekly expenditure on meat increased?

5. The circumference of a circle is πC ins. And its area is πA sq. ins. Prove $C^2 = 4A$. If $A^2 = 4C$, find radius.

6. ABC is a triangle inscribed in a circle. X and Y are the mid-points of the minor arcs AB and AC. XY cuts AB at P and AC at Q. Prove triangle APQ isosceles.

7. Draw a square of side 4 ins. Construct a regular octagon whose alternate sides lie along the sides of the square.

8. AB, PQ are diameters of a circle. AB is produced to D so that BD = AB. QB produced cuts PD in R. Prove PR = RD. (Join AP and PB).

9. Evaluate $3\sqrt{\dfrac{562 \times 0.4607}{642.1}}$.

10. A man does a journey of 240 miles at a certain speed; if he increases his speed by 4 m.p.h. he will save 50 minutes. Find original speed.

J.A.L.C.

*

The final core part of our curriculum was in a set that taught both history and English. In this combined class I ended up in my last year in class A3, most of the year being about fourth in the class. Thus the history paper for classes A1A and A1B would be a little above my level, though later it was history which I studied at university.

Qn. 1. To what do the following phrases refer?
(a) The 7n Years War, (b) The 9 Days Queen, (c) The 11 Years Tyranny, (d) The 19 Long Winters, (e) The 100 Days, (f) The '45.

Qn. 2. What historical personages met violent ends in these years?
(a) 1170, (b) 1381, (c) 1403, (d), 1556, (e) 1649, (f) 1759, (g) 1885.

Qn.3. With what one historical figure do you chiefly connect the following?
(a) The Mad Parliament
(b) The Rump Parliament
(c) Virginian Tobacco
(d) Home Rule
(e) The capture of Calais
(f) The loss of Calais
(g) The Harrying of the North

116

(h) The Bloody Assize
(i) The Coway Stakes
(j) The Angevin Empire
(k) The First Act of Supremacy
(l) The battle of Brunanburh

Qn. 4. From each of the following sets, pick out and write down *the odd one*, stating very briefly what the other three have in common, to show how your choice is made.
(a) 1215, 1314, 1415, 1513.
(b) Richard I, Richard II, Richard III, Edward III.
(c) Marlborough, Wellington, Roberts, Blake.
(d) Habeas Corpus, Pactum Serva, Mortmain, Praemunire.
(e) Naseby, Bannockburn, Bosworth, Culloden.
(f) Matilda of Anjou, Mary Queen of Scots, Sophia of Hanover, Katherine Howard.
(g) Sluys, The Nile, The Boyne, Quiberon Bay.
(h) Tinchebrai, Trpoyes, Versailles, Bretigny.
(i) William III, Edward I, James I, George I.
(j) Limoges, Glencoe, Cawnpore, Plassey.
(k) Peel, Melbourne, Pitt, Walpole.
(l) The New Forest, the Field of the Cloth of Gold, The Tower of London, Berkley Castle.
(m) 1066, 1399, 1588.

Qn. 5. *Either* trace the development of English trade from Plantagenet times, with particular reference to the effect on foreign wars and policy; *or* explain the evolution of our government from the Feudal System to the present day, giving a general outline of changes in class and power.

Qn. 6. Compose a dialogue between any two historical characters, who were *not* contemporary, in which they justify to each other their own beliefs and actions.

Qn. 7. Write a paragraph about *three* of the following.
The Protestant Reformation
The House of Lancaster
Elizabethan successes at sea
The Peninsular War (in Spain)
The Boer War
The Indian Mutiny
The War of American Independence
The main battles of the 100 Years' War

It shows that we were expected not only to know many key facts about English history from the medieval period to the nineteenth century, but also to be able to summarize and explain quite complex historical developments and arguments in short essays. Impressive.

In the other half of a joint class, we did English. This later became my favourite subject at my public school, where I received a distinction at S level. The paper, for A3 and B1–A3 was exactly the level I ended up in for my last year – is as follows:

Qn. 1. 'Falling Asleep' Write a paragraph beginning with the following words, to give the feeling and impressions of someone alone in bed dropping off to sleep, and to describe all the sounds he hears.

'Voices moving about me in the quiet house; thud of feet and a muffled shutting of doors: everyone yawning. Only the clocks alert...'

Qn. 2 Write an essay describing your impressions of:
(1)   A Circus; *or*
(2)   Listening to a Symphony Orchestra; *or*
(3)   A sailing race in a still breeze.
Remember imagination can often be better than mere facts.
Qn. 3
From shadows of rich oaks outpeer
The moss-green bastions of the weir,
Where the quick dipper forages
In elver-peopled crevices,
And a small runlet trickling down the sluice
Gossamer music tries not to unloose.
(*by Edmund Blunden*)

From the above lines:
(1) Give the Subject and the Verb of the two main sentences.
(2) Write down: 2 Adverbial phrase; 2 Adjectival phrases; 1 Adverbial clause.
(3)   What is the ordinary meaning of gossamer?
(4) Now write a careful paraphrase of these lines in clear, good prose. (An elver is a young eel).

Qn. 4. Name your two favourite authors. Explain why you like them, and compare their works.

Qn. 5. The following are quotations from famous poems. Give the name of the author of each one, as well as answering the questions.
(1) 'Then he said "Goodnight" and with muffled oar, Silently rowed...' Who was he?

(2) 'So ---- broke silence with "Yet there is time" ....' Who broke silence?

(3) 'Her hair was long, her food was light
And her eyes were wild...' Who was she?

(4) 'But we left him alone with his glory.' Who was left?

(5) 'He was not of an age, but for all time.' Who wrote this, and about whom?

(6) 'I chatter over stony ways, In little sharps and trebles...' Who chatters?

(7) 'Did he who made the lamb make thee?' Who is 'thee'?

(8) 'The mirror cracked from side to side,
"The curse is come upon me" cried ---- Who cried?

(9) 'So let each Cavalier who loves honour and me
Come follow ----' What should he follow?

(10) '....I have ventured
Like little wanton boys that swim on bladders
This many summers in a sea of glory.' Who is 'I'?

(11) 'He holds him with his skinny hand
"There was a ship," quoth he.' Who holds whom?

Geography was treated in a slightly different way to these core subjects, as it was taught in classes of twice the size and differently composed. But as someone who would later become an anthropologist, and who already had a little impression of distant lands (India), it is worth setting out one exam in this subject.

The exam in 1952 was divided into two parts. The first was done by all the sets, the second was divided into two. One was for all the sets from A1A to C2, the other for C3 to D5. I shall give the version for the top half of the school.

Geography
[question 1 was for all the school, questions 2–4 for the top half]
Qn. 1. On the map of the British Isles, which has been given you, mark and name the following:

(a) Cambrian Mountains, Cotswold Hills, Pennine Chain, North Downs, Southern Uplands, Cheviot Hills.

(b) Severn, Thames, Tees, Tamar, Great Ouse, Trent, Shannon.

(c) Bristol Channel, Solent, the Wash, Straits of Dover, Dogger Bank, Cardigan Bay.

(d) Bristol, Hull, East Anglia, Southampton, Newcastle-on-Tyne, Leeds, Manchester, Belfast, Dublin, Edinburgh.

Qn. 2. Draw a sketch map of *one* of the following areas and describe its main industries: South Wales, Central Lowlands, Liverpool, South

119

Africa.

Or

Write an account of wool growing in Australia.

Qn. 3. Write what you know about the contribution given to mankind by *one* of the following: Ferdinand de Lesseps, Captain Cook, Vasco da Gama, Livingstone.

Or

What do you know about the following:
(a) The Prime Meridian
(b) The Pole Star
(c) How it is proved that there are approximately 69.4 miles to a degree of Latitude.

Qn. 4. Write what you know about *two* of the following: Fiords, U-shaped valleys, fold and block mountains, monsoons, the source of a river, a Mediterranean climate.

Or

Describe geographically a journey down the Nile from Lake Victoria to the sea.

The divinity exam for July 1953 for the middling boys, around my level (Middles 2-7 and Lowers 1-2) gives some idea of what we were covering.

1. Write a short account of EITHER: David's victory over Goliath, OR: Saul and the Witch of Endor.
2. Name the person or persons to whom EACH of the following quotations refers, and write a few lines about ONE of them:
    (a) "Speak, Lord; for thy servant heareth."
    (b) "They were swifter than eagles, they were stronger than lions."
    (c) "And the King said, Bring me a sword. And they brought a sword before the King."
    (d) "My little finger shall be thicker than my father's loins."
3. Describe carefully in your own words EITHER: The Healing of the daughter of Jairus, OR: The feeding of the Five Thousand.
4. Write out our Lord's parable of the Sower and explain the meaning of it.
5. EITHER:
    Give the names of the Twelve Apostles and write briefly what you know about ONE of them.
    OR:
    Write out accurately in the words of the Bible our Lord's Beatitudes from the Sermon on the Mount.

120

What is absent here is as indicative as what is present. Apart from direct lessons drawn from Jesus' teachings, there is little on ethics. Nor is there anything of a vaguely comparative religion perspective. This was a Christian bible-centred course, as one might expect.

We were taught a certain amount of science and particularly biology. Here is one science exam, which seems to have been aimed at the top half of the School, from A1 down to M3 as follows:

1. Give the names and phylum of a one-celled animal and draw a simple picture of it. State briefly how it eats and how it multiplies.
2. Give a list of five different kinds of chemicals or particles which are carried by the blood and state very briefly the main purpose of each.
3. Draw a simple diagram of a Hydra: name its phylum and describe briefly how it eats, multiplies and moves about.
4. Draw a simple diagram of an eye and label as many parts as you can.
5. Name the phylum and class of: a flea, a waterflea, a prehistoric dragon, a modern Dragon.
6. (a) How does a high musical note differ from a low one?
    (b) If we hear the thunder twenty seconds after we have seen the lightning, how far away is the thunderstorm.

[The following questions need not be done by U7, M1, M2, and M3]

7. How does the human eye focus on a distant object? What is wrong if you are near-sighted? What type of glasses will you have to wear?
8. What part do egg-cells and sperm-cells play in the reproduction of animals?
9. Choose one of the following:
    (a) give a simplified diagram of a wireless valve and explain very briefly how it works.
    (b) illustrate the four strokes of a petrol engine with four simple drawings and add a few explanatory notes.
    (c) give a diagram of a cathode-ray tube and explain briefly how it works.
    (d) illustrate with simple diagrams how a steam-engine works.

At the end of term there were prizes for work in various subjects. Taking my last summer, there were a number of form prizes in my class 2B. It looks as if all leavers in the class were given a prize, mine being for Latin, Divinity and French. Special prizes for academic subjects were: Moberly Essay Prize; The Betty Hodgkin Prize for Appreciation of

English; The Gerald Hunt Prize for Scripture; The Ned Morphew Prize for Arithmetic; A.E.L's Latin Prose Prize; Prize for Latin Verse; The Gerald Meister Prize for Mathematics; The William Stradling Prize for Science; The Billy Collier Prize for Science; The Martin Collier Prize for Biology; The School Prize for French; Mrs Haldane's Prize for Geography; The Frank Sidgwick Prize for English Literature; the C.R.L. Fletcher Prize for History. Needless to say, I did not win any of these.

13 KNOWLEDGE

One fruitful approach in order to cover the range of our knowledge in all sorts of fields is to examine the extremely long and detailed 'General Knowledge' papers which were set each summer and printed in The Draconian. There are therefore five of these for my time at the Dragon.

In a letter of 18 July 1954 to my mother I wrote, *I am enclosing our General Knoledge papers this years and last years. In paper 1 (last year's) Questions nos 17 is personal and you would not know it. This year nos 6 you might not know and nos 9. Please will you keep the papers as I collect them.*

Whether I kept the papers so that I could prepare myself for the contest, or as a first sign of my hoarding, I am not sure. The papers were certainly long and difficult and prizes were awarded for the top entries. The Draconian reprinted both the questions and, a few pages later, the answers. As in some other schools at the time, parents were encouraged to pit their wits against their children after the event.

I had always thought that I was no match for the brilliant young Eton and Winchester scholars who won the competitions, and this was indeed generally true. Yet I was amazed to find that in 1955 I have a signed prize for the General Paper awarded to me in my final summer term. It appears that I was not in the top twenty or so named in The Draconian, but since none of them were in my class it may be that I was top of 2B or near to it. So I do not know what my score was or how far down the entries I was. All I have is the prize.

Let me start by examining the structure of the 1955 paper and give the questions and answers. I shall add a rough title to each section to indicate what it seems to be about. I shall also present the answers, as The Draconian did, a few pages further on.

Grammar (20 points)
Give
> *Noun from*: happy; tidy; merry; busy; gay.
> *Plural* of: life, strive; house; mouse; spouse.
> *Past of*: I – drink; think; wink; shrink; blink.
> *Opposite of*: fast; last; early; clever; many.

School slang and gadgets (12 points)
What is: an Atco; a Bounty; a gloat; a Walls; an Osmiroid; a Beano; a

tich frater; a running middle; Mars; a Platignum; a trash; a bish?

School knowledge (12 points)
What is: a Barsonry? Who takes Lower VI? Who takes Lowers in Biology? Who takes Junior Handicrafts? Who captains the Cricket XI? Who is Housemaster of Stradlings? What is taught by Spiv? Name one of the Staff dogs. Give full name of Gunga. Name the river at the foot of the field. Whose boathouse is close to the field? What College is close to the field?

General knowledge (15 points)
How many
   legs has: a biped; a centaur; a tripod; a spider; a titmouse?
   Feet has: a mermaid; a cricket pitch; an alexandrine; the crew of an VIII; a shrimp?
   Eyes has or had: Argus; a needle; a Cyclops; Cerberus; an ounce?

Clothing (20 points)
   On what part of your body would you wear, or have worn a: sombrero; clog; singlet; biretta; boater, Kirby-grip; tarboosh; cuirass; ruff; panama; shako; toupee; ushmak; busby; Glengarry; fillet; greaves; pumps; gives; derbies?

Current Shakespeare Play (20 points)
Give Christian names and occupations of: Starveling; Flute; Bottom; Snout.
Name: Helena's father; Hermia's father; Titania's husband; Peaseblossom's parents.
What did Bottom prefer to new nuts? What food did he say had no fellow? What music did he call for? What bird did he describe 'with little quill'?
What was Puck's other name? Give two names for the flower which charmed Titania and Lysander.

Places and Things (especially round Oxford) (15 points)
What is or was: The Victory; The Parthenon; The Broad; The Jacquerie; The Pelican; The Pharos; The Bodleian; The Rocket; The Fram; The Leviathan; The Mall; The Clink; The Radcliffe; The Oval; The Randolph.

Famous People (15 points)
What name do you generally associate with: Eve; Hare; Watson; Costello; Cavell; Huntley; Thisbe; Jonathan; Sullivan; Botting; Hengist;

124

Juliet; Mears; Dido; Beaumont.

Famous authors (20 points)
What famous author: swam the Hellespont; was 'dull in a new way'; wrote a poem on his blindness; played a flute round Europe; was banished to the Black Sea; distributed stamps; was named 'Tusitalia'; was only 5 foot tall but a good boxer; was 'sent down' from Oxford; enlisted under the name of Silas Tomkyn Cumberbache; was an Inspector of Schools; worked in a blacking factory; was a super-tramp; was a hump-back; invented the pillar box; sailed before the mast; left his wife his second-best bed; was a Controller of Customs; was once a bricklayer; had infantile paralysis when young?

Sport (3 points each, 18 total)
Here are some Headlines from the Sporting Pages of 'The Daily Crackers'. Give them as they should be:
    Compton brakes course record on centre court at Henley.
    Harlequins pip Thames by a Canvas at St. Andrews.
    Stanley Matthews serves two doubles in the Open Championship at Old Trafford.
    Leander defeat Richmond in the Cup Final at Wimbledon.
    Trabert hits century in the 7-a-sides at Wembley.
    Thomson nets thrice against the South Africans at Twickenham.

Geography and places (12 points)
What mount, mountain, or mountains: was home of the Gods; was home of a Poet; was climbed this year; suggests a Musketeer; suggest geography; are mentioned in Pilgrim's Progress; are 'icy'; was the scene of a King's defeat and death; is a Post Office; is a tree; was piled on Ossa; was seen in the New Hall last autumn?

Language (20 points)
What are you if you are: bandy; batey; batty; boozy; cagey; canny; catty; cocky; crabby; foxy; grubby; loopy; potty; sloppy; scruffy; stocky; testy; touchy; tubby; windy?

Famous people (15 points)
Who lives, lived, or might have lived at these addresses: The Castle, Elsinore; The House of Shaws, near Cramond; Lambeth Palace, London; The Palace, Camelot; the Tub, Athens; St. Patrick's Deanery, Dublin; The Cave, Pelion; The Castle, Dunsinane; The Pleasure Dome, Xanadu; The Spy Glass Inn, Bristol; 4 Garford Road, Oxford; The Boar's Head, Eastcheap, London; Tree Top, Never Never Land; 60A Half Moon Street, London; Headmaster's House, Dotheboys

Hall, Yorks?

Poetry (20 points)
Who, or what, in the Dragon Book of Verse: was sent with broom before; sank like lead into the sea; spoke out loud and bold; lies full fathom five; died in the odour of sanctity; sings on the orchard bough; was extremely hungaree; comes silent flooding in; galloped into Aix and stood; shot like a streamer; felt his heart new opened; shook his heavy head; keels the pot; plunged headlong in the tide; was left alone with his glory; was lost evermore in the main; falls like a thunderbolt; at Heaven's gate sings; said he could not rest from travel; swam the Eske river?

School names (20 points)
What boys' surnames are suggested by these clues?
    A relative of Karl and Groucho?
    Curates, Rectors, Vicars, etc.
    Voc. Case of Mr. Sheep.
    Explorer or Novelist.
    Hard to keep on a tightrope.
    Burton's on it.
    Looks like a rumpus in the Courts.
    Three sisters told me I'd be king.
    Spill the beans, hatchet.
    Thisbe thus described her deceased lover's nose.
    Keep on extracting the tares.
    A bog.
    Panky!
    Do in the Irishman.
    Not a heavy better.
    Often goes with Mum.
    Genuine affection.
    Whittington, Deadeye, or Kitcat.
    On Wye or with Cromarty.
    Opposite of define?

The answers are as follows:

Grammar: happiness, tidiness, merriment, business, gaiety; lives, strifes (or none); houses, mice; spouses; drank, thought, winked, shrank, blinked; slow, first, late, stupid, few.
School slang and gadgets: mower, kind of sweet, end of Term 'calendar', ice-cream, pen, 'Trash', small brother, dive, sweet, pen, boys' paper, mistake (Dragonese)

School knowledge: handicraft, Mrs. Owen, Miss Blaikie, Miss Barwell, M. Evers, R.St.J.Y, geography, dogs – Tess, Boz, Bess, Tilly, Flic, Gunga Din, Cherwell, Timms, L.M.H.

General knowledge: 2, 4, 3, 8, 2, 0, 66, 6, 18, 10, 100, 1, 1, 6, 2 (kind of lynx).

Clothing: head, foot, trunk, head, head, head/hair, head, trunk, neck, head, head, head, face, head, head, head, legs, feet, wrists, wrists.

Shakespeare play: Robin – tailor, Francis – bellows-mender, Nick – weaver, Tom, tinker, Nedar, Egeus, Oberon, – Squash/Peascod, dried peas, hay, tongs and bones, wren, Robin Goodfellow, pansy and love-in-idleness.

Places and things: ship (Nelson's), Greek temple, Oxford street, ship (Drake's), French Peasant rising, Egyptian lighthouse, Oxford library, early locomotive, ship (Nansen's), London street, prison, Oxford infirmary, cricket ground, Oxford hotel, sea-monster (Dorm?).

Famous People: Adam, Burke, Holmes, Abbot, Elliston, Palmer, Pyramus, David, Gilbert, Hillard (text book), Horsa, Romeo, Carter (text book), Aeneas, Fletcher.

Famous Authors: Byron, Gray (said by Dr. Johnson), Milton, Goldsmith, Ovid, Wordsworth, Stevenson, Keats, Shelley, Coleridge, Matthew Arnold, Dickens, W.H. Davies, Pope, Trollope, Masefield, Shakespeare, Chaucer, Ben Jonson, Scott.

Sport: Compton – century – Africans – Old Trafford; Harlequins – Richmond – sevens – Twickenham; Matthews – nets – Cup final – Wembley; Leander – Thames – canvas – Henley; Trabert – doubles – Centre Court – Wimbledon; Thomson – record – Championship – St Andrews.

Geography and places: Olympus, Rydal, Kanchenjunga, Athos, Atlas, Delectable, Greenland's, Gilboa, Pleasant, Ash, Pelion, Ararat (in 'Iolanthe').

Language: bow-legged, angry, dotty, addicted to drink, secretive, cautious, spiteful, conceited, ill-tempered, cunning, unclean, dotty, loopy, not thorough, unkempt and grubby, thick set, irritable, prone to offence, fat, nervous.

Famous people: Hamlet, Ebenezer Balfour (Kidnapped), Archbishop of Canterbury, King Arthur, Diogenes, Swift, Chiron (or pupils), Macbeth, Kubla Khan, Long John Silver, E.L.F, Mrs Quickly/Pistol/Falstaff, Peter Pan/Wendy, Bulldog Drummond, Mr. Squeers.

Poetry: Puck, Albatross, Chapman (Keats), Thy father, Jackdaw of Rheims, chaffinch (Browning), Gorging Jack, the main (Clough), Roland, Excalibur, Wolsey, eldest oyster, Greasy Joan, Horatius, Sir John Moore, The Revenge, the eagle (Tennyson), the lark, Ulysses, Lochinvar.

School Names: Marks, Oram, Scott, Balance, Trent, Barrow, Macbeth, Axtell, Cherry, Wheadon, Marsh, Hankey, Kilpatrick, Pennybacker, Dadd, Truelove, Dick, Ross, de Wet.

The possible total was 254 and my friend Philip Steadman won with 174, a remarkably high score in this difficult impromptu test

It is tempting to set out extracts from earlier papers, which show that each year they were very different, but each required a high level of general knowledge in literature, history, geography, sport, music, poetry, local school knowledge and other fields to complete effectively. I am amazed to think that little boys (and the occasional girl) of eleven or twelve were expected to have picked up so much, some of it in class, but much through observation, listening carefully to adults, and then memorizing a complex set of facts which they could quickly mobilize in a long examination. It is not surprising that Peter Snow should describe the boys as having 'the bodies of children but the minds of adults'. I suspect that I have never known as much again in my life as I did when I was thirteen.

*

From time to time there were elaborate treasure hunts. The range well complements the General Knowledge paper – a kind of General Knowledge paper with objects attached. There is Sandy Bruce Lockhart's list from 1955. Obviously the boys were divided into teams and given a list of things to find or to find out, and then pool them with their team. I suspect this was only done sporadically, as in the very cold spring of 1955, when outdoor games of other kinds (or skating) were deemed impossible. Sandy had marked his list with a tick when he found something (shown with an asterisk * below).

LET'S FIND   26 February, 1955

1. The number of this morning's hymn. *
2. A bowler hat.
3. A potato. *
4. The number of Bruno's House in Norham Road. *
5. What has just gone up by one per cent? *
6. The smallest possible conker.
7. The name of the present Vicar of St. Andrew's Church. *
8. The largest possible blown up balloon.
9. A programme of 'Listen to the Wind'.
10. All the Christian names of Mr. Currey.
11. A silver threepenny bit.

12. Whom should the Staff play at hockey on March 24th?
13. An Oxford bus ticket. *
14. A bicycle trouser clip. *
15. A recognisable photograph or drawing of a member of the Staff.
16. A kirby grip.*
17. The date of this year's Boat Race. *
18. The name of the Mayor of Oxford. *
19. An Old Etonian tie.
20. A Christmas cracker.*
21. A golf ball. *
22. The number of soccer colours announced from the platform this term.
23. The name of the captain of this year's Oxford University hockey team.
24. The name of the maker of the new brake's engine. *
25. A Wychwood girl's autograph. *
26. The number of lamp-posts on the East side of Charlbury Road. *
27. What was the School House telephone number in 1952?*
28. A ticket of admission to last term's Iolanthe.
29. The highest number of any house in Park Town. *
30. The registration number of the Bursar's car.
31. The exact number of girls in the Big School this term.
32. Who will open the next Olympic Games? *
33. A sheet (dated) of a January daily paper. *
34. A brazil nut.
35. A remembrance Day poppy. *
36. The number of the nearest pillar box which has an 8 p.m. collection. *
37. Edward Hornby's London address.
38. The name of the Warden of St. Edward's School. *
39. A set of poker dice.
40. A Coronation pencil.
41. The number of courts at Norham Gardens tennis club.
42. A picture postcard of an Oxford College. *
43. What is R.I.K's address in Oxford?
44. The name of the lady who plays the piano for dancing.
45. Who is Mrs. Fernald? *
46. Where was tomorrow's preacher once Headmaster?
47. Today's half-time score in the Scotland v Ireland rugger match.
48. Whom did the Queen honour last night? *
49. The largest possible icicle. *
50. Something which nobody else has got. *

RULES

No Trespassing. New Buildings and Lodge out of bounds. No one is to cross the Banbury Road. No disturbing of private citizens. No one to go upstairs in the School House. Members of the Staff may only give help *five* times during the afternoon.

HAVE REALLY GOOD MANNERS THROUGHOUT.

Group leaders to be ready in their own classrooms with their final sheet of answers and their goods at 4 o'clock sharp.

N.B. Remember to return anything which you may have borrowed.

There must have been some amused (or irritated) Wychwood girls, Mr. Currey, piano teachers and others, and a dripping mass of icicles, bus tickets, trouser clips and burst balloons in the classrooms. But it was obviously fun and again shows that Dragons were meant to retain not only objects – tickets to Iolanthe or poppies or silver threepenny bits – but also to know quite a bit about local adult affairs: what had gone up 1 per cent, who would open the next Olympic Games, the name of the vicar of St. Andrew's. The objects and information were quirky, but just possible. And clearly there must have been much rushing about and fun. This all took place in my last Spring term, but I do not recall the event.

14 GEOGRAPHY

I thought that I had none of my class notebooks for the Dragon and that it would be impossible to say what or how I was taught in any detail. I have, however, discovered that one set of class books, covering a year in geography, have survived. I had for long assigned them to my time at Sedbergh School, where I have other work books, partly because at first glance they seemed rather sophisticated in both content and style.[91] However, on examining a volume, I found that I have placed a coloured label on the outside stating, 'A. Macfarlane Geography, Volumes 1–3', in which there are three separate exercise books, sellotaped together. I have found that these are definitely of the Dragon period, covering the three terms Christmas 1953 to summer 1954, when I was aged eleven-and-three-quarters through to twelve-and-a-half.

Geography was a second-level subject at the Dragon. It was not one of the four key disciplines covered in the fortnightly reports and it was examined in a rather different fashion. Even in the termly reports geography was inserted in a rather abrupt way between major subjects for half my time at the Dragon before it received its own separate place. The classes were often larger than in other subjects.

Geography was one of my middling subjects. I ended up at the Dragon in sets A3/A4, equal tenth in class and twelfth in exams out of 34 with the comment 'Very good'. This was slightly lower than English, history and French and a good deal lower than mathematics. During the three terms from which the work-books survive, my termly reports and marks were as follows.

> Winter 1953: Set B2, B3. Out of 36 pupils in the class, I was placed 13th in class marks and 10th exams. The comment of J.F.T. Copleston, who taught me throughout these three terms, was 'Good'.
>
> March 1954: Set B1. I was 14th in term marks out of a class of 17 and 'keen and interested'.
>
> July 1954: Set B1. I was 13th out of 16 in class marks and equal 10th in

---

[91] A.L. Rowse in his *A Cornish Childhood* (1947), 117–20, describes a similar chance find of a writing book of his elementary school, kept by a teacher. His conclusion is similar to mine: 'from it I see that we were altogether better taught than I had remembered'.

exams. Copleston remarked, 'Much improved: a better understanding of the subject.'

It seems, from the evidence of the exercise books, as well as the comments above, that geography was a subject I enjoyed. My experience of coming back from, and then revisiting, Assam, along with my mother's letters and family reminiscences, may have enthused me, although we hardly touched Asia in this year of teaching. However it was clearly important if I were ever to follow my ancestors and work abroad. So what evidence is there of how I learnt in this accidental survival?

Each notebook is about forty pages long and includes numerous maps, diagrams, lists, etc. Since a complete catalogue of what we did would be tedious, I shall summarize some of the topics covered, and only give a few of the encouraging or critical comments usually attached to my attempts. The book first starts with model answers for short geographical questions: Glaciers, Relief Rain and Rain Shadows, Deltas and Fiords. This is a cyclostyled sheet with brief descriptions of each of these and four diagrams, which I obviously coloured in.

We then dealt with South America, with maps of vegetation, rainfall and temperature. On a world map I filled in world vegetation, animal life and climate. After describing equatorial forests and savannah grasslands we return to Brazil and its industries. All the main features stand out clearly. 'You must however draw your map outline in pencil.' [An inserted piece of carbon paper explains how I must have drawn some of my maps] I continue to describe the timber, brazil nuts and coffee and point out that Brazil grows four fifths of the world's coffee – with a picture of coffee cups. [Comment: Excellent Notes – Keep up the Good work!] There are then other very detailed pages of three maps of parts of Brazil, showing where crops are grown and rainfall occupy a page, and then a diagram in detail of how coffee is grown ['V.G.'] Similar treatment is given to Argentina, and a further page describes the rainfall on the Andes. We moved on to volcanoes, with three diagrams of how a volcano works, for which I only received 5/10, having left out the naming of magma etc. [This exercise is reproduced in the visual essay at the end of the book.] There are a further two pages of cyclostyled maps of South America, with various products and places written in, and that was the end of the work for the Winter term.

*

In Easter Term 1954 I started with North American exploration, where I listed the names and dates of major explorers from Eric the Red through to the Alaska purchase. This was followed by a cyclostyled map of 'N. America: Physical Features', which I filled in. I then described some of the physical divisions, including the Canadian shield, in my own words. The next two pages did the same for climate.

There are then four diagrams of a valley glacier and its features: a cirque, movement of glaciers, erosion by glaciers, moraines. There is then 'Prep' 11 March 1954. 'The Wheat Farmer's Year'. The following page shows in three diagrams and text the three stages of lumbering and then a detailed diagram of a saw mill. I describe coniferous forests and the apples of Nova Scotia. A whole page is devoted to a diagram with annotations to explain 'Why the Grand Banks are the World's Greatest Fishing Grounds' ['Good: A neat diagram']. Inserted loosely here is a cyclostyled description of Tundra, Savannah Grasslands and Hot Deserts, with a world map to show the main location of these.

The next two pages are a cyclostyled map of the 'Dominion of Canada' on which I have drawn the main territories, states and cities. I then drew a diagram to show how Greenwich is the centre of time, followed by a rather strange drawing of a combine harvester. There next follows the prairie farmers' year, with diagrams of the stages.

Three pages are devoted to a Prep I did on Newfoundland. We were given some suggestions for this in the form of 'Prep Hints'.

1. World position – position in relation to Canada.

2. Latitude – N. France.

3. Climate (Damp, foggy cloudy summers, cold winters).

4. Vegetation.

5. Occupations of the people; and why they carry on these industries.

6. Marketing of products.

7. Conclusion.

The essay I produced is as follows. [with Copleston's comments, as he wrote them, underlined]:

Prep

~~New~~ Newfoundland ~~is~~ lies about 45 LONGITUDE west and 48 LATITUDE north. It is ~~fogg~~usually foggy. ~~This~~ is caused by the Labrador ~~and currant~~ cCurrent and the Gulf sStream meeting, one a hot and one a cold current. It has a cold ~~sum~~ winter and cloudy summer. There are ~~timber~~ CONIFEROUS forests and nearly everything is made of wood, including boats, houses, crates, ~~furn~~ furniture.

The main ~~occu The m~~ is fishing. Some of the inhabitants only fish around the coast while others go out in big schooners and fish on the Grand Banks. The Ggrand Bbanks are the best fishing ground in the world and the main fish are cod. This is so because a continental shelf was formed by the iceberghs ~~melting~~ melting. [This sentence has two red ticks against it.] Then planktumon grows on the shallow water and the fish thrive.

~~They are mostly~~ The inhabitants of Newfoundland are a hardy race and they live a hardy life. When the fish and then their liver is taken out sepearately. After this they are stored in crates.

ICEBERGS   PLANKTON   SEPARATELY

7/20 POOR. YOU MUST PLAN YOUR WORK CAREFULLY AND TAKE CARE TO EXPRSS YOURSELF CLEARLY AND ACCURATELY.

1.   YOU SHALD HAVE MENTIONED MORE ABOUT THE LUMBER INDUSTRY.
2.   YOU FAILED TO WRITE ABOUT THE VALUABLE COPPER, LEAD AND ZINC MINES AS WELL AS THE IRON ORE OF BELL ISLAND WHICH IS SMELTED WITH CAPE BRETON ISLAND'S COAL.
3.   CORNER BROOK AND GRAND FALLS POSSESS SOME OF THE LARGEST WOOD-PULP MILLS IN THE WORLD UTILISING CHEAP HYDRO-ELECTRIC POWER.
4.   NEWFOUNDLAND IS AN IMPORTANT INTER-NATIONAL JUNCTION. E.G.GANDER.

I then wrote an essay on 'Lumbering' and then on 'The Tundra'. Then there is a 'Prep' on 'A Valley Glacier', for which I got 15½. The following page is devoted to a Test, with single word answers to 25 questions. I got 15½ right (providing three versions of the spelling of Mississippi).

There is then a two-page essay on the 'Growing of Coffee in Brazil'. This illustrates both my style, and the further efforts of Mr. Copleston to improve my work.

The Ggrowing of Ccoffee in Brazil
Coffee is grown in the south East of Brazil. It is grown on ~~the sides~~ of Fazendas wich are small states (crossed out) LARGE PLANTATIONS owned by Eurapeans the hills. The ground is very fertile due to the fact that there used to be volcanoes. The colour is red and there used to be forests wich have fallen down and decayed. Also there is very good drainage. There is much sun and in the summer there is heavy rain caused by the South East Trades from November to February. There ~~is~~ are no severe frosts and this is ~~exem~~ extremely lucky as one severe frost would kill all the coffee bushes.

[NB: The passage from 'The colour is red to ... coffee bushes' is sidelined in red with GOOD.]

The young ones are sheltered by long huts covered ~~with with~~ with palm leaves. When they are eighteen months old they are transplanted to the ~~hill~~ hillsides. In the summer the work on the fazenda is very hard as they have to weed and prune the land and bushes. The hot sun and heavy rainfall make all the plants grow quickly. At first, ~~they~~ the cherries are green but gradually they turn red then they are called coffee cherries. In the winter they are picked and are put in sacks. As each tree will only produce about ~~a~~ one and a half pounds of coffee so they do not waste any. After that they are ~~the~~ taken to a fast flowing stream at the end they have their outer skin taken off. Then the pulp is taken of by the water. Then it is laid out to dry. <u>The silver on a parchment inner skins are then removed, the coffee graded and sacked, sent to Sao Paulo and from there exported to Europe and N.America by way of Santos and Rio de Janeiro.</u>

<u>17/20 VERY GOOD INDEED.</u>

The book ends with five pages of further tests and short answers to questions.

Stuck in the end is a cyclostyled map of the world showing twenty-five main features and where they are – the comment is 'v.g.'

*

We seem to have been very concerned with the Americas. Book II, summer 1954, starts with a coloured map of North America with a few geographical features, and then another next is a coloured diagram of 'The Importance of Maize (corn) in the U.S.A'. The following page shows 'Work on a one mule cotton plantation', complete with a small sketch of a worker. [This is reproduced in the visual essay at the back of this book.]

There follows a coloured diagram of 'Drilling for Oil', followed by two pages on New York, first an ['Excellent'] map of the site of the city, then a ['v.g.'] set of seven points. We then move to Chicago, with a cyclostyled page of main points about the city, and a map. For this I only received 3/15 and the comment was 'A well carbon traced map. But how does it illustrate the importance of Chicago?' Then on to California, with three pages of annotated coloured diagrams of its climate, products and how the irrigation system works. There is a page of notes with coloured diagrams of what happens in Los Angeles – ['Excellent Notes'].

There is then an interlude on more general tools of geography. This consists of notes on how to draw maps, how to show scales on maps; then three ways of finding north are given, followed by the definition of a contour.

Moving to Europe, there is a map and a page of description of the main physical geography, including main rivers and a further page of the relief and main towns listed. I then traced a map of Europe and coloured in the countries and capital cities of certain countries. Two pages on France show its main geography and various products. How exactly the next items, a cyclostyled page, with two maps I have coloured in, on 'Monsoons', and two further similar pages on Rainfall and Erosion by Rivers fit within Europe is something of a mystery, but we return to ground with a list of the capitals of fifteen European countries.

Again we take a step back to look at more general features of world geography. I list hot and cold currents, naming twenty six out of thirty. [There is a question mark against the 'Irmingher' current – if Mr Copleston had had Google he would have found that this is indeed a current – the Irminger.] Two pages of diagrams then explain the formation of depression, from above, from the side, and how it works. I draw the signs and symbols for roads, railways, and then show the globe with the main seasons and tropics.

Then it is time to move to another major continent, and one of possible interest at the end of the colonial period, namely Africa. I start with a map of the southern half filled in and a further rainfall map. I then list eighteen ports in Africa with British possessions in pink. Maps of the distribution of population in southern Africa and the Natural Regions in the same area receive ticks.

Again it is time for some world geography. There is a list of about thirty rivers around the world, followed by twenty single-word answers to various questions of a miscellaneous kind, for which I received fourteen marks. Half a page describes continental and maritime climates, and then there is a further page of tests. A one-page essay on the use of rivers was 'Good', and received 15/20. This is followed by two further pages of geography tests.

We then wend our way back to southern Europe, by way of a cyclostyled set of notes on coniferous and equatorial forests, and on continental and maritime climates which was followed by a page with some notes by me on 'Mediterranean' climate, and latitude and longitude. I wrote an essay on Mediterranean climates and the kind of industries carried on in the coniferous and equatorial forests. The first part is crossed out with a note 'I asked you about a Maritime climate'. On the facing page is written 'Write out my notes on maritime and continental climates, please'.

Off we go again to the Americas, with a two page essay on cotton, with some quite detailed comments by Mr Copleston and a mark of 14/20. Another essay on 'The Maize Belt of North America' has detailed comments interspersed by the teacher, with the end comment, 'You know a number of facts but you have expressed them in a muddled order. Try to follow some definite plan.' 12/20. We move north again to Canada, with a map of British Columbia and spaces to fill in answers under the headings, 'Use of rivers, climate, fishing, farming activities, most important minerals mined, and two industries of Vancouver and three of its chief exports.' I get 8/15 'Poor' for my answers.

Suddenly we are back in home country, for there is now a cyclostyled map of England, with fifteen cities marked in by me, followed by a cyclostyled work map with ten places and features marked in. This book is clearly not enough for the term's work, for there is then another 'Geog Book (Continued)'. Here we go back to Canada briefly, with maps of Canada coloured in and with some details added by me, but soon switch to the somewhat neglected Africa.

There is another map of South Africa, showing various activities, then some notes on the Union of South Africa which shows its history, climate, population and capitals. For example, I note that the population in 1951 is twelve-and-a-half million, of which two-and-a-half million are European, eight-and-a-half million 'Natives (Bantu)' and one and a half million 'Asian, Malay and Chinese' etc. I note briefly also that 'Native Problem – segregation of the black man.' The various regions with their climate, relief and crops are then described, followed by a map of the 'confederate of Central Africa', ('A good map, but try next time to get everything in' 18/20). A map and details of S. Rhodesia occupy a page. But that is it, and it is time to return to the homeland.

We move to 'The Lancashire Industrial Area', with main activities, towns and zones, which I coloured in. ['v.g.' 14/15], followed by two tests in which I did well. Opposite is a rather elaborate map of England with its coalfields. Now on to tides, and a map of England's geology – but with no names. A note on tidal wave approaches and tides is faced by a coloured map of the Thames basin. The railway network of London in a diagram gets a tick, and opposites a short description with another map of 'The People Coming from Abroad'. Then there is a page on the South Wales Coalfield with various details of exports, imports, etc. A two-page map of some of the features of the lowlands of Scotland gains me 16/20. This is reproduced in the visual essay at the end of this book. We then deal with the main activities and products of Scotland, and probably without ironical intent this is followed by a diagram of a 'Depression', which Mr Copleston notes is 'Not quite finished', but shows it happening over a sketch (reproduced in the visual essay) of the Dragon School.

Having inserted my picture of the Dragon, we officially come back to England again with diagrams and notes on the West Riding woollen industry, with a figure of 'A slice out of the Yorks, Derby, Notts Ind area.' The following page looks at some of the products (with small drawings) of Sheffield, Nottingham and Derby – including a picture of a Rolls Royce.

For an exotic last fling there is then a two-page essay, illustrated with five diagrams, of 'South Sea Isles'. Grimmer, is some advice about the forthcoming Common Entrance exam, headed 'C.E.E. Spot Questions'. This gives suggestions of six general areas which might come up in exams

137

which I would be taking the following year. Perhaps appropriately, but again without intended irony, there is another half-page essay (the third!) on 'A depression' with a diagram.

We end with a miscellany: a 'Prep', with a half page on the central lowlands of Scotland with a detailed map of the movement of commodities, and finally another prep on Ceylon. 'Ceylon – use blue Stembridge, P.172, Ch 14 – read and answer questions 1.2. (P.175)' (If this is Jasper Harry Stembridge, *The World: a general Regional Geography*, we were really up to date since it had only been published by Oxford University Press in 1953.) The volume ends with two unmarked cyclostyled maps of the British Isles and the World which I may have used for tracings.

*

At the end of the school year I moved up into set A3/A4 where, in the first term, I was 15 out of 34 in term marks and 22 in exams, with the comment by 'DP' [D. Parnwell] of 'Quite Good'. I have no further work books from this final year, but inserted into the previous years' volumes is a geography exam for November 1954.

This was set for classes A.3, A.4, B.2, B.C, C.1, C.2 by my teacher, D.P.

I will transcribe this as an indication of what we were expected to be able to know from classes of children roughly from the age of ten to thirteen.

GEOGRAPHY

EXTRA MARKS WILL BE AWARDED FOR GOOD SKETCH MAPS, DIAGRAMS, AND NEATNESS.

Answer Question 1 and *four* others.
1. On the World Map mark in the position of the following, with the NUMBER only (Example: 1 – position of River Yangtze).
Rivers 1. Yangtze 2. Zambezi 3. Nile 4. Tigris
Mountains 5. Atlas 6. Urals 7. Himalayas 8. Appalachians
Capitals of Europe 9.Helsinki 10. Lisbon 11. Warsaw 12. Belgrade
Ocean Currents 13. Kuro Siwo 14. Gulf Stream 15. Peru 16. Benuela
And 17. Suez Canal 18. Kuwait 19. Iceland 20. Tropic of Cancer
2. What do you know about four of the following? (Not more than 10 lines on each): – Monsoons, Latitude and Longitude, Night and Day, a Depression, Dew, the Mistral, Erosion by Ice. [I have underlined Monsoons, Dew, the Mistral, Erosion by Ice.]

138

3. a) Describe carefully the development of a river from its source to its mouth, and

b) select a river and explain its course, system of tributaries, type of mouth, and position of large town on its banks.

4. What do you know about the growth, harvesting, and use of hops?

5. Describe the experiences of a drop of water in the Atlantic Ocean, from the moment it is evaporated by the sun's heat, until it finds itself in a puddle on the Dragon School playground.

6. On a journey along the coasts of France make a list of the ports you see, and describe the different types you find.

7. Why was the Suez Canal built? Tell the story of its construction, and outline its history and geographical importance.

8. Construct a contoured map of an island, about seven miles long and five miles wide. Mark on it the following: -

The scale. Cliffs 300 ft. high in the North-West. A hill over 500 ft. high. A river flowing South-East. Two villages connected by a road. A railway crossing the river and joining the villages by a different route. A church with spire.

Also inserted loosely into the exercise books, though there is no date attached, are two cyclostyled world maps. They are clearly answers to tests, one showing twenty capital cities and their location, for which I received five marks, the other has another twenty rivers and eight sets of mountains. The combined score for all my answers was 27/30.

*

I am surprised and somewhat impressed by the range and depth of what we were expected to learnt at eleven, though I do not know how it would compare to the teaching of students nowadays. It seems to have been based on up-to-date textbooks and helpful cyclostyled notes supplied to us.

I am also surprised and quite impressed by the maturity of my handwriting, though it is not, in essence, different from my letters at the time. I am particularly surprised to find that I could draw quite good maps, diagrams, and small sketches of appropriate objects. My art work here is better than the few traces I had previously discovered illustrating my letters of the period. I seem to have begun to understand scale, perspective, techniques of simplifying down to the essence of a representation. This is not quite up to the standard of the illustration in Tuftes' great works, but it is not bad. I don't think I improved much as the years went on. I would have been able to draw a usable map, a cross-section or plan of a number of things on the basis of this knowledge. I also had a basic grasp of various aspects of climate, physical geography and manufacturing processes.

I am less impressed by my spelling, which starts off as pretty atrocious, though it has improved somewhat by the end of these nine months. Certain words, in particular 'wich', are consistently misspelt. My failure to work out my argument in advance, to plan the logic, is a fault which recurred throughout my schooling and into my years at university.

I am particularly impressed by the attentive oversight of my work by Mr Copleston and my other teachers. Each attempt was carefully scrutinized, most spelling mistakes corrected and bad expressions improved. Arguments were made more concrete and the occasions when there was little plan to the argument pointed out. What I mistook is noted, and omitted facts and arguments are written in. About two-thirds of the comments are encouraging – good, very good, well written and so on. About one third contains constructive comments about what was wrong.

In many preparatory schools about which I have read the system was based on a rather terrifying system of rewards and punishments. If one accumulated a number of black marks for pieces of work, one was punished. I do not remember anything like this and the notes in the geography volumes suggest that the whole system was not based on absolute good and bad marks, but on scores out of ten, twenty or thirty, followed by a comment. It may have been different in more central school subjects such as Latin or French, but I do not remember that it was.

There is also quite a bit of evidence of testing throughout the course, especially at the end of the Christmas and Summer terms. There is a fair amount of essay writing alongside diagrams and maps. The examination clearly attempted to move beyond the repetition of facts, to test our analytic and narrative skills. We were to trace the history of a drop of water (which reminds me of Carlo Levi's carbon atom – which did not end in a Dragon puddle, but in a full stop at the end of his essay), to imagine ourselves sailing down the coast of France, or to design an imaginary island. It is all quite creative and at times humorous and quirky in a way which reflects the exams and general papers described in the previous chapter.

As for the content of what we were to learn, the readers can see for themselves. In this particular year we covered the Americas fairly thoroughly, and also Africa. Within Europe we concentrated on England but also a little on France and Europe more generally. In Asia and the Pacific we mostly noted currents, mountains, rivers and other such features. There was quite a concern with the production of various commodities – cotton, coffee, wood, coal and other such items. There was a little on the population and ethnic composition. There seems, perhaps with unintentional irony, to have been a good deal about the Depression, and it is appropriate that one of my illustrations of the process of this phenomenon had the depression hanging over the Dragon School.

140

There is, of course, no questioning of the prevailing systems. Apart from the note on the colour problem in South Africa, there is nothing on politics, colonialism, imperialism, exploitation of man or nature. I was only eleven and twelve, so I suppose it is not surprising. The questioning of the established system, of why the map of Africa had so much pink on it, would come elsewhere or later.

ORAL CULTURE

The New Hall in the 1940s, with allegorical mural (since removed), the
scene of many performances

15 LECTURES

We were subjected, throughout our time at the Dragon, to various kinds of lectures and exhortations. These consisted of lectures by outside speakers, speeches at the annual prize-giving speech day, and the sermons preached each week at the Sunday service. We were also strongly encouraged to develop rhetorical skills through speech giving ourselves, recitations and a lively debating society. Each of these gives us an insight into the kind of mental and social world that surrounded us in this school.

There were occasional lectures by outside speakers on particular themes that were thought to be useful or amusing – perhaps in giving us ideas for our future careers, or to broaden our minds to take in what was happening in distant lands. The choice of person and subject, a few of which are noted in my letters, tells us a good deal about the kind of world it was expected we would inhabit.

In the Christmas term of my second year, 1951, there was a lecture by a Mr Beckett, summarized in The Draconian (by Mark Elvin, later a distinguished sinologist, when he was thirteen years old) on Kierman's expedition in Persia and the follow-up by Beckett. It was illustrated by slides and Elvin ends his summary: 'They had an interesting conversation with some South Persian soldiers before they left. They discovered that they are friendly, lazy, good-natured, and detest war.'

On 18 February 1953 I wrote: *We had a lecture last night on a expedition to the Arctic and it was very intersting.* Ten days later on 1 March I wrote, *We had a lecture on Saturday about the Olympic games with lantern slides and the lecturer was Harold Abrahams who is a very fine athlete and who won a race a few years ago .... We are having another lecture today about naval aviation and here is a jet or two.* [pictures, obviously traced with carbon paper, of four kinds of plane]; and a week later on 8 March: *We are having a lecture tonight with two sound films on missionary in Africa and china.*

Another lecture occurred at the start of my fourth year, when on October 24, according to The Draconian, Philip Bentlif (O.D.), gave a 'very stimulating lecture' on 'In the New world', an account of his travels across America. The account ends: 'Philip's vivid account made it possible for us to understand the amazing paradox of a highly civilized and artificial society built on the edge of a desert and possessing few natural resources. At the end of the lecture he answered a battery of excited questioners, and sent us all away with the urge to visit the B.O.A.C. or Cunard agencies as soon as possible.'

In the Summer term there was a lecture by a master, Mr Copleston, on 'Takoradi to Timbuktu', travels from the Gold Coast to the north of Africa on a bicycle. The report was written by a boy, Philip Steadman, now a distinguished professor of architecture, then aged twelve-and-a-half. The lecture was accompanied by slides, and ended with a film 'The Tree of Life' on the founding of palm-oil refineries in the Belgian Congo.

I do not note any of these in my surviving letters, but in my last Easter term, on 27 January 1955, I wrote, *In the evening there was a lecture (by an undergraduate from Worcester college) who gave a talk about the Oxford travel club's journey to Angola in S. Africa. And he illustrated it with a coloured film.* Then on 17 March I note, *in the evening their was a talk by a women from the N.S.P.C. (National Society for the Prevention of Cruelty to Children). And it was all very stirring. But next day I was sick.* I was clearly becoming faintly cynical in my old age, or perhaps uncomfortable at a talk which may have been a little close to the bone. Much earlier, on 20 April 1952, I wrote from a summer camp at Milford on Sea, *We had a lucture on doctor bonados and a film on the children their,* another glimpse at another world of children.

The speeches given at the prize-giving in the Summer terms are printed in The Draconian and I will take some extracts and themes from these to see what we were being told. They are particularly interesting since each year a mother and a father of two current pupils gave the speeches, followed by a short speech by the headmaster. So we gain some insight into what parents thought the boys might be interested in, how they should be encouraged in certain directions, and what the assumptions behind sending boys to the school was.

In my first Summer term, 1951, the speeches started with one by a parent, Mrs Dunbabin, who had just given out the prizes. Amongst her remarks, all of them printed in The Draconian, it is worth noting her views on Dragon diaries.

'But the people I really admire are the writers of the diaries. I have always thought diary writing one of the most valuable of all Dragon activities, and when I congratulate the winners I must certainly include their families, because I am sure a good diary must be, partly at any rate, a joint effort... And much more than the prize, the diary itself will be your reward. I know you will enjoy re-reading it and re-living a summer holiday, perhaps in the depths of winter. Best of all, if you do it

year after year, you will have for always a record of your family, your friends, and yourself, and if you watch your ideas changing, and your hand-writing and spelling, you will be very much like looking back and seeing how you became the sort of person you now are.'
'

Alas that I did not take her advice and do not seem to have kept any diaries.

On the subject of diaries, some people did keep diaries, for which they might be awarded prizes. I have read one or two of them. Nigel Williams in Upper 2A, writes: 'My Dragon holiday diaries have survived however, which on re-reading seem to be heavily influenced by Molesworth. The most frequent entry is "Mum in a bate".'

The next speaker was Tommy Hodgkin, another parent. Among other musings in a witty and clever talk, he said

'I sometimes wonder what makes me respect and admire the Dragon School as much as I do. I think that, more than anything else, it is that at the Dragon School one gets the idea of doing what one thinks right and saying what one thinks, and not paying too much attention to whether other people approve of it or not. When I went on from here to a Public School, the first thing people said to me, when they heard I came from the Dragon School, was "Oh, you come from the School where the girls play Rugger".'

Hodgkin, being timid, was at first going to make a conciliatory answer that they never went beyond the third XV. 'Then it occurred to me to reply, "Well, why shouldn't girls play Rugger if they want to?" and I found these people had no answer to that.'

In Summer 1952, my second year, the first speaker was Mrs Hope (whose son Francis, as I recall, was a very successful boy at the school at the time, and who had been a parent of Dragons for twelve years). She proceeded to praise the school, especially for its teachers and for the diverse and often contradictory teaching the pupils received. Ronnie Evers then made a speech. Among other things, he said: 'Lots of things you do here are extraordinarily difficult, but you do them as though they are easy; and you will find, when you go to other schools, that you are much more practised at that kind of thing than other people. You are lucky in being given that sort of training here, making difficult things appear easy. You do not think them easy, but you work so hard at them that everyone else thinks you find them easy.' He then went on to point out that the school motto, 'Arduus ad Solem', was used by Virgil to describe a 'particularly noisome snake'. Yet, 'The Dragon, you see, has taken something ordinary and made it into something rather remarkable, and I should like to think of what this School does for us in that way.'

The final speech was by Joc. He quoted a letter from a Dragon parent:
'My husband and I would like to thank you and your excellent staff on our
boy's behalf. He has acquired an ease of manner and stability of character
– that indefinable something which real Dragons get and which we are
happy to know will last him all his life.' Joc then commented:

'I like to think of this indefinable something as being passed on from
one boy to the next all the time ... And I like to think that this
"something" is based mainly on the freedom which exists here more,
probably, than in any other Preparatory or Public School. But freedom
isn't easy to respect. Indeed, it is far easier to abuse. And the real
Dragon spirit only comes from learning how to use freedom properly
and not to abuse it. It means that every one of us has a much greater
responsibility to the community than if there were more outside
controls, and it means that one of our greatest responsibilities is to learn
how to control ourselves.'

He then drew attention to an earlier address which had talked about
three lamps which the boys should burnish and make brighter. 'The lamp
of friendship – an outstretched hand always ready to help someone in
trouble or someone less lucky than you are yourself. The lamp of witness;
that means the lamp of faith – faith in yourselves, faith in others, and faith
in what is right. And lastly the lamp of dedication – that is, of giving
ourselves up to do what we believe to be right.'

At the prize-giving in Summer 1953, the first speech was by Mrs Backus
and the second by Mr Cartwright. The latter suggested, among other
things: 'The charm of the Dragon School to all Dragons and Old Dragons
is that all change is very, very gradual. Revolutions, whether in countries or
in schools, are very unpleasant for everybody.' He continued, 'Nothing is
ever changed just for novelty's sake. If there is something good, then try to
make it better; and I expect that if you boys think something is bad, you
very quickly tell a master about it, and it gets put right.'

Joc's final speech was mainly a report on how an extremely busy term,
dominated by the Coronation, had gone. Joc ended by noting that the
Ministry of Education had suggested that 'Competence, Curiosity, and
Conscience' should be encouraged in school. To this he wished to add
'Courtesy, Cooperation, and Cheerfulness'. This was addressed especially
to the leavers:

'If, when you leave here, you do so as competent young men able to
do a job well, reliable in a crisis, and able to look after other people if
they need; if you leave here with inquisitive minds wanting to know why
things happen and the reasons for rules and conditions which to you
may not seem to make sense: if you leave here having trained your

conscience to know the difference between right and wrong and having trained yourselves to do what your conscience tells you is right: if you leave here determined to be kind and courteous to all those with whom you come in contact and to co-operate readily with anyone who needs your co-operation; and if you have learnt to remain cheerful always, especially when things go wrong, I reckon that your time here as Dragons will have been well spent.'

At the Summer prize-giving in 1954, the parents chosen to give out the prizes were Mrs Thompson (Penelope Stradling, O.D.), and Mr Stanier, Headmaster of Magdalen College School. Mrs Thompson again praised the value of the holiday diaries and exhorted those who wrote them: 'Don't destroy them or lose them, and don't let your mother tidy them away at spring-cleaning...' – for as you re-read your diary in the future, 'a ghost of your former self will appear before you to remind you'. She went on to say, 'Now I want to repeat what many people have said to you before. You all know you have a big debt to pay for your heritage. It is a debt to a great many people, and one which you will find hard to pay...'

In the final speech by Joc, alongside his usual thanks to staff and account of the term, he said '...I reckon that happiness is rather important. A happy atmosphere is a very important part of any community, and that atmosphere can only be created by the members of the community itself.' He also alluded to the last sermon of term which had stressed how privileged the children were and that this brought responsibilities. Joc added, 'It's not enough to grow up in a happy home and in a happy school and to do your part in making those places happy. It's your responsibility also to find out what other homes are like and what other schools are like.'

At the end of my last term among Joc's observations were some specifically for me and others going off to our public schools. 'Much will be expected of them there, and may I just remind them of what I said about two things, privileges and responsibilities? I always hope that one of the things which Dragons learn here is that privileges are very unimportant things, but that responsibilities are very important.' He ended by saying 'During these last few days there have been some splendid contests in the river and on the fields. Boys have learnt to swim well, to jump well and to run well. But far more important, they have also learnt – I hope and think – to win well and to lose well – to take success and disappointments in their stride. Don't ever forget the importance of these two things.'

*

Each term The Draconian would print a list of the services which were held on Sundays, mostly in the School Hall (since there was no chapel), which all boarders were obliged to attend. The readings at these services are also given and are sometimes revealing. Occasionally, if it was thought to be special, the whole sermon would be printed. Here I shall describe the course of sermons in my first and last years in full, with a few selected sermons, particularly by Joc, in the intervening years.

The first sermon I heard at the school, on September 24 1950, was in fact by the headmaster, Joc. He spoke on 'Orando laborando: how to become good citizens and good Christians, by hard work and prayer'. It was a suitable theme for a school with the motto 'Arduus ad Solem'. The readings went beyond several biblical texts, to something from Ruskin ('Do not ask for God's Kingdom when you do not want it'); St Francis de Sales, 'On cherishing the small virtues'; John Bunyan on 'Let not your left hand know what your right hand doeth' and 'Pray to the Father' by Tennyson.

The next week the headmaster of Donnington School, Oxford, preached on 'The vision of God', and music from Haydn's 'Creation' was played on recordings. There was a little later a sermon by the Bishop of Buckingham on 'Childhood into Manhood; what to keep and what to get rid of: keep trust and wonder; life regarded as a treasure hunt', where the readings included something from C.S. Lewis.

The sermon on 5 November was by the Rector of Lawford in Essex, on 'Trust in God: personal experience of its effects, in India and in war'. At this service the new 1950 Hymn Book was used for the first time. The Remembrance Day service was held a week later on 12 November at the Cross. Various poems were read by boys and the sermon was on 'Friendship; God's Gift to Man'. The following week the Master of Magdalen College School preached on 'Fear – often unnecessary, to be encountered by prayer and faith'.

Among the sermons the following term were the following: The Revd Wilkins on 'Three choices of man – wealth, fame, and service – giving not getting'. This was illustrated by the casket scene in the Merchant of Venice and a reading from Isaac Walton, among other things. Several masters gave sermons and then the Revd Christopher Stead (O.D.) chaplain of Keble College, preached on 'Run the race, looking unto Jesus: looking forward to the goal: perseverance and heroism in man'. The readings included George Macdonald and Thomas Carlyle on the 'Heroic in Man'.

In the Christmas term 1951, at the start of my second year, there were three Bishops preaching. Joc the headmaster again started the year, with a sermon on 'Beginning of Term: happiness, courage, thankfulness'. Most of the readings were on courage. On 9 October I noted in a letter home *We are going to the City church for the service*; as usual, the second service was in the City church for Harvest Festival.

In the Christmas term 1952, the first term of my third year, Joc again gave the first sermon on, 'responsibility: lamps to light and keep burning, and freedom without the abuse of it', thereby continuing the theme of his prize-giving speech at the end of the previous term. On 5 October I wrote to my parents, *We are having the service at the city church and the lord mare will be there because it is harvest festival.* In The Draconian it was noted that this annual harvest festival service at St Martin's church, 'was admittedly rather long, and we hope that some improvement in this matter may be arranged for future occasions'.

On October 26 my teacher Francis Wylie spoke on 'Hope: Mercy even for Pooh Bah'. There were the usual memorial services and readings, and then on November 16, following the performance of 'Patience' in which I had appeared, W.F. Oakeshott, the headmaster of Winchester, preached on 'leadership and true greatness', and the readings included Mencius and Albert Schweitzer. On November 30 the new Principal of Ripon Hall, Bishop Geoffrey Allen, preached on 'the answer to the call', illustrated by his own career as Fellow of an Oxford College, service in China, and as Bishop of Egypt.

The following Easter term we heard about 'Building on foundations, e.g. Dartmoor Stone: Jesus Christ, the Foundation' and two weeks later, 'The extra mile': not content with duty only, the unprofitable servant, which included a reading about Livingstone. The following week we heard about Missions to Seamen. At the end of term I wrote home on 22 March, *We are having our service in St Andrews and we have not much time to write our letters.*

At the start of my fourth year, Christmas 1953, the first sermon was again by Joc, on 'A spirit of purpose and energy, combined with unselfishness and goodwill', and included a reading from Frank Sidgwick, an old boy. In the Summer term, the sermons were started by Joc, who preached on 'the importance of character: the Good Shepherd and the widow's mite', and, as usual, included some poems. The following week the school heard Eric Fletcher, M.P., on 'the use of talent in service to the community'. A later sermon, by Lionel Carey, headmaster of Bromsgrove School, was on 'God and our neighbour: how each individual counts, and yet how insignificant is man and our world'. Lord Hemingford preached on 'Forgiveness', and the Dean of Salisbury on 'Patriotism to God'.

In Christmas 1954, at the start to my last year, Joc spoke in the first week on 'the beginning of term: prayer and work'. On October 17 the Rev. Cragg spoke on 'Finding the way: the need of a compass', and included poems by Whitman and Quarles. As before, one of the speakers was an O.D., a master from Manchester Grammar School. On November 4, my mother and I again attended a service after Iolanthe, where the Principal of Ripon Hall preached on 'Things old and new', with appropriate references to Iolanthe. The following week Michael Gover, O.D., preached on 'Manners', and the service included a reading from Tennyson's 'The Passing of Arthur'. On December 5 Dr Booth, Professor of Historical Theology at Boston University, preached on 'the beginnings of religion', including such items as negro spirituals, which were illustrated by a performance of one called 'Were you there?'. The final service 'was followed by Carols, which were by general consent perhaps the best ever performed at this Service'. Alas, I had already gone home because of flu.

In Spring term 1955, the first sermon was by the Rev. Wilkins, the school teacher of divinity, who was about to leave, on 'It is better to give than to receive'. Dr Booth from Boston returned to give another sermon, 'Abraham Lincoln: a biographical sketch of his life and character'. On 20 February I wrote home *Today the third suppers are going to St Andrew's church and I am in the choir.* The Draconian reported how, 'The seniors among the boarders and some of the day-boys attended Matins at St. Andrew's, where the preacher was the new Vicar, the Revd. F.J. Taylor.'

The following week, the Assistant Bishop of Derby preached on 'The cult of a thankful heart'. Subsequently, the Latin master, L.A. Wilding, preached on 'The importance of the insignificant'. On 13 March I wrote to my parents, *Today there was a service at St Phillips and St James with thousands of long hymns and psalms.* Perhaps even the author of The Draconian account was fed up, since instead of the usual detailed report of what was read and preached, it merely states, 'The boarders attended Mattins at SS. Phil and James.'

In my last term, Joc gave the first sermon, 'Our duty to God and to our neighbour'. On May 22 Peter Marindin preached on 'the standard for living'. Following the Fathers' Cricket matches, Basil Blackwell, J.P. spoke on 'Unanswered prayer'. Blackwell gave a thoughtful sermon, once again accompanied with a long story, which was published. The Provost of Birmingham reflected on 'A Midsummer Night's Dream' which had just been performed. He ended with the sentence, 'For humility and the power to see oneself as the strange creature one is makes for generous tolerance and sympathy for the failings of others, and these are the conditions of being forgiven.' On July 10 Bishop Robert Moberley's theme was 'I serve'. The last sermon I heard was by the Rev. Smith, 'The silent speaking of Jesus, the noise in the world: the still small voice'; it was accompanied by readings which included Wordsworth's 'Lines written near Tintern Abbey', which became one of my favourite poems.

16 SPEAKING

The topics chosen for the debating prize, presumably picked by the boys as subjects they were interested in and could shine with, are revealing. They can be reviewed through the formal reports, which give the names of the boys, their subjects, and a report on parts of their speech and how they were classed. A prize could be won in each term, but no one could win more than one prize in a year and a prize could be held over to the next term if not awarded.

The topics in my first year were: Prep., Korea, Christmas Presents, Holidays, Swimming, The Liberal Party, Anti-nationalization of sugar, Classics to be optional, What School subjects should be taught. And in my second year they were: The advantages of phonetic spelling, Christmas presents, Camping holidays, Trying to be helpful, Shakespeare, Cats, Punctuality, Holidays, Bad habits of the staff. In my third year (the detail of the first term missing – there were only two competitors), Fox-hunting, Learning foreign languages at school, The British workman, The Ideal schoolmaster, School Rules and punishments, Relatives, India, Was the Coronation in London worth it?, Space, Travel possibilities, Mucking About.

Interestingly, Bruno added quite a long note of advice at the end of his Summer 1953 Fitch Prize report, reprinted in The Draconian:

> It is, I suggest, entirely wrong for any speaker to deliver a badly arranged, badly presented, and barely audible speech to any audience – some of the speeches on this occasion were almost completely inaudible. A speech has to be <u>properly prepared</u>. It has to be thought out, arranged, logical (if the speaker is debating some point), well-expressed, well-spoken, and completely audible to every person in the audience. All this calls, not for an eleventh-hour scurry to get something ready, but for hard work well ahead of the time. The speech, when prepared, should be carefully rehearsed, practised, and timed, so that when the moment arrives, the speaker comes to the business confident that he knows exactly what he is going to say, and how he is going to say it. Future competitors, please note.

In my fourth year the topics were: The Pleasures of Camping, The

Attractions of Farming, (Easter 1954, report missing), History is Bunk, Railways, The History of Flying. In my last year the topics were: The Folly of Trying to Reach the Moon (the only competitor, on account of flu), The Value of International Sport, Myxamatosis, Birds, The H-Bomb, The Colour Bar.

Apart from things like camping, holidays, birds etc., two themes seem worth noting. One is that the occasion could be used to make amusing criticisms or suggestions about the school – as in 'The Ideal schoolmaster' and 'School rules and punishments' and 'Bad habits of the staff'. The second is a serious interest in politics and world events – the nationalization of sugar, Korea, the Colour Bar, the H bomb.

I never contended for this prize, and cannot recall whether I ever attended what were, presumably, public performances by the boys who entered. Jake Mermagen, however, writes that, 'In 1955, my last year, there were no entries. Out of a sense of duty I volunteered to make a speech on the life of Hitler. At the last minute someone told me that I could not simply recite historical facts, but needed to prove some point. I hastily changed the title to "Hitler was a great man". Needless to say I did not get the prize!'

*

Perhaps to encourage a love of poetry amongst us, as well as to improve our elocution, there was not only weekly prep in which we had to learn a piece of poetry or prose, but there was also a Recitation Prize. Since in my third year I was a member of the Middle 3 class winning team, I had a special interest in this prize and dimly remember reciting part of Dryden's 'Ode to St Cecilia', which we had to learn. A full report in The Draconian on the event in my first term at the school in 1950 gives a flavour of what it was about. It starts with Mr Bruno's advice on how best to recite.

No one should attempt to recite unless he can do justice to his choice and help his audience to appreciate it, and to do this requires one absolute necessity. The reciter must know his words so perfectly that he speaks them automatically. Then, and only then, can be begin to interpret them. Many poems were ruined by agonised pauses, and tortured groping for words, so that all illusion was lost, and often even the sense. This happened many times when one poem was recited by several different boys, so that the excellent performances of some were nullified by the mistakes of others. When once the words are mastered, then interpretation is helped by the effects of pitch, tone, and pace. Most boys spoke up well and could be heard easily, but too many failed to alter the tone of voice, and few realised how much can be achieved by altering the pace, and by suitable pauses, but not necessarily at the

152

end of the line.

The report details what each year-group performed. The Lowers offered a delightful mixed bunch of poems, including Kipling's 'Hunting Song'. The Middles gave the best performance, including Humbert Wolfe's 'Two Sparrows', and Middle 5 did Belloc's 'Matilda'. In the Uppers, there was a 'Just So' story, again by Kipling, and Goldsmith's 'Village Schoolmaster' and Belloc's 'Food'. Best of all was Flecker's 'Saracens War Song'. This recitation prize for whole forms was only one of those awarded; for example, there were A.E.L's Reading Prizes and the Daisy Pratt Prize for Baby School Recitation.

A revealing account of part of what was behind the recitations is shown in a report in The Draconian of Summer 1954.

'The beauty of Israel is slain upon the high places: How are the mighty fallen!

As Roland Brinton began to declaim the magnificent words of David's lament, the whole audience at once fell under his spell. How the Skipper would have rejoiced to hear him.

Here was Dragon Recitation at its traditional best; first in its choice of a passage which gives such superb scope to the music of the spoken word; second in the way Brinton attacked the passage with such fire and passion; and third in the fine diction and modulation of his voice.

In these days of the glorification of the Common Man, and the needless broadcasting of common ugly voices on T.V. and on the Radio, it was good to hear English at its loveliest, with pure vowels and boldly sounded consonants. Sometimes even Dragons are guilty of slovenly vowel-sounds, due mainly to speaking with their mouths but not with their lips ...

Upper 1 finished the morning's proceedings with great distinction, with Stanier, Beloff, and Jeffery to cap last year's Virgilian success with a beautiful passage from 'Alcestis', in which Beloff was outstanding with his moving and musical speaking of Greek.'

*

Allthough I do not remember attending the debating prize competitions, I did attend the frequent debates organized by the Debating Society. Here we were to learn something about the art of public speaking, of rhetoric and oratory. This has always been an important area in English life since the days of the medieval universities and legal profession. At the Dragon we were being trained to make us leaders of men – and hence the persuasive use of language was an essential craft skill.

This seems to have been an activity I really enjoyed and was probably important in shaping and expressing our views. The few I noted can be supplemented from The Draconian, and the reports on such debates give an insight into the kinds of subject it was thought interesting for children to discuss at the Dragon. It also gives, in the description of the arguments put forward as summarized in the reports – as well as the final vote for and against – an indication of our views at the time. I don't remember speaking at these, but I certainly found them worth reporting.

In my first term, Christmas 1950, there were debates around the following proposals: 'That there are such things as ghosts'. This was carried 43 to 23, an appropriate result for a school which, as I have argued elsewhere, had more than a hint of Hogwarts about it. Then it was proposed, 'That marks should be abolished'. Perhaps not surprisingly, the boys voted 41 to 24 for the motion. Then we debated the hot topic, 'That Rugby Football is unsuitable for boys under the age of 14'. Again, perhaps predictably, the motion was lost 15 votes to 44. On the last Saturday of term there were a series of impromptu debates, that is, shorter debates held at short notice: 'That snow does more harm than good' (carried unanimously), 'That there are such things as flying saucers' (lost by 14 votes to 39) and 'Spare the rod, spoil the child' (lost by 10 votes to 21).

In my second term the motions were: 'That medieval warfare is more cruel than modern warfare' (carried by 40 votes to 16); 'That the amateur derives more enjoyment out of sport than the professional' (carried by 44 votes to 25); 'That a holiday in a hotel is preferable to a camping holiday' (defeated by 67 votes to 10); 'That the written word is more powerful than the spoken word' (defeated 41 votes to 11). Then, near the end of term, there were impromptu debates as follows: 'That tennis should be an alternative game to cricket for all Dragons in the Summer Term' (defeated 22 votes to 29), 'That a good film is more enjoyable than a good play' (carried by 51 votes to 50) and 'That a knowledge of History is more useful in after life than a knowledge of English' (defeated by 48 votes to 27). Debates did not take place in the Summer term.

The first debate I recorded in a letter was at the start of my second year. The Festival of Britain had dominated the summer and the school had visited it. It had been a controversial event, and many critics considered that it had been an economic failure. I reported, on 7 October 1951, *We had a debate and the motion was the festival of Britain gained money. And against the motion one [won] by 43 to 29.* The report states that the actual motion was 'That the Festival of Britain had justified itself'. I did not write about the next two debates: 'That progress had not brought happiness' (defeated 46 votes to 22); 'That films have spoilt the pleasure of reading' (defeated by 44 votes to 22). The end of term impromptu debates were 'That a burglar's life is not a happy one' (defeated unanimously); 'That the spirit of adventure is dead' (defeated unanimously); 'That fat people eat more than thin people' (defeated unanimously).

The following term we had a debate on a subject which reveals something about our views of childhood, where we showed scepticism that these were, as we were often told, 'the happiest days of our life'. On 27 January 1952 I wrote: *We had a debate the motion being 15 is more enjoyable than 50 and against the motion one* [won] *about 12 v 50.* Since this debate, comparing life at the age of fifteen and fifty, shows something about our attitudes to age and the school, I shall give the actual summary of the debate (where no result was said to be available) given in The Draconian:

'The Proposer, P. Swash, said that at fifteen you can play games for Colts or the First XI, but at fifty there are no more team games, only golf, which gets monotonous. Pointing to the playground, Mr. Swash asked if grown-ups would have slides or snowball fights. In the Over 45 Amateur Squash Championship there were only seven entries from the whole of England. At fifteen you have your National Service before you, but this can be enjoyable if you have the right approach. If you lose your job at fifty your chances of getting another are small. At fifty there is the fear of death, but at fifteen life is before you.'

'The Opposer, G. Guinness, said that the House had no idea of life at fifty, when there were different enjoyments and appreciations. At fifty you are at the peak of your life, not a doddering old fool, as the Proposer seemed to think. Perhaps the Amateur Squash Championship had only seven entries, but Squash is not a popular sport. At fifty, his grandfather was an active and efficient Mayor of Maidenhead. Besides golf, the over fifties can swim and go mountaineering.'

'The second speaker, P. Bourne, said that it might be nice to see your family growing up, but your schooldays were the happiest days of your life. At fifteen you had a better sense of humour, and if a snowball should hit you, you would return it, but at fifty you would grumble and take it badly. At fifty you would have financial worries, because no one is rich nowadays. At fifteen one might be starting a job, and it would be fun to be earning one's own living.'

'The fourth speaker, M. Rena, said that his grandfather, at 65, is still able to ski, and go for eight-hour mountaineering courses, and will soon take up curling. People might talk about active sports, but at fifteen you are not really at your sporting prime. At fifty one can understand and appreciate many more books, and can do things (such as driving a motor-car) which are not allowed to a boy of fifteen.'

The names of eighteen other boys who spoke are noted.

The next motion was 'That it is better to give entertainment than to be entertained' (motion carried by 45 votes to 10). The next debate was 'That life in the town is better than life in the country' (the motion was defeated by 23 votes to 8).

In the first term of my third year, Autumn 1952, I noted in a letter on 12 October 1952, that *We had a debate yesterday and the subject was that a athlete gets more enjoyment out of life than a skolar with the motion won by 69-33.* (In fact, the result in given The Draconian is 63 votes to 39.)

The next debate repeated a theme from my first year, though reversing the proposal, namely 'That modern warfare is more cruel than mediaeval warfare'. The outcome was the same, the motion being defeated by 72 votes to 43. The debate about ghosts was also repeated, 'That there are such things as ghosts' and again the school voted for them, 78 votes to 34. There is a very detailed account of the arguments in these debates, and many people spoke in them, including a number of my closer friends and my cousin Jake Mermagen.

In the Easter term of my third year (1953), the report on the debates in The Draconian was unfortunately only a few lines long. It recorded only that among the subjects debated were: 'That all games should be legalized on Sundays' and 'That corporal punishment ought to be re-introduced for crimes of violence'. The arguments and outcomes of these debates are not recorded.

There was also an Impromptu Debate, which is the only one I recorded in my letters under *impromtude* debates. These were reported in my letter of 8 March 1953, with the title of the first correctly transcribed, *the first motion was that a mistress is a better teacher than a master the motion lost 75-25.* My own memory is that the few female teachers I had, particularly my first teacher when I arrived, were kind and protective, but clearly this was not the consensus.

The next recognized the rapidly increasing role of television in our lives. The motion was *Television and the cinema is a substitute to reading.* [The actual motion was 'That neither television nor the cinema can be a satisfactory substitute for reading'.] I reported that *Against the motion won,* though not by how much.

The next, not mentioned in my letter report, and which probed our ambition and feeling of confidence that we could achieve much, namely the motion 'that a bird in the hand is worth two in the bush'. I wrote that, *Against the motion won 100-6.* We were clearly going to go out in the bush and find hidden birds. I also noted another unmentioned motion *that games in the Dragon school should be volentary the motion was defeated.*

At the start of my fourth year, Christmas 1953, the first proposal was 'That the Schoolboy's life is happier than the Master's' (carried by 45 votes to 23). The second debate was on the proposal 'That the inventions of the last hundred years have brought happiness to mankind' (carried by 53 votes to 27).

Unfortunately, there is again only a very small report on debates in the Term Notes for the Easter term 1954. The first motion was 'That the

156

Popular Music of To-day is More Attractive to Listen to Than the Classical Compositions of Yesterday'. The motion was unanimously defeated.

One of the largest divides in the school was between dayboys and boarders. Given the loneliness and separation to which the boarders were subjected, it is perhaps surprising that on 16 February 1954 I reported that, *Yesterday there was a debate the motion was "Dayboys have a more enjoyable time than borders". Against the motion won 59-7.* In fact, the report stated that 'the motion was defeated unanimously', which is even more dramatic. I do not note the series of impromptu debates mentioned in the report.

In my last Autumn term, 1954, the first motion was 'Modern Luxuries are the Cause of Moral Decay in Modern Man'. The outcome is not recorded. There was then something that I described in a letter at the end of October. *There was a new kind of Debat in which there were four boys. Each resembling a famous person 1 Billy Graham 2 Lord Nuffield 3 Prof Einstein 4 Albert Shweitzer 5 Roger Bannister And they were meant to be all in a balloon and two of them had to be thrown out for the other three to be kep in.* Here was a chance to place our priorities, would religion, economics, science, philanthropy or sport survive? Again reflecting the rather academic nature of the school I reported that *1 and 5 were thrown out,* religion and sport. The report on the debate in the Term Notes is as follows:

'R. Burleigh, supporting Roger Bannister, said he deserved to be retained as a great sportsman who might still perform great feats. D. Sherwin-White, supporting Lord Nuffield, said that this great public benefactor and Industrialist had made Oxford what it was, and could not be easily replaced. S. Crossman, supporting Billy Graham, said that this famous evangelist had started a religious crusade which had converted many people. J. Gilman, supporting Albert Schweitzer, said that he had given up a great career to help the Africans. He had won the Nobel Prize. P. Steadman, supporting Alfred Einstein, said that this eminent mathematician had done much work towards the advancement of scientific research. Roger Bannister and Bally Graham were thrown out.'

There was, finally, a last debate at the end of term, the motion being 'Money is the root of all evil'. The motion was unanimously defeated.

In my final term of attending debates, Easter 1955, I wrote on 27 February, *We had a debate on Saturday the motion was that capital punishment ought to be brought back for crimes of violence. The motion won 61-29.* It is perhaps a straw in the wind as to our political and social attitudes.

On 13 March 1955 there were several debates. The first motion was: 'It is better to be an only child than to be in a large family'. Against won 40-15. Most of us, as I recall, had brothers and sisters. Another was 'Atomic weapons should be banned'. Despite our views on capital punishment, we were clearly disturbed by the new weapons and I reported *For won 34-21*. And another one was that *It is better to be good at games than at work. Against won by 54-14*, an outcome which might not have been found in every school at this time.

The final one was a curious topic and had a curious outcome. 'The house regrets the invention of Air Travel.' The motion was carried 45-9. What I thought of this with my interest in jet planes and the way the new planes had brought me closer to my parents in India, I do not know.

The disagreeing figures I gave in the space of a week as to the outcome of the debates suggests that my attention was more on the debate than the votes, but even the topics became hazy after a while, for I reported on 17 March the topics of two out of four of the debates – *on games and work, and atomic weapons, But I can't remember the other two*. Nor did I remember that I had reported all four the week before.

All this debating was clearly a useful preparation in rhetoric and logic and the general arts of persuasion. A number of the boys were the sons of dons at Oxford and elsewhere and would go on to be lecturers, politicians and civil servants, or, it was doubtless still believed, rulers of empire. These were important skills and were clearly encouraged.

It is interesting to note that high numbers seem to have attended the debates. They were, as I recall, entirely voluntary, and probably mainly attended by boarders. That meant a constituency of all ages of about 300 pupils. The numbers attending, from the registered votes, varied from a low of 31 to a high of 115. The normal numbers fluctuated between 50 and 80.

CREATING MEANING

Iolanthe, Christmas 1954, Alan top right

17 ARTS, MUSIC AND PERFORMANCE

Parents and schools attempted to channel our childhood emotions and thoughts through the development of various expressive skills – drawing, painting, crafts of various kinds, dancing and drama. All these existed alongside the main formal teaching concerned with the manipulation of symbolic systems in reading, writing, arithmetic and the learning of languages. I never excelled in any of these artistic and expressive skills, yet the attempt to learn and the realization of a world of painting, music, dance and drama awaiting me had a significant enriching effect on my life. Again there was no hard and fast division between school and home here – my parents, for example, tried to encourage me in a number of these skills. Yet the major thrust was at school.

*

I was just about competent at art but not anything special. I have a number of my drawings and paintings from about the age of seven onwards, some of which are reproduced at the end of this book and in Dorset Days. They were sent to my parents alongside letters, or to fill them out. What I chose to draw – often aeroplanes etc., and how I drew them – very stylized houses, using carbon paper to provide an outline – are all indicative. They hint at a richer world of development than can be retrieved from my handwriting.

My interest in trying to draw and paint was undoubtedly encouraged by my mother, who pointed with approval at my early efforts in my letters. For example, she wrote to my father on 18 March 1948, when I was a little over seven, *I enclose a picture he painted for you. It has got rather smudged, but isn't bad really and completely his own work.*

My mother was herself an aspiring artist and wrote quite frequently about trying to paint. In a letter she wrote to me on 11 December 1949 from a river trip in Assam, *In the afternoon I tried to paint but I'm afraid I wasn't a bit successful and the only thing I could do was this picture of our huts. Not a nice picture but I've come to the conclusion I can't paint! The green sausage-looking things are banana trees!* The picture was enclosed with the letter.

The Chinese and Japanese see writing and painting as one, as in the art

160

of calligraphy. My letters from the ag of seven to thirteen, seen as calligraphy rather than for their content, are revealing in showing the development of my artistic sense.

The way we were encouraged to develop copper-plate writing, given special lessons and special pens (I still remember the pen fetish and getting my first shining Parker set) is significant. Later in life people would read not only what we said, but how we said it, in our handwriting – not just our character but also our education. So learning to write in a good style was a significant form of training at the Dragon.

So I tried out different pens, different colours, different styles in my letters. In particular, the way in which I practised my signature and soon ended up with the form which I still use – with an underlined Alan (ccompare with Roald Dahl who signed himself 'Boy') is worth noting.

My mother does not really comment on my hand-writing or painting very much beyond commending my first efforts. What she thought of them I do not know. But there is one form of external commentary which shows how other people viewed me.

In my first kindergarten, aged six, I got an 'A' for drawing, with an 18/20 for the exams and second in the form. At my kindergarten at 'Southlands' the school reports on 'Art' were fairly bland but favourable, as follows.

Summer 1948	good
Summer 1949	good
Winter 1949	fairly good
Spring 1950	good work this term
Summer 1950	good, some work spoilt by too many minute details

The last comment on 'minute details' ties in with a feature commented on when I went on to the Dragon. The reports on 'Art' are as follows:

Dec 1950	Much improved use of brush and colours. Some good results
Mar 1951	Gaining confidence in his own ability
Dec 1951	Has done well. Will increase quality of his pictures by strengthening his colour
Mar 1952	Is still using weak colour, otherwise sound
July 1952	A careful worker
Dec 1952	He gives good attention and is interested
Mar 1953	Not wholly reliable in either work or behaviour
July 1953	He needs much prompting but there has been

	improvement lately
Dec 1953	Rather bald in statement but has shown a better approach
Mar 1954	Fair: he does not exert himself
July 1954	His small scale drawings are well managed
Dec 1954	Very stiff drawing and very little of it
Mar 1955	Definition good. Avoids colours when he can

There is no report for my last term.

On the whole the reports start reasonably. They decline in the middle part of my time at the Dragon, and then pick up to a certain extent. The internally grey world of loneliness and anxiety which is commented on in other school reports could be thought to have inhibited me. I would not splash out, either with colour or with bold drawing. My work was minimalist, over-detailed, 'stiff' and lacking confidence.

Interestingly, I have absolutely no memories of the art classes, where they were, how they were run, or even of the KRR who taught me for four out of the five years and with whom, at one time, I showed 'not wholly reliable' behaviour. I now discover that KRR was Miss K.R. Richardson of Woodstock Road. Unlike sports, hobbies and games, I do not seem to have found a way to express my inner anxieties or frustrations through art. I did not lay any foundation for art appreciation – there is no mention of going to galleries or looking at paintings, either at the Dragon or from home. I have always thought of myself as visually blind in terms of formal art and I now see the early roots of this.

*

One of the woodworking areas at the Dragon was a small room under the Museum in the centre of the playground. It smelt of wood and glue. I (Alan) remember sawing, making joints and the construction of wobbly bookcases and toast racks. As I recall, I never took to this or any other craft of this kind throughout my life. My hands are nimble enough to fly-tie, which I saw as useful, but I found most crafts somewhat pointless since it was clear that professionals could do things so much better. Nor do I remember modelling in clay or pottery.

I may have learnt to sew and knit – especially French knitting, that is, creating a tube of knitted wool which was, I remember, something of a craze at the Dragon.

My school reports at the Southlands kindergarten under Handwork show a fairly positive picture after a slow start.

Aged 6-7   Summer 1948   Very slow

Aged 7-0 Autumn 1948 Handwork – Very good
Aged 7-7 Summer 1949 Good
Aged 8-0 Autumn 1949 Good
Aged 8-3 Spring 1950 Good

Then at the Dragon under 'Handicraft' the reports were again reasonable.

Dec 1950 Shows promise. Good clay modelling
Mar 1951 Very industrious
Dec 1951 Good. He always works hard

After that reports on Handicraft disappear until:

Dec 1954 Practical work good
Mar 1955 Good
July 1955 Good effort

In the light of this it seems strange to me that despite displaying some enthusiasm and industriousness, nothing remains in my memory. Yet this is one of the features of my childhood. The chosen, voluntary, informal areas of hobbies and games remain in the mind. The formal, repetitive, school teaching has largely vanished except in the reports.

MUSIC

I don't remember music in my infancy in Assam, though, no doubt, there were lullabies from my mother and my ayah.

It appears from the school reports of my kindergarten that I was quite keen on music before I went to the Dragon. The report form had a space for violin and piano, but I clearly learnt neither. The reports for four terms were as follows:

aged 6-7 Singing Quite Good
aged 7-0 Music Most interested
aged 8-0 Singing Very keen, Band – good rhythm
aged 8-2 Singing Very fair

In my last report there is no mention of music.

I have the vaguest memory that at one time I did try to learn the piano, but am not sure where or when this was. Yet there is a notable absence of any music or singing reports for the Dragon. In the almost complete set of termly reports, every other subject is noted. Only the slot for Music and Singing is empty for every term. This confirms my view that I did no

163

formal music learning – whether this was at my own request or because my parents felt it was an unnecessary expense, I do not know.

Apart from formal music lessons and the Gilbert and Sullivan operas, discussed later in the chapter, there must have been singing in the Sunday services in the New Hall and various churches, though I do not remember this. On 20 February 1955 I wrote that, *Today the third suppers are going to St Andres church and I am in the choir*. But this I do not remember.

Nor do I recall something which I allude to in my letter of 2 February 1953 where I stated, after noting *a jolly good sinny show last night called Mad about Music,* that *I always go to the music club wich is a club where you sit down and listen to records being played*. The Draconian report for this term is worth quoting as an example of what this club was about. 'The Club has continued this term, to awake from their Sunday valhalla the residents of Gunga Din with thunderstorms, be they by Rossini or Beethoven, Casse-Noisettes, trumpets (purely voluntary), and other variations on an unoriginal theme. As is only natural, vocal rather than symphonic works seem to please most, though the pianoforte has a great following.

The vocal works played have ranged from Purcell to Ellis, from Handel to Sullivan. Larry Adler, the superb exponent of that sometimes disfavoured instrument, the harmonica, did not go unhonoured. Catholicity was the watchword, though the influence of Christmas Term productions makes the Savoy Operas strong favourites in the popular esteem. It was with this in view that the end of term competition took the form of a quiz based on "Pineapple Poll", the next ballet arrangement of Sullivan's music...'

John Machin remembers that 'the music club was run by Guv in his room at Gunga after Sunday lunch. He had the first long playing gramophone 33 ½ that I ever saw. The prize for sitting through all the classical stuff was, at the end, to listen to Stanley Holloway and his renderings of "Sam pick up tha' Musket" and "Albert and the Lion".'

That report does not give emphasis to the playing of music to which I allude, but the term before the Draconian notes that, 'Nearly all the records played have been the choice of individual boys, and that such fine works as Symphonies and Concertos by Beethoven, Mozart, Mendelssohn, etc., have been a regular feature is a testimony to their good taste. During the term the Club also studied Haydn's "Clock" Symphony with scores, playing a movement a week.'

In Christmas 1953 it states that, 'This term there were altogether forty-one members of the Club with a regular attendance of between fifteen and twenty-five. J. Plewes never missed, and other very regular attenders included P. Green, R. Gadney, J. Gaze, D. Hawley, A. Macfarlane and J. Snape.' In this term, 'As usual our repertoire of records was fairly broad; from Haydn to Sullivan, and from Grand Opera to modern American musical shows.' The following Easter 1954 term, I find that 'The gramophone playing section had a good term...' At the end of term, a competition was held, and among the seven named prizewinners is Macfarlane. A specimen weekly programme, based mainly on the requests of the boys, is given as follows.

Overture: 'Pirates of Penzance' Sullivan
Extracts from 'Swan Lake' Tchaikovsky
Extract from 'Paint your Wagon'
'Jesu, Joy of Man's Desiring' Bach
Harry Lauder singing 'Keep right on to the end of the road'
First Movement of Mozart's Symphony in G minor with scores
First part of 'The Pirates of Penzance'

A similar kind of assortment – Handel, Mozart, Elgar, Liszt, alongside Iolanthe and Larry Adler – was played in Christmas 1954. In my final term of music club, Easter 1955, I am glad to see that alongside Handel, Rossini, Schubert, Tchaikowsky, Chopin and Bach, we had 'Paint your Wagon' and Harry Lauder 'The Road to the Isles'.

I have also discovered that I was a member of the voluntary 'Singer's Club'. Thus in Easter 1955 The Draconian reports: 'The Singer's Club were busy this term rehearsing three songs for the School concert and a carol for the last Sunday service. The songs were 'The Camel's Hump', 'The Frog', and 'Disobedience' from words of A.A. Milne. The Easter Carol was 'This Joyful Eastertide'. The club had twenty boy singers and five masters that term, among whom was A. Macfarlane.

What I do remember was that there was active folk-singing. I used to delight in sitting around in the locker room in School House with several dozen other little boys, singing old rounds, Negro spirituals, folk-songs, and so on – Polly Wolly Doodle, Clementine, John Brown's Body in its shrinking version, Yodilee-Yodala, all these I recall with many others. Jake Mermagen recalls that this was run by R.I. Kitson (Kitkat). This memory is echoed in letter of 2 Feburary 1953. I describe how *We have community singing in the evening we have songs like Campetown races or polly wolly doodle and Old folk at home. This is my version of Old folks at home. Way down upon de dilhi riber far far away, still longing for de old plantation. And for de old folks at home.* [The Dilli was a river I had seen on my trip to Assam.]

At the Dragon I think we just banged spoons and sticks, but the joy of combining voices was intense and some of the best evenings were spent like this. The rhythms and tunes of Scottish and Irish music mainly reached me through the dancing classes, where we heard many famous tunes, and it may have been here that I first heard some country and western music, as well as the exciting rhythms of South America.

165

On 30 November 1953 I noted, *We are having a concert given by all the staff who can play an instrument.* This was one kind of concert, alongside which every term there were 'Home Talent' concerts by various boys and masters. There were also, occasionally, special concerts. One which impressed me was described on 29 November 1954 in a letter I wrote to my father in India: *there is going to be a concert tonight given by a 13 year old boy who plays the piano wonderfully. He started when he was eight and he has not even been Forced to do it he has learnt in his spare time. He has composed lots of tunes and he can play Beethoven without the score. One piece he has composed is called 'The wild train' and it is extremely good.* The Draconian for that term describes how 'On November 28th, the School had the pleasure and privilege of being given a recital by a gifted young pianist, Michael Derry, a thirteen year old schoolboy from Northampton, whom Gerd Sommerhoff had met by chance during the summer holidays. His remarkable technical maturity was combined with the freshness and spontaneity of a child, and he tackled a formidable array of works from Scarlatti to Sibelius with effortless and enviable fluency. Among the things he played were Beethoven's Sonata in G minor, Op 49, No. 1, and a Suite of four pieces he had composed himself, including 'The Bad Tempered Train'.'

*

Alongside such music and theatre, my greatest love between the age of nine and thirteen was for the D'Oyly Carte operas. My uncle Robert was very keen on Gilbert and Sullivan and sang the female lead in 'Yeoman of the Guard' at Sedbergh when I must have been about eight. Thus my grandfather noted on 19 September 1952 in a letter, *Alan is musical and he and Robert are great Gilbert and Sullivan fans.*

The cycle of five Gilbert and Sullivan operas at the Dragon, wonderfully produced by Bruno, in which I was in the second (Patience) and the last (Iolanthe) had a deep effect on me. They took me into colourful imaginary worlds of pirates and gondoliers and Japanese emperors, which added to the delight of the music. The jokes and text, of course, were also teaching me a great deal about the English class system, the political and legal system, even the system of aesthetics (Patience) which portrayed a Britain was still relevant.

I do not note the first, The Mikado, but was keen to be in Patience. On 28 September 1952 I reported, *The play we are acting this term is patience a Gilbert and Sullivan Opera.* There were a number of trials of our voices, and I still remember Bruno coming along the line of the singers listening attentively to each of us and desperately hoping my voice was all right. I could report on 5 October, *We are doing Patience and so far I am in it.* A week later I reported in triumph, *Dear Mummy and daddy I am in patience and I am very exited.* I was a maiden and still remember 'Twenty love-sick maidens we...' I have the programme of the performance, given on November 13, 14, 15, with a list of those in the 'Chorus of Rapturous Maidens'. This includes two actual girls, several of my long-term Dragon friends, and A. Macfarlane. There is also the photo of the cast, and one photograph where I appear on the top left at the front of the rapturous maidens.

The next in the cycle was Pirates of Penzance which I desperately hoped to be in. I note, however, on 27 September 1953, *We are having "Pirates of Penzance" this term. If I am in it I will be a Policeman or Pirate, but I have not much hope as I am two small.* This was indeed the case and no more is heard of this, or of the next year's Gondoliers.

My final chance was to be in Iolanthe in my last year. On 10 October my mother wrote to my father, *My move is complicated by all the children's half terms which happen just about then. I'd like to fit Alan's in anyway if possible as he may be in "Iolanthe".* A week later, on 18 October, she wrote, *Alan is a peer in "Iolanthe" as you probably know, so I must go and see him. It isn't till Nov. 12th which will give me a slight breathing space.* Ten days before the performance I explained on 2 November, *We are rather behind hand with the play 'Iolanthe' in which I am a peer and there are only three more days until the dress rehearsal.*

I remember that I was so entranced by the music and words that I vowed that I would never forget a scrap of Iolanthe and for weeks afterwards sang it through to myself before I went to sleep. The only down side was that in my zeal I decided to add a brilliant touch, namely to have gout as an aged peer – so I hobbled on to the stage on the first night. Afterwards Bruno asked who the boy was who had been hobbling about as a parent had complained that a boy with a broken leg was being put on stage. I was shamefaced. Now I read in one of the commentaries on the performance in the Draconian the comment. 'Some at least of the peers are supposed to be decrepit old men; why, then did they all adopt a stiffly erect posture? More variety here, a few bent backs and shuffling gaits, would have been in order.' So I have discovered that I am vindicated after nearly sixty years! The enormous coronet is well displayed in the photograph of me in the group picture.

The quality of these performances became a bone of contention between my mother and myself and probably show some class snobbery, or at least over-zealous school patriotism on my part. On 27 March 1955 she wrote, *Yesterday afternoon I took them to see "The Yeoman of the Guard" as done by the Windermere Grammar School. It was very good I thought, though a bit wooden in parts – but Alan was most scathing and compared it unfavourably with Dragon School productions, wrongly actually!*

PERFORMANCE

I don't remember that my parents took us to any straight plays during our childhood. Nor did they, as far as I know, go to many themselves. My mother was no doubt a fan of Wilde, Shaw and others, but there is no record that she went to the theatre – which must have existed – in Bournemouth, if not Poole. Certainly London theatre would have been an extravagance beyond normal life, and when she talked about a special treat when my father returned from India it was mostly in terms of a film. So we never went to plays from home.

Acting was important at the Dragon and the highlight was a Gilbert and Sullivan opera which took place every winter and a Shakespeare play every summer. I think I showed no interest in being in any of the five Shakespeare plays though I do remember enjoying some of them, especially I think, 'A Midsummer's Night's Dream' and 'Macbeth'. I do not refer to any of the Shakespeare plays in my letters, which is perhaps indicative of my apathy.

My mother wrote the one account of these Summer term plays in a letter. It is worth quoting in full since it shows a great deal about her ambivalent attitude to the school. It is clear that the play and the service the next morning were intended to impress parents and to show off the self-confidence and upper class airs that we were being taught. But for a struggling relic of a declining post-Raj family, it all seemed pretentious and jarring. Her response is full of contradictions – she was making great sacrifices to put me on the ladder to Oxbridge and the elite, yet she also rebelled against it. On 29 June 1954 she wrote:

> back to the Dragon for "Macbeth", back again to look for supper and finally to bed at 11 p.m. frozen cold as I'd forgotten my bottle! "Macbeth" was very well done really... The boys were word-perfect but fearfully pompous and droney, I was struggling not to giggle half the time and when Lady M. slapped her bony chest and shouted "I have given suck and know how sweet to love the babe that milks me" I nearly collapsed on the spot. Everyone else was frightfully impressed so I fear I must be flippant.

What my mother probably did not know was that part of the bony sound was due to the fact that the boy had broken his arm. As The Draconian's Term Notes put it, 'many of the audience never spotted that Lady M. was burdened with a pound or two of plaster and a stiff elbow'.

My mother continued:

> We went to the service next day and the same lot of little boys got up and droned again, this time they read us Shakespeare's best known sonnet (after explaining carefully what it meant!) and a long excerpt

168

from "Faust" – can't think why, but they were all so pleased with themselves. It was very hot in the hall and several boys were sick so I was glad when the service was over. As usual I spoke to nobody and no-one to me and was quite glad to get away from the place – not a satisfactory school from my point of view.

This sense of being among an alien crowd mirrors that in the account of going to see Iolanthe. Perhaps others also felt awkward. It is clear that there were also other plays and I reported three out of what must have been more. On 11 February 1952 I wrote, *I went to a school play by some boys one was scandal for school and the other two's company threes a crowd.* The following year on 10 May 1953 I wrote, *there is going to be a play done by one of the forms wich is called "The hand and man" written by Bernard Shaw.* Thus we were watching plays by Sheridan, Shaw and others from quite early on, though I don't remember them.

*

In my letters I was enthusiastic in my mentions of dancing. On 30 November 1953 *We had another lot of Scotch dancing last night wich was even more fun than the first lot.*

In the Easter term 1954, there was again voluntary dancing on Saturday evenings. Among the most popular less normal dances, according to The Draconian, were 'the Palais Glide and the Dashing White Sergeant. I hardly dare mention the Hokey-Cokey'. It seems that these were the dances I particularly liked, for the following Christmas term 1954 I wrote to my mother, in a letter that stretched my spelling to its limit, *There was dancing on Friday and Yesterday (Saturday) there was Scottish dancing. Pallez-glyde, Roger de caveleigh. Barn dance, valetta, Hoky polky and the Gay Gordons, Dashing White Seargent.*

In the Winter issue of The Draconian 1954 there was an account of that term's dancing. It mentioned a large number of drummers (staff) alongside the pianist. 'But all this does not seem to have affected the standard of dancing, which has been very good this year, and there seem to have been even more dances to cope with this year than there were last. And we have again had dancing occasionally on Saturday nights, which has been very popular for various reasons, not the least of which was the performance of Gerd's Band...' The end of term dance, we are told, was a success despite rather depleted numbers (because of flu). I was one who missed it.

My last reference was in March 1955 when I recounted that *Their was dancing yesterday evening...* This was different from dancing in the Christmas term, since it seems to have been voluntary. The Draconian mentions that, 'We had four nights of voluntary dancing this term. There were always large numbers of boys present, with some unexpected faces when a rumour had spread of ice creams in the interval.' At the last dance 'there was the added excitement of a real piper in a kilt to play the Scottish dances'. Some boys even introduced coloured bow ties. I have forgotten all this, but probably relished the piper.

The two main types of dance we learnt were Scottish country dances – the Gay Gordons, Strip the Willow, Srathspey and others, and English ballroom dancing, the foxtrot and waltz. There was also perhaps a little Latin American or American dancing as well, Samba, Rumba, Charleston, and so on.

I do remember that I really loved the music played – my introduction to proper Scottish reels and folk-music and to Viennese and other dance music. I also loved the well-organized and communal dances. The Scottish dancing was the greatest delight – the twisting circles and the movement in and out – better than the musical chairs which we played at parties and even better than the Scottish piped band tattoo I once went to in Edinburgh with my parents.

Naomi Mitchison's memory of the school dance also brings back the excitement of the Gallop. She remembered 'the school dance which happened once a year, because of the pattern dances: Lancers and Sir Roger, and still more because of the triumphant final rage of the Gallop when one careered down the hall, bumping as many others as possible and quite likely ending in a joyful heap at the far end.'[92]

Even the ballroom dancing, finding oneself paired with another little boy, having half the time to be the retreating woman, made me realize the gender difference between leading and being led, pushing or being pushed. This was fun. And occasionally one danced with some little boy for whom one felt a certain coy attraction and this gave it a special thrill.

The dances we were taught, and the emphasis on dance, is indicative of the sort of social world we were expected to inhabit later in our lives. We would be dancing our way into the middle class, the world of debutantes, of May Balls, of tea dances. In fact this world was fading and there were few occasions later when I used these skills.

I can now see that dancing was also an important, if minor, part of my education in balance and deportment – alongside bicycling, swimming, running. This teaching of bodily deportment was clearly the equivalent for us boys to the dancing classes featuring ballet, to which my sisters were subjected.

I was also taught how to sit and stand properly at school meals and assemblies. This whole area of the disciplining of the body, which has been a central thread in anthropology, is interesting.

---

[92] Mitchison, *Small Talk*, 61.

GAMES FOR LIFE

The school playing fields, looking east towards the War Memorial
and, behind it, the line of the River Cherwell.

18 SCHOOL GAMES AND SPORTS

As a very small boy in Assam, he writes, I played with my mother and my father (an enthusiastic games player, including an excellent rugby and polo player) and my local ayahs and small Assamese friends.

When I returned to England I was deeply influenced by my mother's younger brother, Robert. He was only seven years my senior and was a passionate games player, despite being blind in one eye and not very strong. We spent our holidays together, he aged about fourteen and at a games-obsessive school (Sedbergh) to which I would later go, and myself aged six or seven.

Robert taught me most of the common games and we played imaginary games with soldiers, cars, horses and meccano. His mother, my grandmother, was also a games fanatic, particularly card games and mah-jong, a Chinese game which I learnt early. (These are described in the companion volume on home life.) So I entered with passion into competitive games, and also watched the obsession of those around me. Robert cut out and collected everything about his favourite football teams and made and played with many kinds of model. There are a number of references in my grandfather's diary to the fact that he went to local grounds to watch football. So I became imbued with games from childhood with a rich set of rules and toys.

Looking back sixty years later, it is difficult to understand or remember the reasons for this passion; a mixture of loneliness, competitive spirit, imaginative wonder, joining a wider world, all these and others no doubt. Each game opened up new worlds, Subbuteo (football), a game of horse-racing, toy soldiers, ball games of many forms. They seemed to give a sudden expansion of the mind as well as the body. Expanding the small models to the large, learning the rules and mastering the skills, it was all exciting. A huge amount of my time and energy was devoted to games, inventing, playing, subverting.

Games shaped the person I am and much of my adult life, both in work and leisure, has been an application of what I learnt in those early hobbies and games. They have clearly been one of the single greatest influences on my personality. So I ran and jumped and kicked and batted and threw vigorously for ten years. Fortunately some natural ability, perhaps inherited

172

from my father, plus the early training from my uncle, combined with determination, meant that I was reasonably successful, though not outstanding.

*

Playing games used to be strongly encouraged in most schools. This is partly to strengthen the muscles and to use up surplus physical energy. Team games are also believed to improve social skills. The essence of a team game is to balance selfishness, the desire to shine and triumph, with sociality, the desire to make one's team win. This balance is also one of the most difficult things to achieve in much of social life. When to keep the ball and when to pass it to another is an art which stretches out into many of our activities. The balance between co-operation and self-assertiveness is well taught within the structured environment of the rules of a game.

It is also believed that games enable people to learn how to demarcate their lives. While the game is on we abide by certain rules. Then the whistle blows and we no longer have to. Learning how to handle defeat (it took me some years not to weep bitterly after losing a game), and feel relaxed with someone who has outwitted or outplayed you, is an important art.

Likewise the subtle art of playing within the rules, but using as much scope and skill within them as possible, is one which is handy in almost every branch of later life. You have to learn the rules of your trade or occupation, but if you just stick to these without creative thought then you will end up as nothing special. If you break them and are caught the result is even worse. How can you keep to the rules yet excel? Skill, personal tricks, long training and perceptive observation of others are among the things needed. The concept of spin, which makes the ball behave in odd ways in cricket and disguises the real motives of politicians when they deal with the public, is one example of this.

People enjoy playing games because they like to compete and dominate; to play, strive, outwit, win, are all important survival tools. But there is more to games than this, particularly team games. Members of a cricket, football or bowls team play together, often socialize together and either create or express their friendship in this way. Friendly rivalry in the squash court may also cement friendship. Matching minds and bodies, or depending and sharing with other members of the team, both give great satisfaction. Friends play together and the stress on learning games at school is also meant to be a lesson in friendship. Like friendship, play is not directed to a practical goal. It is just a game, but to refuse to play is a rejection.

*

Brendon notes the development of the games mania at boarding schools in the later nineteenth century. She suggests that manliness was replacing godliness as the main ideal of boarding schools. By the 1880s the games ethic was dominant in public schools. Brendon commented: 'It also attributed to school sport the peculiarly English tendency "to be willing to sink the personal in the public interest".'[93] It is clearly part of the package of imperial fortitude – team-playing ability and competitive emulation which has so often been discussed.

On the one hand the Dragon seems to have subscribed to the philosophy that games were an important part of the training of a young person. The school song set the tone for what one might expect.[94]

Let us always keep heart in the strife
While our wickets or goals are defended,
For there always is hope while there's life,
And the match isn't lost till its ended!
But whether we win or we lose,
If we fight to the very last minute,
The intent of the game is always the same –
To strive that the Dragon may win it!

When I was there, the same philosophy was present, as suggested by the Term Notes for Easter 1953. The game must go on, for 'the Dragon view is that, come germs, come weather, matches must go on...'

Yet the attitude and treatment was ambivalent. On the one hand sport was encouraged and as at all such preparatory schools a good deal of one's status came from prowess at games. On the other hand there are strong hints that the school valued other things as much or more, and, equally, that the boys did so.

We can see the ambivalence in the school debates during my time in the early 1950s. There were three debates around this theme which I reported (with strange spelling) in my letters. The ambivalence is also shown in the Term Notes which were sent to all pupils and their parents. During my time there, in the Summer issue of 1952 it is mentioned that, 'Dragon cricket had a good season, in that a great deal was played with considerable enthusiasm by a great many boys. But true to Dragon tradition, little or none was watched.... A common query from the Sunday morning letter-writer, hard pressed to make the second page, would be "Who won the match yesterday?" – quite often when there wasn't one.' The same was true of rugger, for in Christmas 1953 it was noted that the rugger team had 'hardly anyone watching'.

There was also pressure to decrease the amount of sport, for in the Christmas term Notes of 1954, 'a Staff meeting discussed and approved a

---

[93] Brendon, *Preparatory Schools*, 52.
[94] *Dragon Centenary*, 30–1.

motion that Dragons play too much rugger, with the result that for all but the top games the four weekly games were reduced to three'. Incidentally, 'Later in the term, at several informal Staff meetings held on the touchline during matches, a further motion, that Dragons do not at the moment play rugger very well, was also passed'. As Jake Mermagen comments, 'Given the sheer numbers, the Dragon should have dominated prep school rugger, but it did not. There were very few international players from the school later in life.'

There also seems to have been a note of cynicism about the values which team sports were meant to be inculcating. Thus in Term Notes for Christmas 1952 when the First Fifteen won the last match of the term and this was announced to the school, 'they were publicly congratulated on their very fine season and some of the older Staff gave a subdued round of applause to the suggestion that success had been largely due to "team spirit", that old-fashioned virtue now almost condemned by the cynics to share the fate of the Old School Tie'.

RUGGER

I will will follow the order in which we played games at the Dragon. The first (Autumn) term was rugger, the second was football and hockey, the Summer was cricket, and competitive sports such as tennis, swimming and athletics. So let us start with the most decisive character-training game of them all – rugger or rugby (union) football.

Rugger was a special game at school in various ways and especially for me. It was a very rough game and taught you about the toughness and hard hits of life, and also taught you could recover from these. It taught one how to play together as a team; everything depended on others whether in the scrum or in the line-out. A lot about a person's character was revealed by the game. It was the most important game in terms of status both at the Dragon and Sedbergh. If one did well in rugby then one's prestige was high. One could not be described as weedy or a fleb or any of the other insulting words. It was the ultimate test of Spartan character.

Personally it was a game I wanted to do well at. I knew my uncle Billy had been a brilliant player at Sedbergh and had played for the army. I knew that my father was an excellent player at school. As late as 1949, when he was over forty, he still played occasionally, as a letter from my mother mentions on 22 May 1949, *You will laugh when I tell you that Daddy is going to try and play Rugger on Sunday. He hasn't played since he was at school and thinks he will probably die starting again in this heat*

175

but I tell him he must get into training so as to take you on, Alan.

It was also a game which my family followed avidly on the radio and occasionally watched. They listened to the varsity rugby match in mid-December each year and on 11 February 1951 my mother wrote to my father, *The wireless is a great joy, we listened to the England-Ireland rugger yesterday – by the way I hope you listened to Scotland-Wales match and swallowed some of the nasty comments you made on Kinninmonth!* Kinninmonth was an old Sedberghian and close friend of my Uncle Billy. Six weeks later she wrote again on 20 March to my father about his future leave, *There'll be the winter to hibernate in and you can get down to your golf and watch Rugger matches in the rain. I listened to Scotland being beaten by England in the Calcutta Cup on Saturday. All Peter Kinninmonths fault according to you I expect?! Actually he played quite well, Billy watched.*

My father did not often watch rugger on his leave (in the rain or otherwise), but my grandfather mentions on 29 December that 'Mac takes Robert and Richard to see schoolboys' rugger international at Richmond'. As my father had himself played for Scotland schoolboys, he had a special reason for going.

Even I went to a match at international level where there was the added excitement that one of my teachers was playing. I wrote on the 11 January 1954 to my parents: *On Saturday I went to Scotland v France pity France won 3-0 my rugby techer (Mr Marshiall) Played full back for Scotland.*

I instinctively knew it was important to shine at rugby, but there were a number of obstacles. Unlike the other three games which I had been able to practise with my uncle and sisters at home, I had never played a game of rugby when I arrived at the Dragon and hence had no skills. The only kind one could reasonably play at home or on the beach was touch rugby – touching the opponent rather than tackling, it being less dangerous. We did play this, but later and not with my uncle Robert who showed no interest in the game. For example, on 11 September 1954 my mother wrote to my father: *We had a day on the beach with the Mermagens before we left, a really warm day and I bathed and we all got very burnt and played rounders and cricket and touch rugger and every other game all day.* [I accompany the letter with a picture of a man converting a rugby try.]

The other problem is that more than any other game, what counts in rugby is size and speed. To run fast with the ball is the ultimate goal. I was always small for my age and a relatively slow runner. What was I to do? I think it was particularly in relation to rugby that I decided I would test the thesis that anybody can do anything. Despite our natural abilities, if we exert huge will power, try really hard, practise, and put all our effort into things, we can attain at least a decent level. Rugby was my life's experiment and fortunately it worked. I learnt confidence that, despite my natural mediocrity, I could succeed against the odds by grim determination. This is picked up pretty well by the accounts of my progress in this game and indeed seems to have been my greatest triumph at the Dragon, precisely the recognition by even the headmaster, as well as the other boys, that I had triumphed over a natural handicap. I was a living embodiment of the school motto, 'Strive to the Sun'.

The first school report on my rugger at the end of my first term at the Dragon captures my effort straight away. It noted, 'Plays Rugger with incredible dash'. I think it was in this first term that I remember one of those flashes. A huge boy (Nick Bullock, now a Fellow of King's College, Cambridge) came hurtling towards me – I was the full back. I threw myself at him and brought him down – and still feel the pain and remember the bruise that lasted for weeks. But I was hailed as a hero and that was enough.

In my second year I seem to have lost heart somewhat. I did not enjoy the game and, though I tried, it was touch and go. The report read: 'He is very plucky, but seemed to lose much of his dash towards the end of the season.' But a year later I was gaining confidence again. My school report now mentioned me as 'A promising player' and the increasing success was mirrored in the letters I wrote to my parents. On 28 September 1952 I mentioned that *We are playing rugger now and I am in fourth game.* I also noted the arrival of my cousin Jake Mermagen who made a good start: *Mermagan has come and he is a very good rugger Player*, another role model, though Jake now writes that 'I was also small and slow and had not played before coming to the Dragon'. I was greatly looking forward to seeing my parents again on a trip to Assam and this may have boosted me. On 20 October I wrote, *Dear mummy and daddy it is only a very little time till I will be seeing you again. We had four rugger matches. The first one won 28-3 and the third 16-11 to them.*

My admiration for good players of my own age is shown in a letter of 3 November where I wrote about my friend Sandy Bruce Lockhart. Interestingly I called him by his Christian name, and wrote *Sandy is in a very high game in cricket too. He is a very good bowler.* I illustrated the point with a picture captioned *He converts it over the post and gets 3 points.*

In my fourth year I had changed my position to scrum half, the kind of position I really liked since one tended to get rid of the ball as quickly as possible. I wrote to my parents on 27 September 1953, *I played my first game of rugger the day before yesterday but it only lasted ten minutes. Yesterday I was scrum half and we had a proper game in wich our side got about 12 points.* The report at the end of term was enthusiastic, 'A very good scrum half – he passes and tackles exceptionally well'.

It was in my last year, aged nearly thirteen, that I reached the pinnacle of my limited success in the game. I did not write about the matches, but there are several independent assessments of that determination and almost reckless enthusiasm which was so highly valued. If the battles of the future were to be won on the playing fields of the Dragon, I would be the sort of man to lead his troops into the guns of the enemy.

At the start of the term my mother wrote to my father on 30 September 1954, *Alan writes to say he is in 1st game at rugger – don't know if that is the 1st XV – and has gone up in form.* A few weeks later she wrote on 18 October,. *He played in 2 1st XV matched and they were beaten 19-0 ("a lot of louts about 2 years older"!) but won the 2nd. Rugger is the game he likes least, but perhaps he'll change his ideas now.*

My overcoming of a natural dislike of the game by sheer effort is referred to below and it is something I remember right through to the end of my boarding school days. Rugby was in many ways torture – cold, painful, miserable. But it made you a man.

My last school report on rugger was unusually long, 'A fearless and intensely plucky full back in 1st XV. His tackling has been a feature of every game and when he grows a bit (and can kick a bit further!) he will be a more than useful player.' When my mother went to see the headmaster Joc Lynam she was somewhat amazed to find that the little boy she regarded as often rude, difficult and unpredictable was so highly regarded by the school. She describes the sherry and then the conversation in a letter on 14 November to my father, *He also praised his rugger, especially his tackling which was marvellous he said, poor Alan, he told me he never enjoyed a game of rugger till it was over!*

My 'marvellous' tackling – the intrepid way I threw myself at larger boys (I was now full back and very small and light for my age) – is the central feature of the unusual eulogy which I have recently discovered in the school magazine and which obviously gave my parents, and particularly my father, great pride as well as earning me the respect of my peers and teachers.

On 11 January 1955 my mother wrote to my father, 'He has had a very good Rugger write-up in the magazine, his play would have warmed the hearts of Old Dragonians! I'll send it out to you to frame.' The account was in The Draconian as follows:

Nor was the size of our full-back much of a deterrent to the opposition. He was, in fact, smaller and lighter than any three-quarter – but his pluck and coolness were comparable to anyone's: what the scores in some of our earlier games would have been if Alan Macfarlane had not been there does not bear thinking about. He is not yet a great 'kick' but his tackling of opponents of all sizes has been a truly memorable feature of the season, and something that Old Dragons of all ages would have very much liked to see... Against Radley, however, we were up against a really good team, and did fairly well to let them through on only six occasions. Indeed, had it not been for a sterling performance by Macfarlane our defeat would have been far heavier. He again played a grand game against Stowe the following week, and this was only not won because a try between the posts was most unaccountably not converted!

The official recognition of this was not just my colours, but also a School Prize for rugger. My diminutive size in all this is well shown in the school photograph where I sit at the end, much smaller than most of the others.

FOOTBALL AND HOCKEY

Of all the team games which I played at the Dragon, I think it was football which I enjoyed most and continued to enjoy throughout my Dragon years (though sadly we only played it in a minor way at Sedbergh). It combined the excitement of rushing around, much less boring than cricket, but without the pain and roughness of rugger. It was on a par with hockey in terms of satisfaction, requiring both skill and thought. It was particularly important to me because it was a game I could, and did, play a great deal not only at school but also at our Broadstone house and my enthusiasm for it started well before I went to the Dragon.

In terms of the Dragon school status system, football was less important than the two games to which a whole term was devoted – rugger and cricket were upper class sports of gentleman played in the Winter and Summer terms, football and hockey games we shared with a much wider swathe of the British population, and even with girls in the case of hockey. Yet it was a game that could be played, in various forms, not only on open fields but also in enclosed spaces such as the covered rink.

As noted in my first school report in March 1951, I arrived as a 'keen and skilful' player, but it was not until the following year that I mentioned the game in a letter to my parents, writing on 27 January 1952, *We had games in the snow wich was nice but when you fell down it was very cold. I scored my first goal yesterday.* At the end of the term I was noted as being 'Very good' in my school report.

The following year I was playing for the third school team. I mentioned the game twice in letters and was obviously able to play informally with a ball my parents had given me. On 27 January 1953 I noted, *I have played two games of soccer this term and my little soccer ball is coming in very useful.* A week later I was less enthusiastic, *I had a game in third game yesterday but I did not like it much as I hardly ever got the ball.* Nevertheless the school report noted me in '3rd game – very good'.

I moved up to the top team in 1954, and my school report noted,

179

'Should be useful next year. Played well in 1st game.' I do not, however, mention the game in my letters. The following year the school report stated, 'Played very well indeed for the 1st XI'. This time, gaining my school colours I gave my only real descriptions of a couple of games and my part in them. On 1 February I wrote, *last week there were the first games of soccer and on Saturday I played in the 1st XI match against Salesian College (Some fluke) wich we drew 3-3 one of our best players headed a goal for them.* [The 'some fluke' was a protection against envy or hubris I imagine]. My mother wrote on the 18th to my father *Alan has got his football colours as you probably know.*

Two days later on the 20 I wrote to my mother in the Lake District:

On Wednesday we played away against Bluecoates school Reading. They are a Public school and play soccer all last term and they only beat us by 3-1 the lowest score against us for about 5 years. On Thursday I got my colours as centre half (Soccer) but I started right half. In the afternoon we had a half holiday and it was lovely weather. Yesterday we woke up to a sprinkling of snow but we played the return match at home against Bluecoates school. In the first half we were pretty equal. Then we kicked off and scored a goal straight away then there was a ding-dong battle in which their were several scrabbles in their goal mouth and in one the ball went over their line but it was quickly kicked out again and the referee did not see it. (I think it is true (I wasn't there) because they admitted themselves that it was a goal). Then in the last few minutes they managed to score and so it was a draw.

The report on football in The Draconian for that term mentions: 'There were four half-backs! In the centre Julian Travis was probably the best equipped player on the side, but when it seemed as if we would have to make use of his versatility in the forward line, Alan Macfarlane moved in from the right and played some splendid games – particularly against the Blue Coat School.'

*

I took to hockey early in my life and always enjoyed it as a game. It seemed to be less aggressive than rugger, and as satisfying as football in its need for strategy and reflection. I came to play, as I now remember, as a half-back, ending up as centre-half. I always liked such a position, and played in the same position in football and the equivalent, fly-half, in rugger, at least later on. I was the communicator, intermediary, the person who controlled the team, moving from defence to attack. I did not need to do too much, but what I did was vital. My great hero in football, Billy

Wright, played centre left, and I knew he was right. I enjoyed the solid thud of a well-driven ball. I adored the version of hockey played on ice, and there was perhaps some distant memory of the version which my father played on a pony: polo.

Later, during my middle years at the Dragon, the shorter, more curly, Indian hockey sticks came in, but I think I stuck to the older kind. These curly sticks, curiously, resembled the walking sticks with which I first played an infant version of the game as described on 19 February 1951 when my mother wrote:

> *Their latest craze is balls, they have three each and a walking stick apiece and they drive the wretched things round the house and garden and take them for walks, each ball has its own name and character and gets bathed and put to bed at night and were even taken to church, though I did insist they should be left in the porch, I couldn't face hockey up and down the aisle!*

Hockey featured quite regularly in my letters from school, always being described for the second term, alongside football. On 3 February 1952 I wrote to my grandparents, accompanied by a drawing of a hockey goal, *I had a game of hokey in wich I hurt my ne but I scored a goal and it was a very nice game.* Towards the end of the month I wrote to them again. *I am playing hockey know and I am in 7th the same game as I was in soccer we have been winning most of the soccer and hockey games We won against st louis 3-1. Hamilton is captain he is very big.* I reported my success to my parents and my mother commented on 3 March *we were sorry to hear you'd been in bed a week, was it your cold or something else? I hope you're quite alright now and getting some hockey, jolly good being in the seventh game.*

Three weeks later, on 22 February, I gave further details to my parents, which illustrate that it could be a dangerous game. *We had a match the day before yesterday wich was a free half and the Dragon won 5-0. The afternoon that was a free half we had a hockey match against another form and we won 7-3.... There was inter games on Wednesday and our game won 3-1 but they had two players missing and another his nose broken.* The school report for March 1951 noted that my hockey was pronounced 'satisfactory', but by the end of 1952 it was 'very good'.

In 1953 my enthusiasm continued. On 22 February I noted to my parents in a slightly contradictory sentence, *We are starting hockey tommorow and I played it yesterday.* The games were not just between forms, or schools, but also between the larger dormitories when I moved into School House that year. On 15th March *There is going to be a dodo v Phenix match. Dodo and Phenix are two big dorms and they are going to have hockey match.* The school report noted me as 'A most promising and

181

thoughtful hockey player'. The element of rational calculation of how best to play reflects what I liked about the game.

In 1954 there are no comments in my letters, though the school report noted I was a 'promising half in the 3rd XI'. In my last year the report stated that I was a 'very useful centre half in the 1st XI'. The question, however, was whether I would get my school colours. My mother wrote to my father on 18 February, *Alan has got his football colours as you probably know, his ambition is to get them all but he is a little doubtful about hockey.* Part of the problem was that this was an especially cold winter. I was also ill quite a bit. As I explained to my father on 13th March *On last Wednesday we played the first game of hockey and it was a 1st XI match against new college in which I played right and left half. We have not played hockey this term hardly but we have had plenty of skating.*

The hoped-for outcome of school colours is described a few days later in a letter to my mother on 17 March.

> *On the Wednesday before last there was the first game of hockey (because of the snow) and it was a match against new college which by some fluke I was in and which we won 3-0. ... Last Tuesday there was a half for games and on Wednesday there was a 1st XI match against Bromesgrove Juniors which we unluckily lost 1-0 but me and another chap called Axtell got our colours. On Thursday afternoon there was another match against Cheltenham juniors which we won 3-0 and three people got their colours including Mermagen...*

The report in The Draconian for the term mentions briefly that 'Alan Macfarlane worked very hard at centre-half and never gave up trying.' The school photograph, with myself, Axtell, Mermagen (interesting that I referred to my cousin by his surname) and others, shows us all with our colours. I continued to play a variant of the game at home, my grandfather noting in his diary on 8 April 1955, 'hockey with children'.

CRICKET

The English love of cricket was once a mystery to the world. Now that it is a passion all over the world, it does not seem quite so strange, though what the attraction of a basically rather slow game is to players and spectators alike it is difficult to say. Much has been written on the subject in order to try to explain the obsession – almost religious – felt for the game. From memory it was a game that my uncle Robert was deeply involved with, which encouraged me. It could, at a pinch, be played by one player – with a good wall to throw the ball against. It encouraged team camaraderie. It called on three different sets of skills, as batsman, bowler and fielder –

and I enjoyed all three. As I was small and a slow runner, it was a game that did not penalize these deficiencies, being largely dependent on a good eye, good body co-ordination and endless practice and commitment – all of which favoured me, at least at the Dragon.

It was also to a certain extent a symbol of both Englishness and middle-class occupations. It required a reasonable pitch, equipment and, above all, leisure. It also linked us to the wider world of Oxbridge, for at the Dragon we were next door to the famous Parks where Oxford University would play some of the best teams in the world. So we had a chance to watch really good cricket – and my letters record that we did. We also had some excellent cricketers among the masters. There were also visiting coaches, including, as I remember well, the handsome and brilliant David Sheppard, who played for England.

So cricket was one of the holy triumvirate of games, along with rugger and football, and it was continued at Sedbergh, though then I tailed off. At the Dragon I was in the top team and remember spending hours in the nets and at a wooden cradle-like device where we practised our catching. Later at Sedbergh I preferred fishing in the Summer term. So, given these few memories, what do the sources tell about my interest and ability at this most English of games?

*

Cricket was very important in my home life around the training and practice with my uncle Robert. When I went to the Dragon I started to play cricket seriously and discovered both the delights and the ennui of the game. In my first summer I mentioned cricket once, writing to my mother during the Summer term, *Dear Mommy I hope you are well. It was intergames yesterday and we one by 4 runs 7 wickets. Noakes who is someone in the house got a new bat with test written on it with Don Bradmans atagrath on it.* My mother thought that I might be watching the game at the Parks, writing to my father on 17 June, *No letter from Alan this week. I always imagine grisly things when I don't hear but I expect he's much too busy watching cricket in the park, they get taken to all the county matches.* I dimly remember such games later in my time at the Dragon – the majestic trees surrounding the huge expanse of green with diminutive figures in sparkling white in the distance. The school report is missing for that term, so I don't know how I was rated.

In my second summer the report noted that I was 'the most improved player in 6 game'. My letters now have quite a bit about cricket in various ways. On 12 May 1952 I wrote to my parents, *we have been playing cricket and last game I was captain and in the first inings I scored 16 and thanks to Miller and Namouk's good bowling and there fielding and crossmans fielding and they are all in my house.* On 8 July I wrote:

> *There was a match against cheltnam junior school they got 61 all
> out. We got 70 for 6 wickets. We are having a house match soon and
> the list of bating is this: A.Macfarlane +, R.Collins o, G.Marsh o?,
> A.Munro, A.Miller o, S.Crossman o?, J.Noakes o *, D.Cooper,
> R.Moulnton, K.Patterson, C. Berresford (+ = wicket, captain = *,
> Bowlers = o) Lots of love from Alan.*

Clearly prowess at cricket was worth mentioning to one's parents as on
3 November 1952 I mentioned that I was going out with a friend from
school, Sandy Bruce Lockhart, *Sandy is in a very high game in cricket too.
He is a very good bowler.*

By my third year I was noted in my report as 'A promising player in 3rd
game'. I now begin to give a great amount of detail about the game in my
letters home. I wrote on 15 February to my parents to commiserate about
some aspect of cricket which my father played in Assam: *I am very glad
sonari won the Roberts cup, but it was a pity about the cricket.* Before the
Summer term I was given the highly esteemed present of a new cricket bat.
I still remember it – small, with the false engraved signatures of a few great
cricketing stars like Len Hutton on it. I remember carefully oiling it with
linseed oil daily and treasuring it for several years. The event was reported
thus. On 30 April I wrote to my parents, *I have got a new cricket bat to
take to sckool and a new watch wich is lovely.* My grandmother explained
the purchase in an appended letter. *I have bought the watch and cricket bat
with the money I got from selling your bits and pieces and a final 24
shilling for Alan's suit. I had meant to buy saving certs: but I thought these
things were as essential and save you the cash!*
On 3 May I wrote:

> *We had a Lovely choice yesterday of what to do. (A) we could see
> the Oxford University Athletics club have a competion against the
> Ameteur England team and we could see people like bannister and
> Baily all afternoon. (B) We could do that for an hour and then come
> back and see the cup final on T.V. or (C) Play vol[untary] cricket and
> watch the cup final on T.V.*

Two weeks later, on 18 May, I wrote: *I saw yorkshire in the parks but they
did not have Trueman.*
The game, though less dangerous than others, had its threats and I
wrote on 18 May, *I have been off games for a week because I was hit on
the eye by a cricket ball.* But I was also proud to report that, *One of our
Masters said that our 4th eleven is equal to an ordinary prep schools first.*
On 2 July 1953 I wrote: *We won the last cricket match by about 80*

runs. I also noted that *The test is not going too badly for England*, a subject which I could share with my parents who listened to the sport in far away Assam.

In my fourth year I had moved up to the top team and was reported to be, 'A much-improved batsman in 1st game, whose fielding close to the wicket was exceptionally good'. In fact, this was the only game at which I gained my school colours in my fourth year. On 18 July I wrote to my parents *By some fluke I have got my tie for cricket.* My mother reported this to my father a week later on my return home: *Alan looks very fit but is slightly husky, he was very pleased as he got his cricket tie before leaving ("by some fluke") and has brought back a picture of himself in his team which I'll send onto you – he looks terribly tough but rather sweet!* The photograph was sent later, my mother noting on 10 October, *I've found the picture of him in his cricket team and will send it separately. I wish I could see him playing in a match, perhaps we will next summer.*

In my letter of 10 July I reported how:

> *I have played in three matches since Wednesday. Firstly I played against Cothill in which we won by about 70 runs I only made 8 runs but while I was in the score went from 44 for 5 to about 85. On Thursday I didn't bat against Cheltenham but we won by five wickets (They scored 98 for 7) and we scored 102 for 6. Yesterday there was 2nd XI match against Salesian College. They declared (very decently) at 120 for 6. As someone was ill I was playing. Our first few batted well. Ellis 8, Scorah 14 Axtell 32. And when I went in it was 64 for 4. Then Wilson was out for 3 and Westrup came in. We began to look as if we would draw when by a fluke I hit 10 in 3 balls then Westrup hit 3 fours. But he was out for 25 but we managed to win with ten minutes to go. I made 33 not out... Today I am playing in a mixed team against the Oxford and Berbonsey club. We have not played yet but I will put the results down. Lots of love   Alan*

Outstanding scores	*Evers 33*		*Mermagen 25*
Our score	*110 for 6*		
Their score	*99 all out*		
My score	*6 (not out)*		
Result	*We won by 4 wickets*		

Two days later I wrote, *We have only got another three weeks until the end of term. There was a match on Wednesday which we won by 50 runs. I batted 3rd but I was run out by the boy at the other end before I had faced a ball.*

The Draconian magazine recorded these games in great detail which gives a flavour of the attention paid to this sport by the school, and my own

185

small part in it. The Summer issue, Number 200, includes all the scores of the 2nd eleven matches, for example, against St Hugh's: A. Macfarlane (first bat) b. Newbury, against St Andrews, AM did not bat, the Father's match was abandoned because of rain. In other games I made lowish numbers, with a highest score of 17 not out. I also caught out two people. At the end of term I received a prize for fielding, which I still have and which has the signatures of all the team, including W. Arber, S. Poulter (Seb), Omer Namouk, N. Raison, J. Mermagen, P.R.N. Travis, Jeremy Noaks.

I already had my colours when I went on to my final year in 1955 and received another prize, this time for both batting and fielding. My school report recorded that, 'His batting improved enormously during the term and I hope he will do really well later on. Can always be relied on to hold a catch almost anywhere.' I do not, however, mention the game in my letters, though by this time they are less full of news as both my parents were home in England. I do remember, however, the pleasure of a last summer term of cricket, the endless practising of catching, my delight in the wonderful spin bowling of Jake Mermagen and the sadness, after all its difficulties, of leaving the Dragon.

SUMMER SPORTS

I do not remember ever playing tennis at the Dragon or even owning a racket, which was, of course, an expensive item. The only reference in any of my letters is ambiguous. On 23 May 1951 my mother wrote, *His letters have been a couple of scrawls saying when is half term and the end of term and could I send him a tennis ball and some lemonade powder!* But tennis balls were coveted for many games, including bad eggs and various games of catch, so this is no evidence that I played. Nor do I remember playing tennis at the Christian boys camp at Swanage to which I was sent in two of my summers, even though its prospectus mentioned, 'other outdoor games, like tennis, padder-tennis...'

*

When I went to the Dragon it was something of a shock to learn that I had forgotten how to swim. I believe that everyone, including myself, thought that once one had learnt to swim, like bicycling, one would always know how. But I did not. So there were sessions in the River Cherwell on the end of a kind of fishing rod contraption – with a rope harness – re-learning. This is one of my most vivid, unpleasant, memories – the water was slimy green and very cold, I often panicked and never really mastered the breaststroke which we had to learn. I would find myself sinking and gurgling in nasty-tasting water and feeling I was drowning.

Gradually, however, I managed to get the hang of it, and my letters chronicle my progress. In the Summer term of 1951 I note in a letter, *We started swimming for the people who had done there river length, and clothes test.* But I still seem to have been struggling with swimming by the start of the third summer at the Dragon, for my mother wrote to me on 3 March 1952 from India: *We're hoping to make a small swimming pool during the summer, Fiona was beginning to swim on the boat and could do half a dozen strokes or so before she finally drank so much water that she sank – and if you get a decent summer you should be flashing around in no time.*

The Summer of 1952, when I was aged ten, seems to have been the turning point for me, perhaps partly because the water was really warm. On 15 July I wrote to my parents, *I have been swimming lately. The water has been 75.* A month later I seem to have been able to dive, as I wrote on 12 August, *I am glad fiona can swim now I will help to teach her how to dive. Lots of love Alan.* Two weeks later my mother wrote to me, *Your school report arrived this week – good on the whole, especially French, Cricket and Swimming – some subjects could be improved upon but I daresay you know them!* Indeed my school report for that term notes 'Swimming: Well done!'

Major events were swimming across the river and back on my own – the river test. And finally the clothes test. I passed these in 1953, aged eleven, noting on 6 July, *I did my clothes Test yesterday wich is swimming across the river and back with some old clothes on.* After that one was deemed to be safe to be in a boat on one's own – though I do record in a letter on 8 July 1952 that, *A boy was drowned in the river yesterday he could swim but the canoe tipped over.* He was not a Dragon pupil.

I also learnt to dive. There were three boards, a very springy one which allowed people to do somersaults, a middle board with a long run to it, and the high board reached by climbing a ladder. This was particularly fearsome and if one dived badly the scorching of the belly flop left a red mark for weeks. On 6 July 1953 I noted, *I did my running spring and my Middle, which is diving off the Middle...*

There were also races – relay races between forms, though I don't remember inter-school competitions. On 2 July 1953 I noted, *We have had swimming relays. I am in our third boat each boat is composed of 4 people and there are 3 boats in our form. There are eleven divisions each division has 5 boats. We were second in the 8th division. Lots of Love Alan.* Four days later I wrote, *We have started relays and M3 did very well.* My contribution was noted in the termly report: 'Swimming: Excellent effort in relays.' In the fourth year the weather was bad in the summer and the Term Notes mention that it was 'not even possible to make a start with swimming relays', an 'ill wind which at least blew some relief for tender ear-drums', which brings back the memory that my ears were indeed tender, one reason I never really took to swimming later in my life.

In my final year, I was clearly still keen on competition swimming, and the Term Notes recorded that 'Swimming relays, which last year never started, this year never stopped'. Towards the end of the term I wrote, *There has been lovely weather lately and their have been swimming relays and our form was top of the river.* My own contribution was noted in my final school report: 'Swam with zig-zag enthusiasm in the 3rd Boat.' This summarizes my memory – I tried really hard, doing an energetic sort of crawl. But I could not work out how to both swim fast and see where I was going at the same time, so constantly bumped into the guiding ropes in the lanes.

One special feature of Dragon bathing was noted in a letter on 6 July 1953, *We have early morning bathing now in the charwell.* This was something I half enjoyed in my last years at the Dragon. One leapt out of bed with just a towel (no swimming trunks or pants) and raced across the Bardwell Road (it would no longer be permitted for lots of almost naked little boys – accompanied by equally scantily clad masters – to do this), and then across the dew-covered playing fields. There, equally surprising to us nowadays, a supervising master might be standing, naked, on one of the diving boards. How times have changed.

The mornings were often beautiful, but the gravel on the road cut my feet. Throwing aside our towels and holding our noses we would leap into the icy waters and swim as quickly as possible back to the shore.

I think that associations – the distinct unpleasantness of the English seaside, the cold baths, the dank river, the nasty taste of chlorine in public baths, the stinging eyes and the blocked ears – taken together meant that swimming became one of the least attractive of my dabblings in the world of water sports, though I am surprised on reading these accounts to find a much more positive picture than I remember.

PRIVATE WORLDS

The Silence Room, where we read and played chess

9 READING AND FILMS

A growing child lives simultaneously in the physical and social landscape on the one hand, and in a world of equally real, yet imagined, events and objects created by art – books, films, museums, pantomimes and other forms – on the other. In some ways this is more vivid than the physical world, especially as in games and hobbies the two become blended. I know that this was immensely important to me, but can only trace a few of the external residues of what most influenced me between the ages of six and thirteen. Nor can I separate these alternative realities into home and school – most overlapped so that, for example, the films I saw in the holidays and those I saw weekly at the Dragon fed into my imagination in the same way.

While I clearly read some comics at school, much of my reading of comics was at home. In fact there is very little reference to specific comics in my letters from the Dragon at all – they were perhaps too prosaic to mention. It may also have been the case that at the Dragon, at least, we were discouraged from reading too many comics. For instance, in the Term Notes for Christmas 1951 it was noted that there had been 'an offensive launched by the authorities against "comics" and "trashes"'. By the 1970s, however, things may have become more liberal. Paul Watkins mentions that 'Thursday was comic book day. 'Beano', 'Topper' and 'Eagle' and 'Look and Learn' arrived rolled up into pipes.'[95]

I must have come under increased pressure to read sufficiently fast to enjoy the process at the Dragon, though I only mention reading a couple of books in all my letters from there. Quite early on in the Summer term 1951 I write that *I am reading a book called the sign of the wolfes head* [a book I cannot trace]. Nine months later, however, it still appears as if it is worth my grandfather writing to my mother reassuringly on 30 March 1952, *He reads quite a lot to himself and has been playing chess with me.* My interest was probably stimulated by listening to stories on the radio, noting on 30 May 1953, *Tonight I will be listening to Treasure Island on the Wireless.* And by this time, aged eleven, people were giving me books as presents – on 18 February 1953 *I got a book from aunt Jean and uncle Alan and a letter from the other granny.* And on 18 May of the same year I wrote to my parents, *Thank you very much for the lovely book.*

As for what we read, either through readings by others or ourselves,

---

[95] Watkins, *Stand*, 79.

there is very little explicit record during school terms. What I read in the holidays is noted elsewhere, including works by Kipling, Arthur Ransome, Agatha Christie, Leslie Charteris and others.

FILMS

When I went to the Dragon my film-viewing was enormously enhanced by fortnightly films during the Christmas and Easter Terms, and occasional films in the Summer. When I first arrived we only had a silent projector in the Ciné Club. The technology was improving rapidly, however, during my time at the Dragon. The Term Notes for Christmas 1952 speak of 'the new talkie now installed in the New Hall' (and in the Cine Club notes for that term this is described as a new Bell, Howell-Gaumont 621 Sound Projector) and the following Term Notes reported that the 'Ciné shows now talkies'.

Likewise at first the films were in black and white, and certainly the films on which I frequently comment in my letters always appear in my imagination in black and white, for example 'Monsieur Hulot', various westerns and school sagas. The first references to coloured films do not occur in my letters until 1955, when I made a point of that fact.

From the letters, it appears that films acted very strongly on our imaginations. They were surrogate worlds, peopling an area today filled with television and the Internet. I never became a film expert, but count amongst the deeper influence on my life some of the great films – from 'Some Like it Hot', to Kurosawa and the 'Studio Ghibli', through to Ray, Bergman and others. Much of this was in my university period but built on the film-watching foundations laid at the Dragon.

All this was recognized by the master in charge of the Cine Club, J.D. Briton, and before looking at films more specifically, it is worth quoting from him. In the report on the Ciné Club in my first term, Christmas 1950, he wrote a long account of film in schools, partly in reaction to a recent report at the time from the Departmental Committee's Report on Children and the Cinema. I quote several paragraphs from this account:

> It is now the common knowledge of a well-informed public that children and adolescents are influenced to an extraordinary degree by what they see at the pictures; and it is also widely known that this influence may be as harmful to a child as it ought to be good. Since we cannot keep children away from the films, something must be done to prepare their minds against the possible evil.

Briton then quotes at length from the Report on how films may affect children, the possible nervous and moral effects. He continues: 'Good parents, who take an active interest in the nervous and moral welfare of

191

their offspring, would have a right to complain if the schools to which they entrust by far the major part of their children's physical, mental, and spiritual nurture took little or no part in combating this "contrary influence" of the public commercial cinema.'

Briton then discusses the relative advantages of silent and sound films, coming to the conclusion that since 'Children of this age are mostly interested in unadulterated action, dialogue is not much appreciated and silent films with music are probably best. Thus silent films with suitable stories are good and sufficient basis for future excursions into the sophisticated world of the sound film, which will be regular fare at a public school.' He continues: 'children prefer straightforward film stories, full of action and the simple emotions of loyalty, courage, and affection (not "love," which is anathema!)... The early silent films have an added advantage of being so far removed from the experience of everyday life of the average boy or girl in their plots and characters that there is little danger of their being muddled up with reality and producing the harmful effects complained of by the Departmental Committee.'

He notes: 'The most popular silent films seem to be Rin-Tin-Tin dog films... Laurel and Hardy, Charlie Chaplin, and Harold Lloyd are popular among the slapstick comedians.' Furthermore 'The tremendous outbursts of laughter and cheering which occur during the showing of these old silent films mean that the impact of the varied climaxes and incidents is immediate and the emotional release absolutely spontaneous and complete.'

Briton concludes: 'During the preparatory school stage, let us try to make the cinema, however it is employed – as entertainment or instruction – the familiar friend of enjoyable and interesting hours. Thus will boys and girls reach adolescence comparatively free from the harm they might have suffered through indiscriminate film-going.'

*

As for my reaction to films during my time at the Dragon, there are a number of hints in my letters. In June 1951 I wrote, *We had a good siny show last night about the making of marionetes and puppets. A funy one about school dogs and a pretend hairdresser which I could not understand it much.*

On 7 July 1952, just before my eleventh birthday, I wrote a somewhat breathless and unpunctuated account as follows:

We had a film last week called the Eureka Stockade it was about a Gold Mining village where a man called bently was accused of murder and a mob burnt down his house and the police were fining them £2 a month for the land and the miners made a blockade but the police attacked and beat the miners but the leader managed to get away and they got a doctor and the docter had to do something that hurt terribly and to drown the noise of the man they sang adeste fideles and it all ended happily, lots of love Alan

In the meantime during 1953 I went to a number of films at the Dragon. On 27 January I reported, *I saw a film last night called bus Christmas, which was about horse thieves.* A week later on 2 February I wrote, *We had a jolly good sinny show last night called Mad about Music.* It is worth pausing on this film since the Ciné Club report by Mr Briton contains a long and mainly disparaging account of it, which does, however, concede that we enjoyed it. He starts by describing 'the sugar and jam-puff stuff' of Deanna Durbin's singing film 'Mad about Music':

> Strangely and excitingly popular, this film had just about everything to ensure its being hooted off the screen; sentimental, artifical; 'Ave Maria' crooned by shiny-faced American choristers, with hazy close-ups of mist-enshrined Deanna dewy-eyed; brash, newly-breeched, dough-brained youths lining up chocolate-sundaes for equally doughy-faced schoolgirls – all this, but the film was a howling success.

He concludes that 'boys are born romancers'.

Two weeks later, on 15 February, *We had a film yesterday afternoon called the tudor rose wich was about history but was very serious and murders and executions.* The report on this by Briton describes it as a 'movingly sad story of young Edward VI and the Lady Jane Grey'. 'This very good film, simple to follow and finely photographed, has taken time to show its reactions. Boys were subdued at the finish – rightly so, at the tragic death of the innocent young girl. This bit of history, however, will remain quietly fixed in memory...' I am not sure, however, that it has, though no doubt if I saw it again it would flood back.

The following week on 22 February, *We had a sinny show last night we had two funny films one was about a spider and a fly and the woman fly got caught but the other one got away and called the other and they mounted on horseflys and some attacked on dragon flys and dropped pepper on the spider. And we had one about the dutch and a charlie chaplain.* Three weeks later, on 15 March, *There was a film on Thursday instead of prep and It was about birds.* All these were in the Spring term.

Finally on 22 March 1953 I reported my first Jacques Tati, 'Jour de Fête': *There was a film last night about a french fair wich was spoken in french but had English written underneath and it was terrificly funny.* Again I dimly remember one or two scenes, particularly one where a postman hitches himself to the back of a lorry and sorts the mail as he is carried along. Briton writes that: 'All agreed – a marvellously funny, brilliantly made film.'

On 3 May I anticipated: *We are going to have a very good film tonight called 'The happiest Days of your Life'.* I noted two weeks later, on 18 May, *We saw a film yesterday on the last Coronation and a Talkie one on the preparations for the next one.*

The following Christmas term on returning to school I noted on 27 September that, *We are having a film called "The man in the white suit" with Alec Guines...* This was a continuation of a spate of films I had seen during the holidays, taken by my grandparents and uncles. I wrote that, *In the hols I saw Genevieve, The Crimson Pirat again, "Call me madame" Peter Pan Natures half Acre "Hans Cristian Anderson".* 'Call me Madam' was originally a musical, and was made into a film in 1953 with Ethel Merman, which is the version I saw.

The year 1954, when I was twelve, was in many ways the high spot of my film watching. Some of these were at the Dragon. On 17 January I wrote, *Today we are having a film called "The Adventures of Hukleburry Finne". Which I think I will enjoy very much.* A couple of weeks later on 2 February, *We had a very good film indeed on India It was called "The Drum" the town where it was all filmed was in Tockut wich you probably know. It was about a rising of the Indians.* This film about the Indian mutiny, I suspect, was probably one which would have appalled my mother who was already very restless about the imperial message. Two weeks later on 16 February, *We are having a very good film tonight called the big store featuring The Marks brothers.*

In each issue of The Draconian under 'Ciné Club' there is a list of the films shown in the term and a note on those ordered for the following term. The Winter Draconian 1954 notes: 'The entertainment film programme for the Christmas term included the following: 'the Lavender Hill Mob', 'The Four feathers', 'The Dragon of Pendragon Castle', 'Vice Versa' and 'Appointment with Venus'. For next term, we have booked, so far, 'The Holiday of Monsieur Hulot', 'Sanders of the river' and 'The Titchfield Thunderbolt'.' This provides an independent check on how full my coverage was. Certainly from this list, I mentioned all of the films except 'Vice Versa'.

The series starts in my letter on 25 October 1954: *We have had some very good films this term the first was "Lavender hill mob" with Alec Guinness. The second "The four feathers". And this week there is "Appointment with Venus" about a petigree cow wich is rescued from the Channel isles.* A week later, on 2 November: *There is a film this evening called 'The Dragon of Pendragon Castle. And a Walt Disney film.* Unlisted above was the fact, noted in a letter at the end of November: *There are some cartoons tonight instead of a long film.*

Back at school in 1955 I wrote home on 27 January: *On Wednesday there were some school films and a film about a storm at sea and then after that there was a bit of Television.* In the same letter I added:

> *In the evening there was a lecture (by an undergraduate from Worcester college) who gave a talk about the Oxford travel club's journey to Angola in S. Africa. And he illustrated it with a coloured film. This evening there is going to be a film called 'The riders of the new forest' and it is about some people (a boy and girl) who live on the outskirts of the New forest and have lots of adventures.*

A week later on 1 February: *on Sunday there was a film 'It's in the Air' with 'George Fawnby' and it was extremely funny.* Whether Sundays were our usual day for films I cannot now remember, though it was the stated date for several films. What I do remember well is the large school hall where we watched the films.

On 20 February: *Last Sunday there was a film The Titfield Thunderbolt which you have probably heard of.* This was one of the films promised in The Draconian; and I mentioned another in an undated letter in early March. *This evening there are going to be some coloured Geographical films ... Last week there was a film called 'Les vacances de M. Hulo' which was about a crazy Englishman who went in a mad car to a holiday hotel in the south of France and the typical holiday camp sort he meets there. And it was extremely funny.* I still remember the collapsing canoe scene from this film. The final film that Spring term was noted on 13 March: *a very good film tonight called 'Sanders of the river' from the book by Edgar Wallace.*

It is interesting that of about forty films whose titles I have recovered from The Draconian, over half are described in my letters. Looking at the titles and subjects of all the films shown it seems clear that the majority were comedies – Tati, Hulbert, Marx Brothers, and Ealing Comedies. There were some adventure or historical films – Tudor Rose, The Man in the White Suit, Captains Courageous, and some others. Apart from the Eureka Stockade, a western, there were really none about war. So it seems strange that by the 1970s the films seem to have become more aggressive, at least according to the memory of Paul Watkins. He remembers a film a week in the New Hall and writes that 'The films were mostly war films – 633 Squadron, Cockleshell Heroes, The Guns of Navarone and also Zulu.' I don't know whether he has just remembered these amongst many others – it would be possible to check in The Draconian. Certainly, even though television was now vying with film, the films had a strong effect on his imagination, as they did on mine, in his case causing fear and anxiety among other things.[96]

---

[96] Watkins, *Stand*, 82–3.

*

Several of my school letters mention visiting dayboy friends or friends in Dorset who had televisions at this time. The school itself also started to put on special television events for the boys – there seems to have been some way to project television since I seem to remember the 1953 Coronation on television. My parents express envy of this in their letters, but the home television era for our family would come much later. The early days of watching the Potter's Wheel, Muffin the Mule and Bill and Ben largely passed me by.

I first mention television on 17 February 1952. *I am going out with a friend to his birthday party he is Dunken Cooper grandson of frank cooper who is the owner of coopers marmalade factory and I am going to see the tellivision.*

It was in the early months of 1953 that television arrived at the Dragon. On 22 February 1953, I wrote, *We have had television brought into the school and probably we will be seeing it soon.* It was only two weeks after this that we had the debate on the motion that 'Television and the cinema is a substitute to reading'.

Both the arrival of television and the ambivalence towards it of many of the older staff, is referred to in the school's Term Notes: 'During the following Easter Term a Television aerial appeared above the eastern end of the New Hall, and got a somewhat mixed reception. "Moron's morphia" was Ted Hicks' comment...'[97] A number of older staff thought it, 'one more victory for the Passive over the Active'. The comments on the televising of the Coronation the following term show both what the impetus had been, and how some of the opposition was undermined. 'And for the rest of the morning the television screen in the New Hall was the focus of attention, and in excellent focus too. And a good many of us were soon feeling a little uncomfortable about the lukewarm, or even hostile, reception given to television on its arrival last term.'

By the following school year, my last at the Dragon, television was obviously installed in the school and become more common. On 27 January 1955 I wrote that I went to a film *and then after that there was a bit of Television.* A month later, on 20 February, *Today is not very interesting except there is no work and there is going to be T.V. this evening.* On 3 May one of the choices we had on a special day was, *watch the cup final on T.V.*

By the time of Paul Watkins, twenty years after I was at the Dragon, he notes 'The corridor led to the TV room ... We could only watch TV on Saturday afternoons and evenings.'[98]

---

[97] Jaques, *Century,* 195.

[98] Watkins, *Stand,* 29.

20 ENTERTAINMENTS AND CLUBS

The one performance that lies on the boundaries of musical and pantomime which I remember from the Dragon is mentioned in a letter of 1 February 1955: *Then on Thursday afternoon we went to 'Listen to the wind' wich is a very funny Musical Pantomime and I think it was the best I had seen.* The Term Notes give the following account of this event, 'Listen to the Wind', the Christmas play at the Oxford Playhouse ... Joc ... now persuaded the Company to give a special performance for Dragons...' The account continues, 'The two ladies received their admirers, and their boxes of "Dragon" chocolates, seated decorously on their Victorian sofa'.

*

There is a report on the visit of The Hogarth Puppets to the Dragon on 15 November 1951. I made no mention of this in my letters, though on the preceding 30 June I had written home that *There was a puppet show last week with had the hoagarth Ochastrer, the flower ballet, two plays one was fly by night and 2 kings.* The Christmas Term show is described at some length in The Draconian, including 'The Hogarth Puppet Circus' featuring Hoopoo, the Clown; his Mysterious Excellency the Grand Turk; Colonel Poonah with Bulbous; Flash, the Cowboy, with Sparkle; Muffin the Mule, etc.

*

A form of educational entertainment which again had great force in the pre-television age was that of museums and displays. My interest in collecting things, described elsewhere, may have partly been linked to the growing realization that there were people who had Cabinets of Curiosities: this is exactly how I remember the little museum at the top of the stairs in the centre of the playground at the Dragon. I remember the collections of butterflies, beetles and eggs, supreme among them a huge and wondrous (part of) an egg supposedly of an extinct species or even a dinosaur. On a recent visit, the egg seems to have gone, but the old drawers of butterflies are still there. Jake Mermagen remembers 'The waste paper basket made out of an elephant's foot'.

*

There seem to have been two expeditions a year. In the mid-term break of the Christmas term the boys were given a choice of various places each year arranged for boarders by the school. The records I have from The Draconian suggest the following choices. In Christmas 1950 the choice was the Tower, the Mint, the G.P.O., the Navy at Greenwich, the Palace at Westminster or a nerve-centre of British Railways. The following Christmas of 1951 it was Imperial Tobacco, a visit to Bath, the Severn Wildfowl Trust, and Brabazon air-liner (Bristol Aeroplane Factory). In 1952 there were whole day expeditions to the Tower and London. In 1953 it was to Cadbury's chocolate factory, a marmalade factory, Severn Wildfowl, etc. The Draconian in Winter 1954 noted the 'mid-term expeditions', gave accounts of visits to, The Mint, the G.P.O, the Houses of Parliament, Guinness, The Imperial War Museum, Harrods, the Tower, Slimbridge (Wildfowl Trust). Reports on all the expeditions were written by boys.

Only on this last occasion, as far as I can see, do I mention the expedition. In an undated letter towards the end of November I wrote to my mother. *I spent a very enjoyable week end, and on Monday I went first to the Imperial War Museum which was extremely good also I went to Harrods which was also good.* These expeditions thus covered a whole range of subjects: finance, communications, politics, business, the army, retailing and conservation.

In the summer we tended to go elsewhere. For example, in 1952 there were whole-day expeditions to the river or Whipsnade, and another excursion to the Bradfield Greek Play. In 1953 I mention, in a letter of 6 July *We had a lovely time at Whipsnade and I took 8 photographs.* Then in summer 1955 there is mention of visits to the Royal Tournament at Olympia and Whipsnade. The school also made its first overseas expedition, to Paris, but I did not go on this. The river expedition, I now discover, consisted of hiring a flotilla of boats and going up the Thames from Port Meadow to Wytham Woods, Godstow. There was a great deal of bathing, special teas, various games, and masters and pupils participated. On the expedition on June 29 1953, the headmaster, Joc, was 'armed with cine camera and portable wireless set', and some film taken by Joc survives and is being restored.

*

There were a number of activities which because of their seriousness and the fact that they were often done with other friends, were to lay the foundation for some of the passions of our adult lives. They were encouraged at the Dragon and by our parents and would train us in the art of hobbies, often institutionalized in later life in clubs.

One of these was gardening. In the section on gardens and gardening in

'Dorset Days', I explain that gardening was an important part of my life at home. This continued in a minor way at the Dragon.

Perhaps as something partly left over from the war, I do remember that the Dragon had allowed the boys to dig up part of a bank near the road opposite to School House and above the sports sandpit. Here we were encouraged to do a little gardening, planting both flowers and vegetables. I remember that I was quite keen and had a small patch with carrots, the great standby, and perhaps some mustard and cress. I don't remember ever winning any prizes.

My memories are supplemented by reports in The Draconian, which show that gardening was seriously encouraged at the school. For example, in the summer of 1952 we are told, 'There have been four outstandingly good gardens this year...', and various boys are named as outstanding gardeners. 'There was such a demand for gardens earlier in the year that the flower beds on the Silence Lawn have been divided up and allotted ... The perpetual shortage of tools has been relieved by some trowels manufactured in the Handicraft Hut.' The following year there is an even longer report since the weather had been good and ten named individuals won prizes. Thus it was obviously something which was valued alongside other arts and crafts with special prizes.

*

Chess was considered very important at the Dragon from the founding of the school. Both the Skipper and his brother Hum had played chess for the county and it was widely recognized that it was extremely good for the brain. I was never much good at chess, but in my letters I refer to it once or twice. On 7 April 1952 my grandmother noted, *He reads quite a lot to himself and has been playing chess with me.*

In the Term Notes for Christmas 1952 it is mentioned that the first ever award of ties for chess was made, putting it on a level with other serious sports and games. The chess team regularly appeared in photographs in The Draconian.

A useful overview of the game at the school is provided in the report on the Chess Club in Easter 1952.

> The headquarters of Dragon School Chess is the Silence Room, around the walls of which are the results of competitions. Here, due to instruction from members of the Staff and to much competitive play among themselves, the Dragons have now reached a standard of play comparable with the great days of Swinnerton-Dyer and Galbraith. As proof of this the Oxford City team stated that on all boards the School team put up a very good performance against them.

Perhaps the most encouraging factor in Dragon Chess is that the enthusiasm and initiative for the game, to a great extent, come from the Dragons themselves. In some continental schools to-day chess is directed by the State and has become part of the school curriculum.... Here we stoutly defend the amateur and voluntary status of the game, but perhaps one day a sound knowledge of chess will be an essential qualification for a scholarship, and our headquarters will become the classroom of some Russian or Yugo-Slav chess master. Incidentally chess 'prep' might give rise to some interesting diversions.

Two books well worth reading are: British Chess by Kenneth Matthews and How to Play the Chess Openings by Znosko-Borovsky.

The School team was: W. Johnson, P. Palme, R. Hoare, M. Elvin, W. Turney, D. Wisset, N. Marston, A. Montgomery-Smith.

Results:

v. St Edwards's School	Draw 3–3
v. Oxford City	Lost 0–6
v. Magdalen College School	Won 6–0
v. Salesian College	Won 4–1
v. Staff	Draw
Senior Tournament	1. P. Balme; 2. W. Johnston; 3. R. Hoare
Junior Tournament	1. A. Montgomery-Smith; 2. D. Morgan
Draughts	1. E. Auckland; 2. D. Balme.

A special event, which was repeated on a return visit, is mentioned in one of my letters home. On 8 March 1953 I wrote, *There is a chess match this after noon against the champion of Isreal.* This is described in the Chess Club notes.

'The highlight of the term was the visit of Mr. Persitz the Israeli champion, on Sunday March 8th. Mr. Persitz played a simultaneous match in the New Hall against fifteen Dragons, and, without any delay whatsoever, won all matches in an hour and a half. He then astonished us by playing Paul Balme, without looking at the board, and beat him without any difficulty. It was a new experience for all of us who watched Mr. Persitz playing blindfold chess...' Despite these defeats, the school was excellent at the game. Thus the Christmas 1954 Draconian noted that 'Since March 1951, the School has played 25 matches, of which 21 have been won, 2 have been drawn, and 2 lost, in each case to Teddy's'.

The only other board game I mention while at school was one called Dover Patrol; writing on 15 February 1953. *I plaid dover Patrol yesterday wich is a game wich you have two navies and you do not know what the other persons piece is and the higher one wins.*

*

Finally, a special club at the Dragon, of which I was not a member but whose activities influenced us as they did many others, was the Ciné Club. An interest in film and film-making seems to have started early at the Dragon. In 1938 it is reported:

> This Autumn term saw one innovation come to stay, the Cine Club, which, with its own projector worked by the boys, turned on a Cine Show for most week-ends ... The Cine Club survived the war years, and then, guided by Jim Britton, made great strides, setting up its own Film Unit which attracted the attention, and the cameras, of the B.B.C. With the help of more than one Dragon parent in the business it gained access to some of the big Studios to study film-making at first hand...[99]

One such expedition is noted in the Term Notes for Christmas 1953: 'Jim Britton and the film Club break new ground with a visit to Pinewood Studios'. The activity was unusual, and a year or so after I left the BBC came down to film the Science Club and later to make a film of the Dragon film unit making a film.

Looking through the reports on the Ciné Club by Briton, I note that between 1949, when the film-making started, and Easter 1954, they note that some nine films had been made (seven or eight of them clearly in my five years at the school). In the Christmas 1950 report there is reference to an earlier film, 'Angus McBrainstorm's Brainstorm' about a mad scientist at the school. In 1951 there were 'Father's Welcome' a comedy, 'Pardoner's Tale' (Chaucer), 'The Last Ten Days' (of a Dragon term), 'Bright Star' (the first sound film) and 'The Adventures of Jan Storm' (another about a scientist). In the Christmas term of 1952 the thirty-seven members in the club made 'Struwellpeter'. In 1953 they continued with this film and made 'Little Johnny Head in the Air', and a short comedy called 'Pickeled Parents', and visited Pinewood studios. In 1954 they made a film about school activities during the last fortnight of term, including a cricket match, drill, swimming, athletics and other things. This film was shown in the Summer term 1955, where it is noted that it was hoped to show it with some additions in September. There was also a modern version of Guy Fawkes.

---

[99] Jacques, *Centenary History*, 149.

RECREATION

Skating on the School House tennis court, Easter term 1955

21 AUTUMN

One of the best ways into childhood worlds is through children's play. The world of imaginative play was not strictly separated between home and school. The Dragon, however, was the place for particular games and crazes.

As I look back upon this phenomenon, I have come to realize that this only very partially recoverable world was enormously important in my development. As a retired Dragon master, Bev MacInnes, noted after describing some of the games in the playground, 'My travels in the playground are the most important part of my journey. Again the Headmaster took the risks and left play to develop and become a central part of what the children learned and retained when they left us.'[100]

The scene can be set by a description of a piece of the playground in the Christmas 1952 issue of The Draconian by M.J. Harrison, aged thirteen-and-a-half and in class A.3, entitled 'The Playground'.

> The playground is void of boys. A gentle autumn breeze softly carries the leaves, which kick and struggle, to the tarred surface below. Those on the ground run along, trying to get back into the friendly branches of the surrounding trees. The dragon sunning himself on top of the Old Hall smiles down on the school. A tom-cat eats out of a dustbin.
>
> Suddenly someone is fool enough to ring the bell. The golden silence is shattered. Out come hundreds of very noisy little boys, all shouting 'Roll up, non-swindle marble show', and 'Anyone on conkers?' The dragon puts his hands over his ears. The wind carries the leaves back up again. The cat runs away.
>
> At last some clever person rings the bell again. After about five minutes, all is quiet. The wind knocks the leaves down again. The cat resumes its meal. The dragon smiles down. Suddenly, without warning, a P.T. class comes out to do its exercises in the playground. The cat is sick. The wind goes elsewhere, and the dragon looks at the scene below in disgust.

*

---

[100] Bev MacInnes, *A Sense of Purpose* (no date), 138.

There were two Autumn term games which were special and deserve separate treatment. Marbles was the most interesting and obsessive of games. I don't know of any serious anthropological study of marbles, though there is a good deal on the Internet describing the history of this most ancient of children's games (dating back to the Egyptians and beyond, and famously depicted in one of Brueghel's paintings), and we learn from examples the fact that over 400 million people in the world, apparently, collect marbles. It is curious that so much effort has been devoted to describing how you play the game, and so little paid to why people play and what functions marbles can have in the education of children.

In my letters to my parents during the 1950s there are two references to marbles. On 20 October 1953 I wrote: *We are playing marbles this term and I have got quite a few in fact I have got 16 big marbles* [picture of marble diameter about an inch] *and 50 small ones* [picture, diameter about half an inch] *which I will be able to show to the girls...* The following year I wrote in another letter on 27 September, *The craze is marboils this term.* Behind these brief references lies a world of activity and excitement.

The marble season was circumscribed to part of the winter term. It was initiated by a number of boys who had brought back bags of marbles after the holidays. Those who had failed to do so would spend time in the ditch behind the fence (which is still there and where marbles are still played I am told). An assiduous hunt would usually uncover a few, often chipped, with which to start one's game – or, I imagine, one could borrow a few from a friends and then return them (with interest, perhaps) later on. Jake Mermagen comments: 'I think the main source of supply must have been the day-bugs, particularly if the market needed an infusion because of hoarding. I still have letters to my Mum asking for supplies, which of course weren't forthcoming as the postage would have been more expensive than the marbles.'

Marbles were graded in a complex system of value based on an intersection of their beauty, size, rarity and condition. There were many varieties – at present I remember just a few. There were bottle tops, transparent green, blue or with no colour and for the most part worthless. Yet Jake Mermagen remembers that they 'were initially worthless, but at a certain point, for a reason no-one could understand, certain bottletops, possibly because of their colour or perfectly unchipped condition, became incredibly valuable.' In hindsight, this suggests that an older player had managed to manipulate the market by rumour, suggestion or cunning.

There were agates, or aggies as they were called, including those with a streak of red in them (blood aggies), but mostly a milky white. These were the humble pawns or main playing marbles, known as 'titches'. There were French or semi-spirals. Jake comments that they were 'quite valuable, but then Woolworths started to produce them and they became common trash'.

There were water glasses, which became valuable if they had some pattern inside them, but their value was disputable, as Jake describes. 'There were plain glass marbles with the minutest wisp in the middle which would classify as a spiral and be worth several hundred ordinary marbles, but without the confirmation of the wisp by the crowd, they were almost worthless.'

At the highest pinnacle of value might be a huge spiral – the size of a golf-ball, beautiful, unchipped, worth hundreds of ordinary marbles. These were graded according to the number and beauty of the colours that curled like the double helix of DNA round each other. (Did Crick go to a marble-playing school, I wonder?) Yet if these majestic marbles were badly chipped they immediately lost much of their value.

Marbles could be swapped and exchanged off the site of the game – and exchanged for other things as general purpose money (as anthropologists call it). But the main activity combined two principles which immediately links the activity to adult play, namely the capitalist market described by Adam Smith, (I wonder whether he too played marbles?)

Marbles required a combination of physical dexterity and skill, temperamental control and perseverance, self-confidence and self-belief. Jake Mermagen had to perform the difficult adjustment of coming into the school as a boarder about half-way through the normal five years. He comments, 'It really was a very good forum, in which boys could mix and gain their self-confidence. I remember as a newboy first finding my feet on the marble ground.' It was also a place where one learnt the arts of making an assessment of risk, profit and market value. Above all, it encouraged the desire to accumulate in order to gain status with others.

Our first account of marbles was written before an article by Lucius Cary, who was a year or two behind us in the school I believe, came to our notice. It gives an excellent account of marbles as 'an almost perfect market'. Since our account may have still left some readers slightly confused about how the game was actually played, and Cary gives an excellent sketch of the scene, let us start by quoting part of his description.

The currency of the game was the titch, the smallest common marble available (more formally a titch semi), and all more valuable marbles were described as being worth '25 titch', '48 titch', etc. To play the game, a seller would set out a 'show', the most common of which was a titch pyramid, consisting of three titch arranged in a triangle with a fourth balanced on top, and would inscribe a chalk circle around the show. He would also inscribe a line on the ground at about one large pace from the titch pyramid. To play the game a buyer, having first selected which of the many shows to choose from, would 'roll up'. He would stand feet apart behind the line, and selecting a titch from his marble bag would bend down and take careful aim, usually swinging his right hand several times back and forth between his legs before launching his titch at the show... If he succeeded in hitting the show, then the shooter would be entitled to receive his own marble back, plus all those which he had succeeded in knocking out of the circle. But if he missed, then the owner of the show was entitled to keep the shied marble.[101]

The aim was to make profits, in other words accumulate. One way was to set up a stall or shop in the market. Instead of putting out shoes or vegetables, we would put out one, or an array, or heap, (there were many combinations possible) of marbles. What we put out – how attractively it was displayed, the shop window, as it were – was important. There were other games, where the marbles were put in a ring drawn in the dust and one had to hit them out, or one person would throw and the opponent try to hit them, chasing all over the playground.

The main action took place along the fence where up to thirty boys, as I recall, would have their stalls. The pricing, that is to say the setting of the intersection between risk and reward, was done by working out how far the 'customer' had to throw from, calculating the value of the marbles on display, and the skill of likely players. If it were set too far, people would not be enticed to throw at the target. If it were too close, then one would soon lose all one's marbles (to lose one's marbles is an interesting expression, meaning to go mad). Another variant is described by Jake, 'I recall that some people made "houses" with doors, through which the marble had to pass to get a prize, rather than striking other marbles'.

Once the distance (and price) was set it could not be arbitrarily changed to reflect the customer's skill until play had stopped. I remember several skilled throwers and if they approached my stall I trembled and foresaw disaster. Particularly formidable, as Jake confirms, was Julian Travis, nicknamed (like his father before him) Pickles. He was a demon player, and it appears that his skills carried on to his younger brothers.

Lucius Cary tells a nice anecdote about his brother Mike, as follows: 'as in other markets, collective madness could suddenly strike, and very large prizes were available to those with initiative. On one occasion, the acknowledged marble king came back to school after half-term with what must have been a large Victorian doorknob, an enormous hunk of glass, which I guess had no intrinsic value. But he kept his treasure in a sealed box, and allowed only occasional glimpses to a select few. Within hours, all the talk in the school was of this monster marble. 'I haven't actually seen it myself but Colchester says that Travis's brother has seen it and it is huge.'

---

[101] Lucius Cary, 'Finding your marbles', *Spectator*, 22 May 2004.

In no time at all it had acquired a mythical status akin to the Koh-i-noor diamond (also of no intrinsic value, and valuable only because it is prized for its rarity).'[102]

The distance varied from a few feet, if one had just put one or two common marbles, to up to fifty yards if the target was a huge spiral of the best kind. Only a brilliant shot could get these – someone armed with a large bag of marbles. In pursuit of one of these, fortunes could be gambled and won or lost.

So the whole process combined several human desires: aesthetic appreciation of the miraculous colours and shapes; greed and avarice; the pleasure of making collections; the honing of skills; the excitement of the chase; the pleasure of taking risks and succeeding. It also included concentration and skill.

And, of course, it was educational – which perhaps the staff realized. It taught me things such as the assessment of risk, the quantification of chance and probabilities, scales of comparison between valuables, the function of bargaining and exchange, the social bonds created through competition, the delights of acquisition, sharing and abandoning valuable objects, competition for status in a hierarchy, the laws of supply and demand (sometimes a boy would flood the market and a certain kind of marble would rapidly drop in value). I also learnt when to hoard and when to distribute, conspicuous consumption, and prestige gained through giving things away.

Ultimately it taught me how to lose without losing myself, how to distance myself from objects, how to come to terms with winning and losing and, most importantly, the transience of worldly goods and their ultimate worthlessness. For, at the end of the brief rush of enthusiasm – as I remember the craze would only last six weeks or so – suddenly it was over. Then, since such transitory gains cannot be stored up, like Big Men in New Guinea who have a large feast with their pigs, or the Potlatch of the North West Coast Indians, the custom was that the most successful would announce that they were going to throw away all their marbles. At an appointed time they would go to the top of the steps outside the old museum in the centre of the playground and cast their marbles off – and the attendant crowd of boys would rush for them.

All this was a child's world – and largely limited to school. I don't remember playing much at home. And I don't think that the masters played any part in this, although Paul Watkins notes that saw masters rolling marbles in the 1970s. It all took place, and all the rules were worked out, by the boys. This was one of its most important features – it was an informal, almost black, economy, beside the formal one of the school and it taught self-reliance, self-organization and the ability to police

---

[102] Cary, 'Finding your marbles'.

and adjudicate without the use of formal sanctions – all useful skills for supposed future rulers of an extended Empire with a minimal enforcement capacity.

Some extra details on Dragon marbles are given in Paul Watkins' autobiography of the 1970s. Interestingly, marbles features more than any other craze or game. He notes the way in which marbles acted as a convertible currency, 'Everything had a value at the Dragon. Each marble, each piece of toffee and each chair in the TV room. You knew how many toffees it would take to buy a Medium Triple Treble marble and how many Triple Trebs it would take to get you the best seat in the TV room. None of this was written down, but everybody knew.'

He also notes the way in which there were fluctuations in the value of marbles relative to other commodities due to emotion and fashion, just like the apparently crazy swings in the Stock Exchange, 'Crisps were currency. For a bag, you could trade Big Treb marbles ... in the frenzy of handing out, the crisps would grow in value. It was like a documentary on the Stock Market ... all the hands raised and faces twisted with want. You could sit back and watch the frenzy and make it work for you. I had sacks of marbles to prove it.'[103]

Watkins also notes the fluctuations in the values of articles relative to each other. The various crazes were complex and separate, 'because each carried its own language and its own sets of values for objects. A bag of marbles that would not get you a cricket ball in trade one week would get you a whole set of cricket equipment, bat and pads and ball, two weeks later. There was no telling what the next craze might be or how long it would last.'[104]

Watkins suggests that the marble season was in the Spring rather than the Autumn term, and gives a vivid description of the game which amplifies but overlaps a good deal with what I remember, though there are names of marbles, the medicine boxes instead of bags, and a version played with dustbin lids which I do not recall.

'In the spring time we brought our collections of marbles – Triple Trebs and Spirals and Big Reds and Big Blues and Big Greens. We kept them in military medicine boxes lined with cotton wool to prevent chipping. When class was over, we ran like hell to claim our spots in the playground and set up our Shows. We set the marbles down on a shallow bed of sand gathered from the sandpit and drew a ring round them. With a piece of chalk stolen from class, we marked out the distance that the rollers had to stand. Then we yelled across the asphalt –"Roll up, roll up, two Spirals and a Jumbo Treb out!" When the boys

---

[103] Quotations from Watkins, *Stand*, pp. 26–32.

[104] Watkins, *Stand*, 65.

came, and they always did come, they either knocked the marble out of the ring and kept it, or they didn't and they lost what they bet. The more valuable the marble, the more chances they had to roll ... Or we dragged out one of the dustbins and flipped over the lid. We set a marble in the middle and let people roll their own marbles around the edge, to see if they could knock our marble out of place. If they did, they kept it. You could lose your whole damn collection in one Bun Break. I did it a couple of times.'[105]

It appears from the Term Notes that marbles were seen as something of an addiction by the authorities and if the frenzy grew too great, or lasted too long, then playing was prohibited. It also appears that the playing of marbles was at its most passionate in my first three Christmas terms, and that the craze began to decline in the last two years. This may be partly connected to the rise of other crazes, especially five-stones, and also possibly to the degrading of the value of some of the marbles alluded to above through their mass production and sale in large stores. What is obvious, from the attention given to the subject in Term Notes, is that this craze was recognized to be special – receiving three or four times more words than conkers or any other craze.

In my first Christmas term 1950 it was noted that, 'Marbles had the mortification of seeing the umpire's finger go up before they had even taken guard'. The following Christmas, the Term Notes mentioned that 'Marbles were given rather more rope than usual with which to hang themselves, and the announcement of their demise provided the only sensation of the term, revealing as it did the hitherto undreamt of depths to which human depravity, as represented by the marble addict, can sink.' At Christmas 1952 it was noted that 'It is of course the "Marbles Term" and the 1952 marbles season had an unusually long run, dying in the end an almost natural death, so that the official ban, when at last it came, sounded more like a polite valediction. But there was an ugly rumour of an iron hand inside the velvet glove, and a plan for a drastic offensive next year.'

My first mention of marbles had been in Christmas term 1953, when the craze was already starting to diminish according to the Term Notes, 'the marble fever seemed to be a less serious disease than in recent years, with its victims running rather lower temperatures than usual'. In my last Christmas term it was noted that, 'marbles can be said to have passed their boom and be heading for a slump; they still need the eye of authority, but can now be left to die a natural death about the end of October'.

*

---

[105] Watkins, *Stand*, 66.

There are only two references in my letters to conkers, both at the start of my third year. The first was on 5 October 1952, writing to my parents before my anticipated visit to India in December, *It will soon be guy falkes day and all the shops have fireworks. I have got thousands of conquers I will bring out a few big ones and I will bring out a catapult.* Two weeks later on the 20th I wrote, *I have got hundreds of concquers this season and I have got up to a 86. Then it was smashed by a 4.* I know that playing conkers, or the more appropriately spelt conquers, was always a major occupation for a few weeks of each year.

The Term Notes for each Winter term mentioned conkers as one of the crazes, though not in such detail as the marbles which accompanied it. While marbles were disapproved of, the school authorities seem to have approved of conkers and it is implied that even some of the masters played. The first reference in the Christmas term 1950 notes, 'any conkers present at the Hymn that morning must have blushed glossily at hearing themselves described as a game of skill in the finest amateur tradition, untainted by sordid financial transactions...' and the headmaster even offered to lend people skewers to make holes in them.

The following Christmas, 'Conkers still exercise some aesthetic attraction for the collector, but as a game they can not be described as moribund...' It appears that a television company came to the school to film the sport the following year, so we read, 'The despised conker acquired some much-needed glamour from being televised'. In 1953 it is merely noted that 'Conkers had a short season', and in my final Winter term: 'Conkers continue to appeal to the more discerning boys and the less hard-working masters.'

The nuts of the horse chestnut had to be ripe and falling, so conkers could only be played from October onwards. North Oxford and the area round the Dragon were, as I recall, well supplied with beautiful horse-chestnuts (though walking down behind the classrooms recently, where I remember a number of such trees, only one remains). I still remember the joy of the progression of their growth – the sticky buds even before the winter ended, then the candled flowers, then the hedgehog balls on the trees. And when they fell and split or were opened like magic caskets, inside was the magnificent chestnut colour, so brilliant and glossy and set like a jewel in its little nest of white softness. To watch the chestnut trees through the year and to gather the chestnuts and to begin to wonder about their future success was part of the pleasure.

Once gathered, the chestnuts were prepared for battle. It was no use putting an entirely fresh conker on to a string (through a hole bored with a meat skewer of which there seemed to be a large supply) for it would split on being hit. Minimally the conkers should be left for a week or two when they would lose their sheen but become harder. The process could be amplified by various techniques. One was to heat the conkers – leave them on a school radiator or even contrive to put them in an oven at the school or at home. Or they could be heated, as I dimly recall, by being held for long, uncomfortable hours in one's armpit. Or, I seem to remember, they could be made rock hard by leaving in vinegar for a few months. Afterwards one took off the skin and left the wizened, miniature, brain-like conker kernel exposed.

When ready they were pierced and put on a string and we would challenge or be challenged. Here that was some option. One did not need to accept a challenge – if one were a venerable hundreder it was hardly worth while to accept the challenge of a oner or two-er – I obviously regretted, as an eighty-six-er, being defeated by a humbler four-er, as recorded in my letter. The numbers were reckoned by adding the total of the two conkers in combat, plus one for the victory. Thus a fiftier beating a thirtier would become an eighty-oner. I don't remember ever getting to more than a one hundred-er, but I think that there were quite a few conkers with several hundred wins attributed to them.

Yet the question of when a conker ceased to exist, which echoes many adult debates about angels on heads of pins, was present. Jake Mermagen wrote:

'I do recall disputes as to whether a conker was still a conker. Some were damaged to the point that there was only a fragment left – which became harder to hit because it was smaller. But so long as there was a visible fragment it did qualify. The disputes arose over whether a fragment was indeed still there! Bits became embedded in the string and were claimed to classify as a conker. I don't recall microscopes being used in the analysis but it sometimes came close to the point where they were needed.'

Of course, the game was based on trust. It would have been relatively easy to add a few victories and proclaim one had a much higher score. But such 'cheating' would have been pointless. As with all school games, there were rules and if one got the reputation for cheating that would have been disastrous as no-one would have played with you again. The kind of trust in the maintenance of internal rules – upon which civil society and a capitalist economy rests – was being taught to us in this, as well as in other games.

This must have been one of the main lessons I learnt at school. My mother recounts that I wanted so desperately to win at anything I undertook that I would, before I went to the Dragon and in the family circle, cheat to do so. My wider family, especially my uncles, began to wean me off this a year or so before the Dragon. But when I found myself cheating in a game at the age of sixty-seven the other day, I realized that the cure was not yet complete.

I do think that in marbles, conkers and other such games at school I found that honesty was the best, and indeed the only, policy – a valuable lesson. One learnt to separate oneself – one's reputation, honour and integrity were bound up with the small object on the end of the string, but they would survive its destruction. It is possible to hazard oneself in public contest and to win, or to lose, without one's own inner *amour propre* being destroyed.

I also learnt a good deal about others by how they played – just as one can learn about people by how they drive a car. Normally mild people became almost vicious and highly competitive when a small nut was tied to the end of a string – other large and threatening boys became courteous and almost timid.

Conkers, like marbles, was a game of skill as well as of chance – indeed it was the blend of these which anticipated much of future life. A good player knew exactly when and how hard to hit the opponents, often after a careful examination of the opponent's conker for tiny cracks or weaknesses. I became reasonable at hitting, but not outstanding.

I went on playing conkers, I think, after the Dragon. But I don't remember the same deep excitement. And again I learnt that the game itself and the competition were the important things – the small, brown conker had no intrinsic value, the history of the object being exchanged and potentially destroyed became a legend and the holder of the object accrued status. In the highly communal school world, ways of externalizing, negotiating and playing with status in games such as conkers and marbles were invaluable. It would be interesting to know what the modern analogy is – and what games children play that fulfil a similar function nowadays. It may be that the iPod and virtual games on the web may have more or less privatized play and destroyed such actual, real, communal activities.

Paul Watkins only mentions conkers once, but gives quite a full description.

In winter, you brought out your radiator-hardened, two-year-old Conkers. You drilled holes in horse chestnuts and hung them from pieces of string. You found yourself some Little Man with a big fat, new and shiny conker and challenged him. He'd hold up the string and let you take a swing. You watched his face as your shrivelled rock-hard Conker blew his prize into white chips across the playground. When he cried, you'd tell him – "don't Blub, Little Man". But then you'd meet a senior whose Conker looked strange and transparent. He had hollowed out the middle and filled it full of glue which hardened into something stronger than rock, but you didn't know that yet. Your conker disintegrated when he swung at it. And he told you not to Blub even though you weren't Blubbing – you were tougher than to Blub – at least in the middle of the playground.[106]

This account shows the more aggressive side of the game (toughening up the character), which was part of it but certainly not all. I am pretty sure that the technique of putting hard glue into the centre was not done in my day – and would, by turning the conker from a natural to an artificial object, have been considered cheating. It takes away the element of sport. A game that apparently started in France using snail shells needs to be played with something which is not too strong.

---

[106] Watkins, *Stand*, 66.

22 WINTER AND ALL THE YEAR ROUND

On 20th October 1952, at the start of my third year, I wrote to my parents. *We are playing a jolly good game with search lights.* Behind this lay many evenings spent either in the school hall, or out on the playing fields, with huge torches or even semi-professional spot-lights from army and navy stores which consisted of a separate light, a large box of batteries, and a device for sending Morse code messages in light. The two teams would have their lights and others would try to creep up on the opposing team without being spotted.

I still remember the joy of holding a monstrous long silver torch which was fed with six or eight batteries, the beam of which could reach trees at the other end of the large playing field. I also remember the terror of being picked up by the lights and 'deaded', or the thrill of picking up some crawling figure. The game played into an undercurrent of memories, evoked through stories, told by relatives and returned teachers to the Dragon and Old Boys who came to the school, of the Second World War, which had finished only five years before I went to the school, and was still shaping our lives in numerous ways.

Guy Fawkes was, of course, an event shared with most children around the country. On 5 October 1952 I noted in a letter, *It will soon by guy falkes day and all the shops have fireworks.* Whether the last was a hint to my parents, I am not sure. Nowadays, of course, boys would not be allowed to let off their own fireworks due to health and safety regulations, but during this period it seems there was a more ambivalent attitude, with a major display run by the masters, but groups of boys letting off some permitted fireworks.

In the Term Notes for my second Christmas Term in 1951 it was noted 'This year the night is moonlit, frosty and still. As soon as the school bell gives the signal, from each of the countless crouching groups, dimly torch-lit, dotted about the two fields, comes a bang or a flash, or both.' The following year the authorities were more severe. No boarders were allowed to light fireworks so, according to the Term Notes, 'a Day-boy firework party in a garden opposite the School entrance drew a capacity crowd...' The following year the Term Notes mention that 'Fog threatens, but fails to blot out, an evening of post-dated fireworks...'

In my final Christmas term I noted in a letter of 2 November that *Guy Fawkes day was yesterday*. We clearly held it on a week-end rather than necessarily on November 5. It was back to the arrangement of allowing the boys some minor fireworks of their own. The Term Notes mention that 'Right up to the final bell crouching figures can be seen all over the field, oblivious of the display, bent low over the last of their squibs as it lowly expires in the mud.'

Gerd Sommerhoff gives a summary of some of the features of the fireworks displays.

> To illustrate the school's policy of fostering a sense of responsibility through freedom, I should mention Guy Fawkes night. Whereas most schools choose their autumn break so as to be rid of the boys on that hazardous night, the Dragon School actually welcomed the event, partly as an exercise in responsibility. On the morning of November 5th, the school's Tuck Shop would have small fireworks on sale to the boys. Days before we had already manufactured sparklers and "jumping jacks" in the Science Club. At Morning Assembly the boys would be given a talk about the necessary precautions and warned to behave responsibly. After dark, then, they would flock onto the main playing field and light their bits and pieces. At the same time the official school fireworks were run at the end of the field by the school prefects, who were allowed to smoke at those occasions 'since they need the cigarettes to light the fuses'.[107]

To us, today, this seems incredible and indeed at the time smoking was, normally, strongly forbidden. But it seems unlikely that Sommerhoff was mistaken.

*

*

Three of the winters in the first half of the 1950s were very cold ones, and so keen on skating were the Dragon masters, in particular the headmaster, Joc, that in the big freezes we were given a succession of half or full holidays for skating, and other winter sports.

The earliest mention of winter sports is in a letter I wrote from the

---

[107] Sommerhoff, *Consciousness*, 81–2.

Dragon on 27 January 1952 to my parents who had just left for India.

I hope you are enjoying the trip and it is not to rough. It has been snowing quite hard and on Saturday we had half a inch of snow and we had some nice slides and it has been nice. I am keeping my diary up so I can tell you what is happening when I come out. We had games in the snow wich was nice but when you fell down it was very cold.

This does not seem to have led to skating, but the following winter was one of the two really cold ones I experienced at the Dragon and the Term Notes give a vivid picture of how the whole school schedule was adjusted to this. The temperature began to drop in late November and 'The snow began in earnest at mid-day on Saturday, November 29th'.

The icy weather gave time for the skates to be got out, and Operation Wintersport to be set in motion, in short for the clock to be put back to February 1947. For it was now obvious that from an academic angle the term was wrecked beyond repair. The labour of slide making in the playground was lightened by the momentary thaw, which converted the whole area, and most of North Oxford into one vast slide. The tennis court was trampled, hosed, and skated on, all in the space of some sixteen hours. And then came reports of many acres of perfect ice on Port Meadow, and for nearly a week morning school ended almost as soon as it begun.

The next spell of skating was in the early part of 1954. In a letter on 2 February 1954 I wrote to my parents from the Dragon, *Dear Mummy and Daddy, we have had freezing weather. And I have not played any games (except ice hockey)... We have been doing a lot of skating lately and I am absolutely thrilled I can go quite fast, faster than most people could run... I am going skating this afternoon.*

The Term Notes for this term describe the background to this: 'Hoses and floodlight appeared round the tennis court... The Port Meadow season opened on 28 January, and the lawn was "isolated" and ready for use only one day later.' The effects were dramatic, and I wonder how many preparatory schools would have reacted in this way. 'A skating season means disorganisation; but this time the disorganisation was rather well organised. School stopped at eleven on each whole-school day, and skating followed till lunch. From lunch till 2.30 furious inter-form ice-hockey matches were played on the lawn, then some more school (when everyone was asleep) later.' 'Skates were available for all, better skates and more of them than ever before...– Joc-skates.'

A year later I wrote on 1 February 1955, *On Monday Teusday*

216

Wednesday and Thursday morning there was skating. Three weeks later I wrote to my father, *The weather here is pretty awful snow every day and then it thaws in the afternoon. But today the latest news is that there is skating this afternoon,* and on 13 March I wrote: *We have not played hockey this term hardly but we have had plenty of skating.*

The Term Notes mention that at the end of the school holidays there were hard frosts but no snow, so newspapers were laid on the tennis court and soaked in water. Then other opportunities opened up in the first spell of icy weather. 'The ice on Port Meadow was unsatisfactory, but Dragons settled down to a good spell of skating on an adjoining field placed at their disposal by a kind farmer called, believe it or not, Giles. Meanwhile the School House lawn had been made ready in record time by laying trestle tables on the snow and getting the staff and the more circular boys to jump on them.' After a while 'skating faded and soccer faded in'. But there was a blizzard at the end of the fifth week, 'And this turned out to be the opening of the term's second Ice Age. – but in this second spell of cold weather skating was confined to the lawn' in the period before bun-break. Furthermore, 'the playground offered a very good official slide...'

The events around skating are amongst my most vivid flashes of childhood memory. We used to go down to the seemingly endless flooded fields of Port Meadow by the Thames and I remember first awkwardly trying on my skates and flopping around, and then gaining confidence, as described in my letters. As I did so, I moved out with my friends over a magic landscape, studded with little islands, but full of lagoons, narrow passages and great expanses of ice. Often I could look down through the ice to see the frozen grass, or an ominous deep blackness below.

A teacher had invented the method of laying down newspapers and soaking them and then the water froze so that an ice rink was formed on the large front lawn at School House. This meant that we could skate at night with torches and lamps and perhaps some food – a particular pleasure, almost carnival-like.

The additional joy of skating was ice hockey. I particularly remember the serene wonder of sailing along with the puck (if that is what it is called) on the ice. The weightlessness and mastery is the closest I have ever got to flying. It was totally entrancing.

There were also other winter sports, in particular sledging, snowball fights and making snowmen. I wrote on 27 January 1955 to my mother, *On Thursday it snowed hard and there was snowballing on the field and people made forts and giant snowballs.* Strangely, I do not remember this at all.

ALL YEAR ROUND

There is practically nothing in my letters about other playground games, but I know there were many other crazes and games. I don't remember elastic, which may have been more popular with girls than boys at this time, and I don't remember skipping ropes, which may also have been thought sissy. But I think I remember a craze for yo-yos, and perhaps for spinning tops.

A game that took up a lot of time was bad eggs. This was played with a tennis ball or a softish ball against a wall of the old school building – the one facing towards the games pitches. I seem to remember it had no windows, but certain pieces (possibly a chimney) stuck out, so that a good thrower could get the ball to bounce in odd directions. Assembling several boys, you would throw the ball and either shout the name of a boy or a pre-assigned number, and that person had to catch the ball, either with both hands before it bounced, or with one hand after it had bounced once. If he failed he lost a point. After a certain number of points he became a target for the bad eggs. This meant that he would have to go to the wall and bend over so that his backside would become a target. From about twenty yards each of the players would throw the ball at him. Obviously the trade-off was whether to throw very hard to sting the target, and risk retribution later, or be moderate ('Do as you would be done by').

I seem to remember we played this for hours, but I noticed recently that the wall has now been swallowed up in a new extension so I don't know if the game is still played. It also appears that the school authorities were ambivalent about this and other such games, for in the Term Notes for summer 1952 it is noted that there was a 'gradual whittling down of those areas of the School buildings against which tennis balls could legally be thrown'.

Another game that we played incessantly was tig, or catching another boy, exclaiming 'Tig' as one touched them. Someone was 'he' and the boys scuttled off. It could be played with one other player, and tig formed one of the moments of lightning memory of my life at the Dragon: I was playing tig with another boy and he started to run round a clump of bushes and fence near the entrance of the school. He was a faster runner than I and I chased him for what seemed hours, never able to catch up. It was like a terrible nightmare that would never stop, and I still remember the panting exhaustion and the sweat trickling down my legs and the dust. Finally I had the brilliant idea that I would run round the other way. So I suddenly met him head-on, looking as exhausted as myself. Perhaps I learnt a lesson about counter-intuitive or lateral thinking to solve a problem from this.

One could opt out by saying 'pax' or peace. A variant was off the ground tig, where one could find refuge on some branch or wall. I still remember playing blind man's bluff, where one boy was blindfold and think I remember that part of our teasing of a wheelchair-bound boy occurred when he was the 'blind man'. There must also have been 'sardines' where one person hides, to be joined, crammed like sardines, in his hiding place by others as they find him.

Finally, there was a popular game called lurky, which I had forgotten until I was reminded of it by Jake Mermagen who described the game to me as a variety of hide and seek. 'A piece of wood, usually gleaned from the Barsonry, [woodworking room] was placed inside a circle. Someone was chosen to be the guard of the block and everyone else went and hid. The game was for someone to kick the lurky block out of the circle before the guard got to them – or something like that.'

Another description by an old boy, Andrew Hunt, describes it thus: 'Of course I must not forget Lurky, that matchless game which depends for its success on a yard containing dustbins, piles of planks and other builders' debris. As these are cleared, the game becomes duller ... The idea is to lurk unseen by the He, then to rush out with a cry of joy and kick a tin out of the ring before He can spot you and get back to the centre to call out your name. If you do this, all the previous prisoners are released and rush away before He can "lurky" them back again.'[108] This clearly put a large strain on shoes, for as Term Notes for Christmas 1953 mentions that, 'the steady popularity of Lurky can be gauged from the entry under the heading "shoe repairs" in any Boarder's House account'.

Three other crazes not mentioned by me are noted in the Term Notes. In Christmas term 1952 '"Handkerchief parachutes" occupied one of the wet week-ends, but by bed-time on the Sunday matrons were in full cry, and the kill followed at 9 o'clock next morning.' In Christmas term 1954 there was '"I spy" – fairly solid through the year'. And finally, in my last term, summer 1954, the Term Notes mention that 'the one noticeable "craze" of the term was stilts'.

Andrew Hunt mentions two other crazes which occurred after my time. One was 'bombs. These were lead balls, cut in two, quite small, and you inserted a "cap", as used in toy pistols, between the two halves. The two sections had a groove in which string was fixed, so that you could hold the bomb and swing it. When you dropped it sharply on a hard floor, the cap exploded with a satisfying bang. This craze was ultimately outlawed as the staff got tired of the bangs. Another craze which was eventually put down was flying propellers. These were about the size of a saucer: they were pushed up a twisted rod and whizzed off into the air unpredictably, occasionally hitting someone rather hard.'[109]

---

[108] Andrew Hunt, *Oxford to Zimbabwe,; A Life's Recall* (1994), 4.

[109] Hunt, *Oxford to Zimbabwe,* 4.

23 CRAZES AND HOBBIES

The school playground with boys doing physical education. The building at the back was the old hall. The building with weather vane was the school lavatory and to its left the fence against which we played marbles.

Watkins wrote that 'At the Dragon there seemed to be about one craze every week. Sometimes you would have to have a Rotring. They were drafting pens which used black ink that never washed out. Then over the space of a few weeks, Rotrings went out of fashion. ... Instead all they heard about were Yo-Yos, especially the glow-in-the-dark kind, because it had become the latest craze. Stamp collecting took hold one spring ... Skateboards gave us permanently bloody knees and elbows. ... Then the interest had gone and we moved on to gliders.'[110]

In my letters I only mention one or two crazes that involved collecting and swapping things. One was the keeping of white mice. My mother wrote

---

[110] Watkins, *Stand*, 65-6.

to me on 3 March 1952 asking, *Are you going to get your white mice next holidays?* I am not sure whether I took any action, but a year later I wrote from the Dragon on 22 March 1953, *There is a craze of white mice in the school and I might buy one in the holls and I will call it Donald.* [Donald was my father's name.] I remember the excitement of owning my own pet, the strange smell of mice in their nest, the delight of feeling their tickling exploration under one's clothes, and the amazement of seeing the tiny, blind, pink, slug-like new-born mice. They became part of the currency, like marbles and conkers. One advantage (as my wife Sarah discovered in her first ventures into capitalism through the keeping, breeding and selling of guinea pigs) was that one could make profits by expanding the stock through breeding – something one cannot do with a conker or marble.

It appears that the teachers knew about the craze as the Term Notes for summer 1953 noted, 'Life in fact went on, and nowhere more noticeably than in 2B cricket pavilion, where it included mice, golden hamsters, and even a rumoured guinea-pig or two'. I was on the edge of this, for in a letter on 10 May 1953 I wrote home, *One of my friends bought Two mice and a hampster and I am having lovely fun with them...* The breeding of mice seems to have been tolerated, for the headmaster Joc even mentioned in his Prize Day speech in the Summer term that while the staff were to be thanked for many things, they could not be held responsible for 'the multiplication of white mice'.

Another craze was for making little tank-like devices from cotton reels. The cotton reel had a rubber band threaded through it with a piece of candle and a small piece of stick at one end. One wound it up and then it trundled along. Some had the wooden edge cut into a zigzag pattern. Others had rubber bands or tyres. They would climb steep slopes and could be made to fight.

The only other craze I remember was rather odd. There were obviously some entrepreneurial boys at the school. One of them somehow got hold of what looked like small diamonds – little crystals. They were dazzling and we were convinced they were real. So we desperately tried to acquire some, but when we proudly showed our hoard to grown-ups at the end of term we were mortified to hear that they were fakes.

There is also a description of a new craze which arrived in my third Christmas term, 'five stones' or knuckle-bones. I remember playing it a great deal with little wooden coloured squares and other objects. It seems to a certain extent to have usurped marbles as the main craze of the Winter term, and the authorities appear to have seen it as amusing rather than, as with marbles, a threat. From the Term Notes for 1952: 'then came "Five Stones" one of the oldest games in the world but a new line in Dragon "crazes", which, despite the fact that it contained no suggestion of any threat to either morals or property, took such a grip that it saw the term out, by which time the real addict could clean his teeth with one hand while proceeding from one-sie to crinkle-sie and beyond with the other.'

The following Christmas it was noted that 'the closing weeks saw another big run of Five-Stones'; then, in my final Winter term, 'And Five Stones, coming in about the middle of November, get such a grip that by the end of term quite a number of boys cannot be handed anything at all, from a face flannel to a second helping, without throwing it up and catching it on the back of the hand.'

REFLECTIONS

School Leavers 1955 – Alan six from right, second row from front

24 REFLECTIONS ON MYSELF

My overlapping life at home is explored in 'Dorset Days'. Here it is worth noting a couple of particular features. One concerns the fact that my parents were in India for the two years before I went to the Dragon, and for most of the time I was at the school. Their absence, and the knowledge of how long it would take my letters to reach them and a reply to come back, added to my loneliness – though, as explained elsewhere, my mother's love and the warmth of my grandparents greatly mitigated this.

The second is the nature of the Dragon school. The particularly open, relaxed and familistic atmosphere that the Skipper had initiated in the school meant that even though I clearly found life a strain and seldom smiled for several years, in the end it was a positive experience. The Skipper was right about hindsight in a Speech-day address in 1900. 'I am delighted to feel that one of the chief features of the School is the affection which the old boys retain for us. I am not sure if they do not like us better after a few years of absence, when distance has lent some enchantment to the view, than when they are actually here as present boys.'[111] My letters indeed do suggest that I did enjoy a good deal of my time there and, by the end, was smiling quite a lot.

This, in fact, seems to me to be one of the main psychological devices which bound us to the system and resulted in a deep internalized loyalty and ultimately self-confidence. We would start at the bottom of the heap. Gradually, as in some long tunnel, the light would appear, then flood in. By the end we loved it. This happened to me three times in my life – at the Dragon, at Sedbergh and, to a certain extent, as a teacher at Cambridge University.

That this was what was happening to many of us is shown by Paul Watkins. He started in tears, misery, loneliness and desperation. Much of his book is somewhat negative. At the end, however, he realized how much the Dragon had meant to him,

I knew that I would probably never return ... The places we had owned and called secret would now be secret for somebody else. ... the smell of everything that kept us warm and fed and clothed would be bitter and strange in our nostrils the same way they were for the parents.

---

[111] *The Skipper*, 43.

... I realized too, that I would miss grumpy Pa Vicker, and the boggy-smelling river-bank and the peg-legged shuffle of M Blek coming to wake us up in the mornings.'[112]

Watkins continues:

In the farewell ceremony, as I collected my Leaver's Book from the Headmaster, I still couldn't believe it was ending. Something caught in my throat in a way that had never happened before, the morning that I woke early to be on the bus that went up to Heathrow Airport.'[113] When he returned a couple of years later, 'It seemed to me that in the time between, the Dragon School had faded to a mass of echoes in my head. But when I got there, I realized it was not the Dragon which had become an echo to me. It was I who was now nothing more than an echo in the school.'[114]

I have felt the same. We end up as ghosts – and we feel the same way when we go back to other places which have deeply affected us. Jan Morris is right to describe the school as a place with 'a personality so pervasive that when its old boys grow up to be Hugh Gaitskells or John Betjemans, you can still see its stamp upon them'.[115]

*

The enchantment that grows after one leaves takes many forms. It has even, perhaps, fuelled my love for a projection of this crazy world of North Oxford into one of the richest seams of English literature, namely children's fiction. The area is associated with Lewis Carroll, J.R.R. Tolkien, C.S. Lewis and Philip Pullman. The intensity of this world, its strong rituals, the clashes between powerful ideologies which are reflected in it, the encouragement to independence go into the mix which led to 'Alice in Wonderland', the hobbits, and the Narnia heroes and heroines. I realize now, towards the end of writing this book, that in the fantasies and friendships from my time at the Dragon I was constantly slipping into parallel worlds, and was then dragged back into this one.

*

It is strange to look back through the reversed time telescope at myself

---

[112] Watkins, *Stand*, 87.

[113] Watkins, *Stand*, 87.

[114] Watkins, *Stand*, 88.

[115] Morris, *Oxford*, 160.

as I moved from the five-year-old who arrived back from India in 1947 to the nearly fourteen-year-old preparing to go to his public school at Sedbergh in 1955. The evidence for my shifting and sliding identity and personality is contradictory and patchy. There are the impressions of others. There are photographs and a few paintings. There are my activities and enthusiasms.

Looking through my letters complements, from the inside, the observations from outside of my parents and teachers. In using them to jog my memory, of course, I am fully aware of the various forms of distortion that occur. Orwell is at least partly right when he comments, 'Not to expose your true feelings to an adult seems to be instinctive from the age of seven or eight onwards.'[116] Yet, allowing for all this, I still think that there are often some unintended clues to my developing character in those letters from which I can draw some conclusion. Again, although some of this has been quoted before, nevertheless it is worth repeating it here as part of the final portrait of my character and its development at this time.

There is a certain amount to suggest a sense of humour, including the use of irony and mild invective. I clearly found certain films and books amusing, for example, on 17 January 1954 aged twelve, *I have read an extremely funny book wich I advise you to get. It is called down with school or your might get "The Horror of St Trinians". They are very good and I think the girls would love them.* It is obvious that these famous characterizations of boys' and girls' boarding schools exactly captured the kind of humour I tried to emulate.

There are examples of my attempts at humour on 10 May 1953, when I was eleven. I wrote about playing against *Radley Midgets but Realy they were much bigger than our side.* Eighteen months later, on 25 October, I had improved this to: *another against Radley Midgets (Jolly big midgets!).* Somewhat clumsy, Molesworthian humour led me on 17 March 1954 to write, *By some bad luck I am in the sick-room because I was sick on Friday morning but I have been perfectly alright since but the old hags (Three witches from Macbeth) have been trying their foul concoctions on us in the form of many coloured gargolls (of course I have not got a sore throat).* This is, incidentally, as far as I can see, the only indirect hint of any class, gender or age snobbery in my letters.

I attempted self-mockery or irony of a kind from about the age of twelve. For example, on 18 July 1954 I laconically remarked *I haven't killed anyone with that dagger* – obviously referring to some dangerous instrument my parents were aware of. I sugared my requests to my parents by turning them into semi-humorous exchanges. Thus, when I asked for pin-ups and some more tuck for my prefect study when aged just thirteen, I wrote on 20 February 1955:

---

[116] Orwell, *Essays*, 450.

By the way if you have not sent the tuck could you cut the front Pictures of the 'Picture Post' and the big double page ones inside of film stars and send them along some time next week because we stick them up on the walls of the Dark-room (the special room of the prefects) Lots of love Alan
P.S. don't forget the tuck?
P.S.S. Don't forget the pin ups?
P.S.S.S Don't forget either?

In the following letter in March, I wrote:

I am not spending any money on the tuck shop and so I am nearly out of tuck (just dropping a hint). I know if you have nothing to do I expect you like to make stations and tunnels for Hornby I have a terrific craze for electric trains and I am going to make some electric signals they cost about 8/- in the shops and about 4d in the science club I hope you will make some things that I can look forward.

I doubt whether my mother, though perhaps amused, rushed to start making me Hornby add-ons.

As an example of the humour I enjoyed in films, I wrote in March 1955, *Last week there was a film called 'Les vacances de M.Hulo' which was about a crazy Englishman* [sic] *who went in a mad care to a holiday hotel in the south of France and the typical holiday camp sort he meets there. And it was extremely funny.*

Then again, of course, we were great fans of Gilbert and Sullivan. Singing in Patience and then Iolanthe must have helped to give me a sense of that irony and teasing satire which is the basis of both of these shrewd observations of English pretensions and class snobbery.

There are two other occasions where I am not certain whether I was being deadpan humorous, or serious. Both were in my last year. One was on 13 March: *Today there was a service at St Phillips and St James with thousands of long hymns and psalms.* A week later, on about 17 March, I described *a talk by a women from the N.S.P.C. (National Society for the Prevention of Cruelty to Children). And it was all very stirring. But next day I was sick.* I suspect that I was being mildly cynical, though the deadpan juxtaposition was probably unintentional. Finally, I was not beyond teasing my parents. In an undated letter of July 1954 I wrote to my father, *I hope you are not getting too fat*, which I accompanied with a picture of an obese gentleman.

From these hints, it looks as if I had developed the usual arts of irony, satire, self-mockery, exaggeration and all the elements of English middle-class humour by the age of eleven or twelve. One final example of this is the mock school report which I wrote and which is reproduced in the visual essays at the end of the book. The report was supposedly written in May 1953 and states that A. Macfarlane, aged 11.2 is a scholar of incredible talent. From the contents and the hand-writing it is clear that I got one of the little report forms and filled it in a 'Down with Skool' jokey way. Whether I sent it to my grandmother or parents I don't know. What interests me about it is that it showed a clear understanding of what I should be aiming at – and I even used the initials of the principal teachers in the top classes.

*

A good deal of the humour depended on seeing the situation from the outside, from the point of view of both myself and the person to whom I was writing. I never remember having letters vetted by staff so I must have impOSED constraints on myself. This is perhaps what strikes me most about the letters, namely that my sense of self-awareness, combined with an awareness of the other – the recipient – and their needs and lives was advanced. My letters seem to be carefully crafted to focus on my parents and their well-being. None of my letters ever reflect any strong negative or unhappy feelings of my own, except through humorous asides.

From the very start when I was aged seven I was showing interest and often polite concern for the recipient. A letter on 14 July 1949, when I was seven-and-a-half, started *Dear Mummy, Much love for your birthday.* This was perhaps prompted by my grandparents, but this may not have been the case in the very next letter to my parents, starting *I liked your nice letter.* I then wrote to wish my father *Many happy returns of your birthday. I hope you will have a very happy day,* in October 1949 when still aged seven.

The concern for the other and his or her life is one of the central features of my letters. Aged just nine I wrote to my father at the end of February 1951 after my mother and sister came home, *Dear Daddy, I hope you are very well and you are not so lonely without mumy and ann.* I was constantly asking after the health and well-being of my parents and sisters, as well as politely thanking them for gifts. In the following month, March 1951, for example, I wrote to my mother, then in Dorset with my sisters:

> *Dear Momy and Ann and fiona, I hope you are better know after that flue. I love the comics and are enjoying your letters. Thank you very much for the lovely sweets you sent me. The time is flying I am looking forward to the hols and Daddy coming home. I am just recovering from flue myself. It will be quite write to come on the second thank you. I am very sorry that I didn't send this sooner than this. We are lucky because we are going to have three birthday partys in a week. This is the kind of [? boat] I would lik to go on the Broads in*

[picture of a very smart sailing boat]. *I am afraid I havnt any more time now I will be writing soon I have just joind the cubs club lots of love Alan.*

Other examples of my projection through empathy and sympathy, particularly into my parents' life in Assam, are scattered throughout the letters. When aged ten, on 11 February 1952 I wrote, *I hope the girls will enjoy you teaching them.* On 7 April 1952 I wrote *It must be awful with all that lightning tell fiona I could not give her anything but I will bring something for her when I come out to you ... I expect Daddy was furious about the 2-1 defeat of Scotland yesterday lots of love to fiona and Anne and all of you Allan.*

When my mother had a rabies injection, I wrote on 29 September of the same year, *Dear Mummy, thank you so much for your letter. I am so sorry to hear that you had to have injections and that they made you feel ill I hope you are better now ... I liked to hear about the Performing elephants. I wonder if daddy saw any more wild ones. I am getting excited about my trip to India. How nice it will be to see you all again. Best love to you all Alan*

After I returned from the trip to India my interest and queries about the parallel life in Assam increased. In my first letter afterwards on 18 January 1953 I wrote *I wonder how mopsy is getting on and candy too ... I hope you are well and everything is going well. Lots of love Alan.* In the next letter on 27 January I wrote I *got your letter today and I hope Fiona's finger will get better quickly. And I hope your cold will get better. It is a pity Sonari did not win but I hope they will have better luck next time ... I expect mopsy will be growing into a big dog now.*

There are many such enquiries and comments which show clearly that the life so vividly kept alive by my mother's brilliant long letters from Assam was indeed a parallel world for me throughout my time at the Dragon. When the two worlds suddenly merged, I was intrigued. Thus on 29 April 1953, *Mr Swift came today and gave granny the passel you sent. Its funny to think I met him in India and again here.* The following year, on 17 January 1954 I wrote, *How are the horses getting on? I hope they are still in favour. I wonder whether you have started the holidays. I should think it is the cool wheather still but it will be the monsoons fairly soon.*

Likewise the world in Dorset remained alive during the term time, and in my less frequent letters to my grandparents, or to my mother when she was home, I enquired frequently about how things were going. For example, on 17 February 1952 I wrote, *Dear Grany and Grandpa, I hope the chickens are getting on okay and no more hens have been caught by fox.* A month later I again wrote to them *Dear Granny and Grandpa, I hope the chickens are getting on allright and none of the chiks have died. I wonder wether any of the chicks have been caught by pudy yet or wether pudy has caught any mice yet.*

The competitiveness of my life at the Dragon, the other side to empathy and concern, comes out indirectly in the accounts of competitions and sports, but is not phrased in an aggressive way in the letters. The passionate personal desire to win has become muted into a hope that we would win games and regret at losing. An interesting feature of my socialization into becoming a 'good sport' is the way in which I was inculcated into the habit of avoiding boasting by making any success into an accident or, in Dragon jargon, a fluke. This was especially marked when reporting high honours, like school colours.

Thus on 18 July 1954, aged twelve-and-a half, I wrote, *By some fluke I have got my tie for cricket.* Earlier that year on 17 January 1954 I had written about football. *I have been back at school two days and so I have not much to say I am in 1st game and with considarable luck I might get into the first 11.* The following year, on 1st February I wrote: *last week there were the first games of soccer and on Saturday I played in the 1st XI [football] match against Salesian College (Some fluke)* ... and in March: *On the Wednesday before last there was the first game of hockey (because of the snow) and it was a match against new college which by some fluke I was in and which we won 3-0.* And concerNing a cricket match, on 10 July 1954, I wrote, *We began to look as if we would draw when by a fluke I hit 10 in 3 balls then Westrup hit 3 fours. But he was out for 25 but we managed to win with ten minutes to go. I made 33 not out.*

Games are perhaps the most widely described feature of my life at the Dragon, almost every letter having some account of some sport or other. It was on that subject that I knew my own interest would coincide with that of my parents, particularly my father. The other major themes which obviously both interested me and I thought would interest the recipient, were the weather, health and frequent references to films and outings.

*

There are signs in the letters that my self-confidence, as well as my happiness, was increasing all the time. One thing which encouraged and reflected this was travel. That I went on my own by train to school from Dorset and also up to Scotland, without any indication that I saw this is as anything of a problem, is interesting. For example, when aged ten-and-a-half, my mother noted in a letter of 6 May 1951, *Anne and I took him by train to Bournemouth station and he didn't seem at all worried at the thought of the 3 and a half hour train journey.* Such a journey would have presumably involved going to London and changing at Paddington on to the school train to the Dragon.

Or again, at the end of my tenth year, I travelled alone to India and back by air. I wrote a postcard to my grandmother from the flight as follows: *Dear Granny this is the Argonaught I am flying in it is very comfortable and we get wonderful food. We are about 2 hours travelling and I have not been sick we got a shower bath at Karachi and I am feeling nice and cool lots of love Alan.* There is no sign of anxiety, though I was told later that I went missing and held the plane up for a while on one of the stops.

There is very little sense of fear or anxiety in my letters – about things that might happen to me in the future, of dread of any kind. Oddly, the only thing which really worried me, and practically the only example of any mention of national events (apart from sports), had to do with two notorious murder cases. On 25 March 1953 I wrote, *I have been rather frightened the last few nights as a Mr Cristie has disappeared from a place where a man knocked down the wall and found 5 women and the Police dug up the garden and found two more women on[e] of witch was Mrs Cristie.* The other was a year earlier, when on 18 February 1952 I wrote, *Last week there was terrific exitement because Bentley was hung because he helped Craig Murder P.c. Miles Lots of Love Alan.*

Apart from this, the only other events outside the family or school to be mentioned was in a letter on 27 January 1953, when I noted, *A jet plain crashed into a pylon last night and the lights went out.* This was, of course, something which affected me directly. And on 11 February 1952 I wrote, *Jock made a very good speech on the day the king died and he was nearly crying and he was faltering. And lots of people were crying.* It is worth noting that I called my junior headmaster by his nickname to my parents.

*

Much of life in a boarding school revolves about friendship (and enmity). Learning about how to make and break friendship, how to cultivate it and what it means, is one of the most important things which a school imparts. Watkins, writing of the Dragon some twenty years after I was there, notes, 'It seemed to me that you had to figure out people pretty quickly at the Dragon School. Who you could trust and who not. You measured them up fast and went with your instincts. And you knew that at the same time, people were measuring you up and it would take a lot to change their opinions.'[117] This is something I remember too.

Being a boarder, with my parents away in India, I was particularly dependent – as my mother pointed out – on friends who would take me back to their homes for a few weekends. Some of these events are mentioned in my letters. I remember being very close to a few boys, including Arber and Mermagen and a few on whom I suppose I had minor crushes. With them and with others I began to develop that ability and

---

[117] Watkins, *Stand*, 7

pleasure in discovering an equal, mutually dependent and voluntary relationship.

The threat that I would not develop the ability to make friends and be absorbed into a wider world worried my mother when early on she seemed to think I had few friends. In fact, both at home and at school, it is clear that I had a number of friends. An early letter to my parents, when I was aged seven-and-a-half, on 14th July 1949 mentions, *We are in Scotland and I have a boy friend. His name is John.* And there are quite frequent references in the Dragon letters to friends with whom I would do things or who took me out to their homes. For example, on 17 February 1952 I wrote, *I am going out with a friend to his birthday party he is Dunken Cooper ... and I am going to see the tellivision.*

I clearly selected my friends sensibly. I commented on Jamie's younger brother Sandy on 3 November 1952, *I am going out with Sandy Bruce Lockhart who is a very nice boy.* Another friend's background I quickly sketched in for my parents, on 16 February: *I was asked to a birthday tea on Thursday and the same person is asking me out today his name is David Walters and his father owns a silk factory.* On 1 February 1955 I mentioned: *on Sunday I went out with a friend and we played with his trains ... Yesterday I went out again and had duck and roast potatoes and peaches. We mucked about with his air rifle and his Trix trains.* That Joc should tell my mother when she went to see him that I was a very popular little boy may be true.

Towards the end of my days at the Dragon my mother described the deepening friendship with Stephen Grieve (mentioned above). He did not feature in my letters, but nor did many others whom I now remember as friends – particularly when I look at the school photographs.

*

From my letters, I seem to have been fairly balanced and to have lived within a social world in which space and time co-ordinates were pretty well adjusted. I knew where my parents were and what Assam was like; when at school I could visualize their world and that of my home. I was well aware of time, how long they had been away and when I would next see them, and how long it was to the end of the term or holidays. I lived much in the future and the past as well as in the present. All this would have helped to mute any sudden conflicts or pressures from school and reminds us that for perhaps most, at least at the Dragon school, the supposedly closed physical world of the boarding school was not really a prison. Our minds could travel freely in all sorts of directions, not merely into sub-worlds of friendship, games, fantasies, literature and films, but away to our families and friends.

One letter in particular shows my awareness of what was going on around me, of future time and a wider world of India, of hopes and dreams and parallel lives of relatives and friends. On 12 August 1952 when I was ten-and-a-half, I wrote:

> *Dear Mummy and Daddy, I hope you are not feeling the hot weather too much. I am so looking forward to flying out to you in December. The other day Richard drove me in his car to Swanage and we had two bathes wich I enjoyed. I have been having good rags with Robert. On the 15th robert is taking me to London and is putting me in the train for SCOTLAND. It will be fun seeing the Cowans again. Granny has just got a new lot of baby chicks and last night she won first prize for her eggs. We are hoping to hear the result of Roberts Exam this week. Richard cut down a big tree at the bottom of the Garden yesterday and I cut down a small oak. I am glad fiona can swim now I will help to teach her how to dive. Lots of love Alan.*
>
> *

It is worth noting the growing maturity of my style and observations in the letters, even if this means repeating a few extracts. I notice the improvement and some rather more adult ways of writing things from about the age of twelve. On 11 January 1954 I wrote to may parents from Scotland: *I went out to a pleasant little town in Peeblesshire and a 6 course dinner.* That autumn in an undated letter at the end of November, *I spent a very enjoyable week end* at school. Perhaps one of the best graphic pieces of writing was on 20 February 1954.

> *In the afternoon we had a half holiday and it was lovely weather. Yesterday we woke up to a sprinkling of snow but we played the return match at home against Bluecoates school. In the first half we were pretty equal. Then we kicked off and scored a goal straight away then there was a ding-dong battle in which their were several scrabbles in their goal mouth and in one the ball went over their line but it was quickly kicked out again and the referee did not see it. (I think it is true [I wasn't there] because they admitted themselves that it was a goal). Then in the last few minutes they managed to score and so it was a draw.*

This was beginning to be dramatic writing and the use of the word 'sprinkling' is apposite.

The letters and the occasional paintings or drawings are contemporaneous instances of my voice, however stylized. The photographs record my growing up and facial expressions. My speech, however, is not recorded at all except in my letters. This makes the very few instances of my recorded conversations in my mother's letters even more tantalizing, though all of them, fortunately, occur in the few months

233

before I learnt to write and my first letters survive.

On 13 April 1948 my mother wrote to my father, *Alan and Fiona have met some children up the road and are picking up dreadful habits, they come back chanting "Ha, ha, hee, hee, you've got a face like a chimpanzee" and then shriek hysterically!*

At the end of the same month, on 30 April, when I went to my first proper kindergarten aged six-and-a-quarter my mother reported *he said he told the small boy next to him that his daddy had shot a tiger, to which the boy replied that so had his Daddy.* "Ah" said Alan after a moment's thought "but my Daddy's tiger was a mad tiger". A month later an aged aunt came to visit us and my mother described the occasion on 6 May:

> *She is a nice old thing, large and rather downright, Alan followed her round everywhere, he even went to see the people next door with her, and came back with his eyes popping out of his head "D'you know what happened to her sister?" he said "She had three-quarters of her stomach took out" and then as an after thought "But I suppose they put it back again"!*

In the same letter she described how,

> *He came back the other day, bristling with pride because he had been made Captain. "Captain of what?" we asked. "Oh nothing". "But you must be captain of something – what do you have to do?" "Oh nothing". "Well why are you captain then?" "So that when I go out of the room somebody else can be vice-captain". Quite logical to him!*

*

One of my central characteristics was a desire to excel, or at least to win and succeed in whatever I was doing. This had the good effect of making me persistent and determined in certain respects, as can be seen in the accounts of learning to ride a bicycle and playing rugger. Later I applied this to my academic work. I really tried, and knowing myself to be very small and not particularly intellectually talented, I came to believe that effort could overcome this lack. I was ambitious, keen to prove myself, and never really contented with what I had achieved.

There were negative sides to this. One was that I was a bad loser – I minded too much. There are a number of accounts of this, of sulks and tears in various games. I did gradually learn the art of losing and this was particularly something which a boarding school like the Dragon drummed into one – being a good sport, modest in victory, resilient in defeat.

Another negative feature was that if I could win by dominating I was prepared to use all my weapons, including physical force. I am not sure that I either bullied or was bullied at kindergarten or the Dragon or with

234

any of my friends. But there are a number of accounts of me bullying my sisters – lamMing them up, as we used to put it – and this continued right up to my thirteenth birthday. On the other hand there were quite long periods of contented play, and my sisters seem to have been fond of me, which suggests it may not have been seen by them as malicious – more a matter of trying to assert superiority.

The fact that neither Jamie BRUCE LOCKHART nor I remember bullying as a serious problem at the Dragon may be because we were lucky. My own character no doubt helped. My friend Stephen Grieve remembers me as like a terrier dog – small, but not to be messed with. And Jake Mermagen remembers me as serious and slightly set apart, but not someone who was picked on. Probably most important, I suspect, was that the delicate mechanisms evolved in the relations between boys and teachers, and between younger and older boys, made it a rather unusually bullying-free school.

The absence of serious bullying may again be partly explained by the Lynam headmasters. The Skipper set his face against it and realized that part of the solution might be to encourage the boys themselves to stand up against it. In his 1908 speech he said that teachers had failed if they let the boys 'take refuge in that cowardly subterfuge of "schoolboy honour" when they see bullying or cheating or vice, without protest'.[118] Yet there must have been some bullying and a friend of my own age mentioned recently to me that he remembers standing up to and fighting 'the school bully' in the playground, watched by over fifty boys – and winning. Yet it is not something which, unlike the vcase for many unfortunate children, deeply affected my life.

*

The desire to do well which led me to concentrate hard on sports and games does not at first seem to have extended to academic work. My mother frequently described me as intelligent, but unable to concentrate or work hard at things like reading and writing. What I do remember is that I had a rather short attention span, and when I moved on to something new, threw over the old quickly. For example, I hated clearing up the toys I had been playing with before I went on to another game.

I gained much of the sustenance and models for my imagination from things other than books, although it is clear that I also enjoyed being read to and later reading for myself, despite my mother's impatience with my slowness. The radio was important, but it was the imaginative worlds created by pantomimes, musicals (including Gilbert and Sullivan) and above all films (TV only came in late in the period) that stimulated me in my games of King Arthur, pirates, and so on.

---

[118] Jaques, *Centenary*, 48.

My social attitudes seem fairly predictable and conventional. There are no signs of being a particular snob, though my derisory comments on the Windermere Grammar School production of 'Yeoman of the Guard' may have had something of snobbery behind them. My attitude to women seems pretty standard. My remarks about the school matrons who looked after us when we were ill and we termed the old hags or some such was a rather feeble attempt at humour. My attitude to girls seems also pretty standard, though slightly puzzling. There were girls at the Dragon but I can't ever remember particularly noticing them.

My first, unexpressed and unrequited love is described by my mother – a little girl I wanted to sit next to. I seemed happy with little girls I met until I was about twelve. Then I thought them fleb – weak and unexciting – and made sarcastic remarks about them. But this was the time when I was also asking for pin-ups for my study wall and noting how pretty pantomime chorus girls were. I suspect, however, that being brought up surrounded by a number of strong and intelligent women – grandmother, mother and sisters – made me respect and feel at ease with women.

*

The theme through much of this seems to be one of contradictions, hence my delight, even at the Dragon school, in Pope's 'Essay on Man' – 'to deem himself a God or Beast ... his mind or body to prefer', etc. I was often in the realm of both/and, having to deal with warring sides – as my mother often commented, partly sweet, charming and gentle, partly a brute. Even in my worst offences – for example, when I repeatedly stole – it was often for a good reason (to buy a stamp for my mother's letter to my father, to buy plants for my garden), and I would genuinely share my pocket money with my sisters.

Another contradiction concerned the fairly aggressive sports I liked – air-guns, archery, fishing – and the fact, as my mother noted, that I was really too soft-hearted ever to want to kill an animal or bird. In fact I seem to have been fond of animals and there are accounts of my relations with rabbits, white mice, Puddy (the cat) and other animals, which later would turn into a deep affection for various dogs. I fed wild birds with pleasure when I was little and seem to have been unusually enthusiastic about gentle pursuits like gardening. The model of my courteous and gentlemanly, poetry-loving anddistinguished military grandfather, no doubt helped.

*

Travelling to and reading about Assam gave me a sort of pride in India, and in the same way our summer trips to Scotland, my Scottish relatives, my father's stories of how our family was descended from Rob Roy McGregor, and hearing about the family tartan, homeland at Loch Morar, war-cry ('Loch Sloy', after which I named my first sailing boat) all emphasized my pride. My name, Alan Donald James Macfarlane, was Scottish to the core.

It is clear that I identified with the Scots and not the lowly Sassenachs around me. In the summer of 1954, when I was twelve-and-a-half, my mother notes my pride in Scotland. On 16 August she wrote about a country show:

> The jumping was very feeble but Anne was entranced, and afterwards we had a display by the Dagenham Girl Pipers, they weighed about twelve stone apiece and were incredibly plain poor things with enormous chests and calves due to blowing and marching I suppose but were quite good, a small boy in front greeted them with the remark "Oh lor, here comes the cats chorus" which made Alan white with rage but he consoled himself by saying that they were mostly English anyway in a tone of unutterable scorn.

Two weeks later on 30 August she wrote, *The children are very pleased with the idea* [of a trip to Scotland], *Alan feels that he will at last be among his own kind again instead of the weedy English whom he has to put up with so much of the time.*

I am reminded that my pride was linked to my feelings for my father, whom I believed to be a true Scot (though only now do I discover that he was in fact brought up in Texas until the age of twelve). Sent home to a boarding school in Scotland, my father emphasized his Scottish roots, and I identified with this. The enthusiasm was particularly marked in sporting events and there are quite frequent references to shared delight (or irritation) when Scotland was playing its various foes at rugby or football. My mother, I suspect, was ambivalent about whom she supported. She was mainly English, but as I grew up I was relieved to find that her middle name was Stirling which was linked to Scottish ancestors. She used to say that she was a quarter Scottish, which was better than nothing I felt.

*

It is difficult to tease out my belief and attitudes towards religion. I dwelt much in the imagined worlds of 'The Jungle Book', 'Puck of Pook's Hill', 'The Meeting Pool', various types of fairy stories, and the adventures which my mother used to write and send to us – and which later became partially incorporated into her 'Children of Bird God Hill' and some other of her unpublished works. All this was much stronger and more meaningful, it would seem, than anything formally religious, which was rather unexciting.

In holidays I was sent to a number of boys' Christian camps on the south coast, starting when I was about ten. I don't think this was because my mother was particularly keen on organized religion, though she clearly went to church with us. Rather it was because her brother Richard, my uncle, was a devout Christian and a master at such camps. I needed to be sent somewhere in the long summer holidays to take the pressure off my grandparents and these camps were a good solution for a time.

Yet there is no sign of enthusiasm for religion in my writings. I note visits to various churches from the Dragon, but without comment except to say that some of the services were too long. I did quite well in divinity, according to my school reports, but this tells me little about my faith. In all, I suspect I was quite unquestioning and still believed in fairies, Father Christmas, the tooth fairy and magical worlds through much of my time at the Dragon. Enchantment has been a theme which has interested me all my life, but it is the enchantment of poetry and stories rather than the rather un-magical version of protestant Christianity which was my environment at home and at the Dragon.

25 REFLECTIONS ON THE SCHOOL

The overall objective of my school education was that I should become, over a period of twelve years or so, between the ages of six and eighteen, an effective adult. What I was learning was how to survive and, it was hoped, to survive successfully, in any situation in which I found myself. This was an explicit goal of both my family and schools. Yet I don't recall ever finding a detailed checklist of what it was that others thought I should be learning. Nor do I recall seeing any explicit account of where and how I would learn these qualities, especially the more ephemeral ones.

There were various ways in which I was to learn how to become a reasonable and responsible adult. There was the formal classroom teaching, first at kindergarten and then at the Dragon School, and later at Sedbergh. These were the lessons and preps where I would learn skills and information which it was thought would help me. I was to learn to read, write and do arithmetic. I was to develop my abilities with foreign languages, to start to understand the history of my country and other parts of the world, to learn to appreciate literature, to learn the basics of geography, of science and divinity. This was what school was officially about. Yet this is only a tiny part of what it was really doing.

There were several subjects where I was not only formally taught in class but also learnt informally outside the classroom both at the Dragon and at home. These included drawing and painting, musical appreciation and singing, dancing, making things in wood and clay, acting and making speeches. Some of these were subjects on which I had termly reports but others were practised in a semi-formal way.

Much of the application of what I learnt was in the playground or other public space, in the arena of games and sports, and at home. So I was to learn to be persuasive – rhetoric – to be analytical, to be able to compare and contrast, to summarize and synthesize, to be logical, to concentrate for periods of time on a problem. Many of these skills were as useful in marbles as in Latin.

I was to learn a number of skills and virtues which were encouraged and practised in all of the settings I inhabited. I should be self-confident, but not arrogant. I should be ambitious, but not too directly assertive. I should

239

be full of hope about the future, whatever my experiences of the past. I should be filled with curiosity and delight, but also prepared for long periods of tedious and boring effort and patient waiting. So I should be dogged and persevering, yet realize when further effort was futile. I should be resilient, so that minor and even major setbacks did not destroy my will. I should strongly desire to win and conquer if I could, yet I should also be prepared to concede defeat graciously and without bitterness or self-doubt. I should be ingenious and original, yet be aware of the rules by which effort in any sphere must be guided.

I should be highly individual, self-aware and confident in my own judgement. I should keep my private counsel, not dependent on others to prop me up. Yet I should also be a good team-player, sociable, affectionate, knowing when to share and when to keep to myself. I should be serious about serious matters, but also have a developed sense of the ridiculous, a humour which could tease and reduce tension, and acquire an ability to attack power or stupidity through irony and satire.

I should be charming when charm was needed, but also be prepared to be stern and to say no if that was required. I should be certain of my own values and priorities, but also tolerant and understanding of others who did not share them. I should manage my time carefully so as not to waste it, yet also be able to relax, to conserve energy and re-charge myself, to forget the internal clock and to enter timelessness. Thus I should learn how to save time, and how to spend it, how to prioritize what was important, how to do several things quickly, one after the other, or even at the same time.

I should learn to appreciate beauty in all its forms – in art, poetry, music, nature, and people. Yet I should not be dismissive of the poor, the ugly, the deformed or the miserable. I should value people for themselves and not for the externals, whether of wealth, success, force of character, family background. I should acquire the art of friendship and the judging of character, and how to face the loss of friendship. I should treat people as ends and not as means, learn to separate head and heart, how to tell the truth, but also to refrain from telling the truth or to tell lies with good intent.

I should learn how to handle relationships with people who were very different from me – girls, adults, foreigners, and people from other social classes or different occupations. In these I should show generosity, courtesy without condescension, interest without prurience. I should not think of myself as either superior or inferior, but equal, though through pure chance I might have more material and social advantages.

I should be able to assess the likely outcomes of my actions, the general degree of risk in any activity and whether it was worth taking. I should be courageous and ready to do dangerous things, but not foolhardy to the extent that I put others or myself in unnecessary danger.

So, to summarize: we were to be filled with good emotions. This was especially important. Good emotions included things like self-confidence, cheerfulness, overcoming of loneliness, the art of attracting people to one's personality, and of being attracted by them, the arts of love, hate, detachment and attachment. This is a complex web and particularly difficult because the natural place to develop these emotions, the family, was largely replaced for boarders in an artificially generated setting, the new 'quasi-family' of the school. Something which was constructed so that non-family had to take on some of the warmth and intensity of the blood family.

*

Given the huge emphasis on the physical disciplining of children, the games, sports, toughening up and occasional physical punishment, it is clear that much of school life was to do with toughening the body. This made sense in a world of pre-modern medicine, inadequate heating or cooling, and limited food in many remote parts of the globe. This meant that the body had to be really tough and inured to pain to survive. We should strive hard to be good at games, and respect those who were. But again we should keep this in moderation. Modesty in our achievements, putting more emphasis on commitment and effort rather than attainment, was encouraged. Sport and games were a necessary part of growth, but they could be over emphasized.

I should learn a certain class style of deportment. Of course, almost all children were taught these things at home or at school, but we were being groomed for an elite bodily discipline. Thus there was sometimes overt but often indirect instruction on how to swim, how to run and jump, how to walk, how to sit, how to sleep, how to go to the toilet, how to wash and keep myself clean. I should learn to be nimble and balanced, poised and resilient. I should learn how to eat properly and to speak properly – that is, speak appropriately for my social background. But equally I should not scorn those who did these things differently.

I should learn how to shoot, how to boat, how to ride a bike and many other practical applications of bodily skills. I was to learn how to face pain and sickness without flinching, how to accept nakedness and being with others when I was naked.

I should learn how to compete fiercely, to defend myself, to fight and to conquer. I should become physically strong, yet gentle with it, not be a bully or too competitive. I should learn how to give and to receive graciously, and with gratitude. I should learn to share my good fortune with others, but also not to boast or triumph over those around me. I should learn not to envy others or feel hurt by their successes, but rather enlarged by their happiness. I should learn how to say no and how to say yes, without giving offence or causing jealousy. I should learn how to mourn my losses, to feel grief deeply, yet also to be brave and able to comfort others.

I should learn how to remember things that were important and practise the art of memory, but equally I should be able to forget – or at least lock away – what I needed not to remember, a kind of constructive amnesia. I should learn to see no evil, hear no evil and speak no evil, like the three wise monkeys. Yet I should also enjoy the pleasures of gossip and shared intimacies.

Complementing all of this, though different, was the good spiritual life to which I was being gradually introduced. This was wider than formal Christianity, though that was a part of it. We were to learn to believe in the value of the human spirit, wherever it was manifested, and to ponder on the meaning of life. We should try to spread good Christian values through practice rather than precept, or as Gandhi would say, a rose does not need to advertise itself, it just smells sweet.

So we should espouse a set of broadly gentlemanly, Christian, ethics and moral standards. We should learn love, hope and charity, turning the other cheek, honesty even when no one was looking, doing 'small, unremembered acts of kindness and of love'. Our moral system should be within us and not followed because of fear or external controls. This might lead to loneliness, but we should learn to face loneliness. It might lead to lost opportunities for gain and advancement. But we should remember that our rewards were a better sense of self-worth, as well, perhaps, as in heaven. So we were being taught the deepest qualities – how to love, how to hate, what to value, what to scorn, who we were and what we should become.

In all this striving and balancing of contrary ideals of feeling, thought and action, we should never lose the ability to slip off into the delights and ecstasies of imagined and imaginary worlds that had been created by a host of great thinkers and artists. This was a land of delight which we could also learn to create for ourselves through our developing skills, whether a beautifully executed football shot, a small fish extracted from a stream, or a moment when we wrote something of which we did not think ourselves capable.

*

Several things surprise me about what I now realize we were absorbing. One is the degree to which many of the values and goals clashed and therefore how much judgement had to be exercised. One should be strong and competitive and brave and forceful, but also not bully, not worry about being defeated by someone better, be co-operative and kind. This is just one amongst many of these clashes alluded to above. So we were always learning how to walk tightropes, the sorts of middle way between unacceptable extremes. 'Placed on this isthmus of a middle state ... created

242

half to rise and half to fall, great lord of all things, yet a prey to all, sole judge of truth, in endless error hurled.' We were indeed, as I learnt from Pope's poem in the 'Dragon Book of Verse' in these years, 'the glory, jest and riddle of the world'.

Another thing that strikes me is that we were learning all these skills simultaneously, in so many ways and in so many places. A game of football taught honesty, co-operation, courage, humour, risk-assessment, logic and perhaps even rhetoric, just as much as playing marbles in the playground, taking part in a Gilbert and Sullivan opera, learning in our formal classes, or listening to sermons and lectures. And what happened at school was complemented by our home life, where we would practise and develop many of the skills – bearing pain in illness, bicycling, shooting, dealing with girls, learning friendship and how to deal with adults. So it was a very complex package, where the example of others, the ethos and ethics of the institutions, the organization of different activities, the encouragement and disincentives we received, all influenced us in a multi-dimensional way.

At that period, of course, I had little idea of what was happening. I just lived the experience and did not have the leisure or wider knowledge which would have made it possible for me to understand the pressures exerted upon us. Only towards the end of a life studying different societies and how they educate their children, and with hindsight, can I begin to disentangle some of the deeper currents which affected my life. As I start to understand more, I realize that I was in many ways very fortunate. I was probably being given as good an education as was available in those days.

On the other hand, I can see why I wandered around with an anxious frown, small and quite shy and quiet, except on the rugger field. I had rapidly to learn new ways of thought and action through intense concentration. For me, in the end, the effect has been mostly positive. But some boys who went through what was a crash course in the creation of imperial rulers found it too much and never recovered. Probably I was saved above all by the warmth and support I received from my family, especially my mother, grandparents and my young uncle Robert. So I survived – and here I am.

In these and other areas the child at the Dragon was being shaped into a sort of model of the English gentleman. The Dragon was to be tough, trustworthy, humorous, self-deprecating, clever, a leader of men, individualistic yet a team player, able to overcome obstacles in the most difficult situations, a survivor and a true Christian knight. Bits of these models occur in Chaucer and in Shakespeare, and through our teaching in literature we were given instruction. But much was to be instilled into us more indirectly. And against all of these models we could set the model of the bad life – the bad sport, the liar, the fanatic, the bully, the libertine, the toady, the swot, the cheat...

As for whether my family and the Dragon succeeded in filling me with these lofty ideals and emotions – many conflicting and some of dubious value – I leave others to decide. Certainly it was a compelling vision of the supposed good life, and one which would continue, in somewhat different forms, into my public school and university education.

It was clearly a school which, along with the public schools, had grown up in a period when the British were training an elite to run the largest empire the world had ever known. The strangeness of the 1950s and 1960s was that this function was being eroded so fast. Yet even a decade after I left the school, the novelist Pico Iyer remembers that 'When I was at school, it was always assumed that all the years of quasi-military training ... were meant to teach us how to rule the Empire and subdue the natives around the world. When we graduated, however, we found that the Empire was gone, and the only natives visible were ourselves.'[119]

*

Looking back at my years at the Dragon, I believed until recently that I had been unhappy for much of the first half of my time there. I thought of it as similar to the Catholic view of the afterlife, my school experience being divided into Inferno (two years), Purgatorio (two years) and Paradiso (one year). If asked, I would have said that though the school had a good reputation, it suffered from most of the faults of boarding education of that time; it was snobbish, complacent, put too much emphasis on games, was geared to the academically exceptional and not well suited to average boys such as myself. In other words, I have often wondered why my parents sent me to a boarding school at all, and why to this rather elite and expensive one in particular.

As I read through the letters and other sources and tried to organize them into a serious analytic account I soon realized that almost all of my unquestioned assumptions and memories were distorted. I was seriously homesick and lonely at the start. I was wary and anxious and seldom smiled. Even my friends were worried, they now tell me, at my serious expression. Yet it is quite clear from the contemporary materials that I also enjoyed much of school life throughout my time and particularly in the last half of my five years.

The school was indeed an elite establishment and mainly catered for children from upper middle class families. Yet I never found any problem in being the son of a tea planter or coming from a family that was clearly financially struggling. It is difficult to trace much snobbery or complacency in any of the remaining materials, either those of the school or in the letters. I realize that the Dragon was based on a relatively liberal

---

[119] Pico Iyer, 'The Playing Fields of Hogwarts', *New York Times*, 10 October, 1999. More generally on the relationship between boarding schools and empire, see Kathryn Tidrick, *Empire and the English Character* (1990)

244

philosophy, in many ways well in advance of its time. The curriculum was broad and we were given great encouragement to develop our talents, whatever they were. Basically we picked up the message that almost all the teachers liked and trusted us and wanted us to do as well as we could. This confidence in us was one of the central features of the school, dating back to the Skipper.

The teachers were, almost without exception, excellent. Given the difficulties of the post-war years they gave us the best education they could. Most of us left the school at an educational level well above the normal intake into secondary education. In fact a number suffered from the excellence of the school because they found their public schools a great disappointment, as I have learnt from talking to a number of Old Dragons. Thinking about the education system that is constantly being discussed in modern Britain, America, China, India and elsewhere, I am increasingly persuaded that the way the Dragon was run would provide some useful hints as to how to provide excellent schooling, even today.

My mother was clearly ambivalent about the school when she visited it, feeling an outsider and rather overwhelmed by the self-confidence and self-regard of the boys and teachers. Yet she never considered taking me away, or confided any of her concerns to me, as far as I can remember. The endorsement of the school was evident by the fact that my parents made a huge sacrifice to send me there, especially as they were constantly worrying about money at this period. They were unable to afford many other things – a house of their own, a car, help in the home in England, foreign holidays. Yet they spent over three hundred pounds a year on my schooling, which was a great deal of money in those days.

There are few hints as to why they chose this school, but having lived in north Oxford for a while when they returned from Assam in 1947, and having a cousin sending her children to the school, must have been among the factors. They undertook the sacrifice to buy the best education they thought available, and boarding was essential as they were away in Assam for most of the time I was at the school.

I conclude, on the basis of this attempt to relive my Dragon Days, that the school was exceptional. Not all the boys and girls who went there will feel the same, and I have talked to a number of old boys who feel angry or bitter about parts of what they remember. Perhaps, like me before I looked at the contemporary documents, they tend to remember the painful parts more clearly; the humdrum pleasures are forgotten. As far as I am concerned, however, the Dragon took an average child and inculcated a strength and self-confidence that helped me to survive and enjoy a largely fulfilled and happy life. If I had gone to one of the awful preparatory schools that I have read about my life would have been very different. I am deeply grateful to those of my family, friends and teachers who gave me so much and whose effort and care I have only now begun to appreciate.

*

Let me draw right back now and see both my experience and the Dragon School in a much wider context. As far as I am aware, the practice of sending small boys (and girls) away from home to boarding schools from the age of about eight is unique to England (and Scotland). It is a very old custom and as early as 1800 there were many thousands of private preparatory schools in England.

Looked at from an anthropological point of view it is clearly the first of the three phases of the 'rite of passage', or transition, analysed by Arnold van Gennep. In his schema, the first stage is separation off from the normal world. An individual is taken out of his or her institutional setting and moved into a space which is outside the usual constraints and customs. This space is termed liminality, the crossing of a threshold (*limen* in latin) into a parallel world.

This separating process is what the Dragon and other preparatory schools specialized in. They performed the extremely difficult task of taking us from our homes and families and settled us with strange adults and other boys. It was a very painful process, which is why I remember it as starting in Inferno, even if it was not, I find as I study the sources, as bad as I remember. Yet it was considered essential for it transferred us from the family to society. It moved us out of our birth group into a world where we were competitive individuals within an association. The preparatory school was precisely the preparation for the next stage.

When we moved on to the fully liminal or out-of-the-normal and cut off world of the boys public schools, there were five years when we were subjected to the full force of the English elite educational system. We started right at the bottom, as 'fags' or menial servants for older boys, and worked our way up to become prefects or minor rulers in our houses. We learnt how the English system of power, class and wealth worked through our progress up the various ladders of games, studies and classes. We internalized the mental, moral and social rules which underpin the kind of individualistic and capitalist system which we would have to operate in when we were adult. We learnt the rules of the game we were to play through our lives.

At the end of these five years of seclusion we needed to be re-integrated into the world, but at a different level. Through going to Oxford, I was re-absorbed into the wider upper middle class society. I would take a general course which would polish me and prepare me for whatever profession I entered after University. I began to return from my parallel world into the fully divided adult world of English society.

It now seems to me that this rite of passage lies at the foundation of the peculiar English world of individualism and capitalism which has interested me throughout my academic life. I have found late in my life that a study of the three stages of my education is a useful way to understand the construction of the world views of the civilization into which I was born. It is normally difficult to understand one's own prejudices and blinkers, or the unspoken assumptions which construct our lives. By using the contemporary account I have deposited of my voyage through this ancient yet modern form of initiation, I can begin to understand myself a little better and also the way in which the first modern nation was constructed.

26 AFTERWARDS

So what happened to the three of us after the Dragon – what did we make of this privileged education in our later life? In September 1955 I went on to Sedbergh School in Yorkshire, where my three uncles had also been. This was a tough northern boarding school with a tradition for rugger and running, set in magnificent country near to my relatively new home in the Lake District. At Sedbergh I changed again. I grew by a foot, broadened out and my calf muscles expanded. I soon found that effort alone was not enough to take me to the top of sports, and after the age of sixteen devoted less energy to rugger and cricket and dropped into the second stream. Instead I developed passionate hobbies, in particular fishing. I could fish both in the Lake District and Sedbergh and learnt the joys of fly-fishing and the excitement of the deep shaded pool and the struggle with sea trout.

I also learnt the guitar. These were pivotal years with the end of post-war austerity and the rise of electronic music and the start of youth culture. All was changing and I became an enthusiastic part of it, playing rock, skiffle, blues and folk in a keen, if amateurish, way. In parallel I started to love classical music.

My academic work suddenly took off too as I began to be involved in poetry, drama and history. I had wonderful teachers, especially in my last two years in the Upper Sixth, with Andrew Morgan and David Alban. They opened magic casements on the past and parallel literary worlds. There seemed promise of university entrance and perhaps more. I began to organize my work meticulously and to hoard my paper archives, throwing away very little from the age of sixteen.

The joy of living in Esthwaite Dale, Wordsworth's childhood valley, and wandering where he had experienced the scenes described in the 'Prelude', and then at seventeen following his footsteps on the continental tour to Italy, added to my widening sensibility. So did a second visit to Assam for my seventeenth birthday, to visit my parents who were still away for the majority of these years. I saw the horrors of Calcutta and the beauties of tribal India and both altered my life, bringing back memories of my infancy and the earlier visit from the Dragon.

With my two sisters at home, our grandparents' house became a social centre for the new pop scene and when I got my first motorbike I started to feel the excitement of adult freedom. The search for young love added spice and I began to go out with girls. My grandparents, loving and energetic, gave me a solid home environment.

In 1960 I went to Worcester College, Oxford, to read history. If the Dragon and Sedbergh through much of their time were purgatory, or preparation, then Oxford was paradise. I made my own choices, had my own room and coffee set, was treated as a young gentleman, had my first serious girlfriends. And the world of the Dragon slightly to the north of the college fused back into my being. I tried to retain something of the innocence and delight of pre-adulthood by reading a great deal of poetry and children's fiction. But I also began to be interested in international affairs and politics. The religious enthusiasm of my last two years at Sedbergh increased for a while and then began to fade.

Through the winter of extreme cold (1962–3) and the fears of the Cuban missile crisis and the imminent end of the world, I kept my head down and continued to work in a highly organized and intent way. I just missed a first but did well enough to win a county exhibition to do a doctorate in history. So I stayed on another three years and under the superb guidance of Keith Thomas wrote a thesis on witchcraft prosecutions in Tudor and Stuart England. I started to attend anthropology lectures and at the end of my doctorate felt that I should add to my training by doing a two-year Master's in anthropology – which I did at the London School of Economics.

Then came the time for my final training in anthropology – intensive field research in another culture. As I had always wanted to return to the India of my infancy and two subsequent visits, and Assam was closed because of political troubles, I went to spend fifteen months in a high mountain village in Nepal. There I studied the culture, economy and demography of the Gurung peoples – original work which was turned some years later into a second doctorate at the School of Oriental and African Studies.

A year after my return in 1970 I was elected to a Research Fellowship (in history) at King's College, Cambridge, so in 1971 went to take up my Fellowship. In 1975 I started work as a Lecturer in Social Anthropology at Cambridge and subsequently became a Reader and Professor of Anthropological Science. I moved to our fenland home outside Cambridge in 1976 and have lived there ever since. I remained a Fellow of King's College for most of the period from 1971 and am now a Life Fellow.

In the forty years in Cambridge I published nineteen books and numerous articles. I taught generations of undergraduates and graduates from many countries and played my part in the administration of my department and college. Sarah and I have been involved in many research projects. We undertook the reconstruction of the history of an English village over five hundred years from original records. We made an exhibition, videodisc, database and book on the Naga peoples of the Assam-Burma border. We continued documenting the social history of the Gurung community of Nepal, using film, photographs and diaries and based on eighteen visits. We visited Japan and China at least half a dozen times each. We worked on computer retrieval systems and visual anthropology. We interviewed over 180 leading thinkers in a series of films and developed a large personal website. The period between 1990 and 2003, was in many ways the most exciting of my life owing to my friendship with Gerry Martin, with whom I spent many hours discussing history and anthropology and co-wrote a book on glass. I wrote a book on tea with my mother and a set of 'Letters to Lily' for my step granddaughter.

Now, at the end of all this, it is time to return to the beginning. The papers I have hoarded since I was sixteen, including additional archives from my family and particularly the writings of my mother, have waited all this time to be read and absorbed. Through them I am beginning to understand something about my past and that of the various family strands that meet in me. So retirement is a mixture of sorting all these out, trips down the willowed river in our small boat, wandering through the large memory garden, and enjoying our friends, family and trips to China, Nepal, Japan and elsewhere. Sharing all of this with Sarah over the years has been my greatest pleasure.

BIBLIOGRAPHIC NOTE

Books and articles:

Berners, Lord, *First Childhood* (reprint, 1998)
Betjeman, John, *Summoned by Bells: A Verse Autobiography* (1960)
Brendon, Vyvyen, *Prep School Children; A Class Apart Over Two Centuries* (2009)
Bruce Lockhart, Jamie, *Different Days* (2012)
Cary, Lucius, 'Finding your marbles', *Spectator*, 22 May 2004
Dahl, Roald, *Boy* (1984).
Devitt, Desmond (ed.), *A Diversity of Dragons* (2003)
Frayn, Michael, 'Festival' in Sissons, M and P. French, (eds), *The Age of Austerity* (1964)
Hunt, Andrew, *Oxford to Zimbabwe; A Life's Recall* (1994)
Iyer Pico, 'The Playing Fields of Hogwarts', *New York Times*, October 10, 1999
Jacques, C.H., *A Dragon Centenary, 1877-1977* (1977)
Karleka, Malvika and Mukherjee, Rudrangshu (ed.), *Remembered Childhood; Essays in Honour of André Beteille* (2010)
Lambert, Royston, *The Hot House Society: An exploration of boarding-school life through the boys' and girls' own writings* (1968)
Macfarlane, Alan, *Dorset Days* (2012)
Macfarlane, Iris, *Daughters of the Empire* (2006)
MacInnes, Bev, *A Sense of Purpose*, no date
MacInnes, Bev, *An Independent School* (2005)
Morris, James, *Oxford* (1965)
Mitchison, Naomi, *Small Talk: Memories of an Edwardian Childhood* (1973)
Orwell, George, *Essays* (Penguin 2000 reprint)
Rhodes James, Richard, *The Road from Mandalay* (2207)
Rowse, A.L. *A Cornish Childhood* (1947)
Richardson, Maurice, *Little Victims; Prep School Memories* (1968)
Snow, Peter, *Oxford Observed: Town and Gown* (1991)
Sommerhoff, Gerd, *In and Out of Consciousness: The Intimate History of a search for Certainties* (1996)
Stallworthy, Jon, *Singing School; The Making of a Poet* (1998)
Stell, Helen, *Our Father, Pat Cotter* (2005; Dragon School Archives)
The Skipper : A memoir of C.C. Lynam (1858-1938)(Dragon School, 1940)
Tidrick, Kathryn, *Empire and the English Character (1990)*

Trotter, Jacqueline (ed.), *Valour and Vision: Poems of the War* (1920)
Watkins, Paul, *Stand Before Your God* (1993)

Other sources:

I am grateful to the headmaster of the Dragon School for his kind permission to quote from sources in the Dragon School Archives.

Most important of these are the series of articles in The Draconian. These include some older volumes, but particularly those for the years between 1949 and 1956. Especially useful were the Term Notes compiled by C.H. Jacques.

I have also reproduced a number of photographs from the School Archive, particularly a number of postcards, leaver's photographs and other pictures. I am grateful to Gay Sturt for considerable help in locating and copying these and to the headmaster for permission to use them.

The Dragon website and various articles on the Internet have also been helpful.

VISUAL ESSAY

Cover of The Draconian; the bathing area and fields bottom right

The School

Some of the pictures come from old postcards, and others from the Draconian. All the pictures are reproduced by kind permission of the Headmaster of the Dragon School.

*

The Museum as it was when we were at the Dragon. Somewhere is the dinosaur's egg which struck us so forcefully.

The carpentry shop under the old Museum, or 'Barsonry' (after the teacher, Mr. Barson). Here we made wobbly toast racks and book shelves amidst the smell of glue and wood shavings.

The Silence Room at the end of the New Hall

The huts were still up when we were at the Dragon and Alan ended up in class 2B, which was at the far right, he believes. All of the masters here taught us in some way or other.

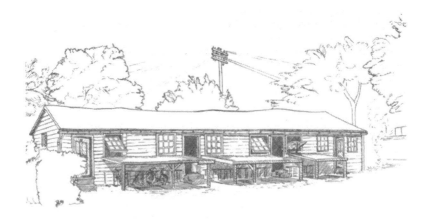

and

Their Oldest Inhabitants

School sports 1951

RELAYS

(Photographs by J.D.B.)

Trial by Jury, Easter 1952, Joc as Judge

257

Patience by Gilbert and Sullivan, Winter 1952, Alan is in bottom row, four from left

Pirates of Penzance by Gilbert and Sullivan, Winter 1953, Jamie is there somewhere under helmet

Coronation Day 1953

'Come to the Fair'

Bicycle Parade

The Emett Train

Bike-Football

The Middle Board and main bathing area.

The Spring Board and Top Board

Easter 1955

R. Moggridge, P. Wheadon, S. Poulter, D. Parfit, W. Arber

GROWING UP

In Oxford when we returned in 1947, aged about six and a half.

Scruffy and losing teeth, with sister Fiona, aged about eight in 1949.

The 'Cup Final' in 1949, uncle Robert, Fiona, Grandpa and Alan

Aged about nine and at the Dragon School, end of 1950 or early 1951.

Aged about twelve in 1954 sampling the joys of uncle's new motorcar.

Dressed in casual Dragon mode, with the characteristic school snake belt, in the summer of 1954, aged twelve.

SPORTS TEAMS

1954 Rugger Colours at the Dragon – Alan far right

Hockey Colours 1955, Alan bottom left

1955 Football Colours, Alan bottom left

1955 Cricket Colours at the Dragon – Alan far right

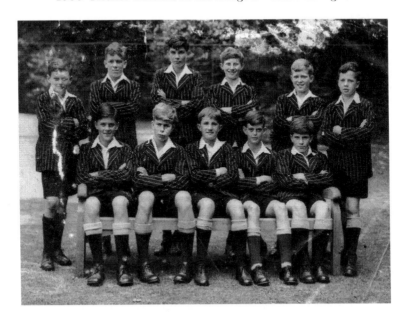

DEVELOPMENT OF HANDWRITING

My first surviving letter; aged nearly six, December 1947

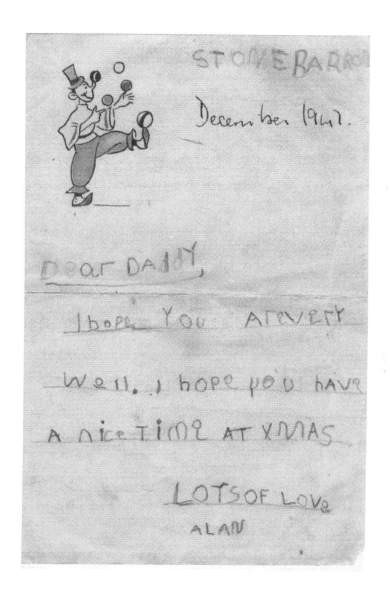

July 1950: two months before Dragon

Dear momy and .... off corse. I hope you are all very well. I am looking forwod to when you are coming Back. I exspect I will like the dragen it sounds lovly. I wish dady could come too and we could have lovly fun. I am very keen on airplans I think I will be a airman. it is a exiting life. The deans have been very very kind

March 1951, after two terms at the Dragon, aged nine

TELEPHONE
OXFORD 47079

6 BARDWELL ROAD
OXFORD

? 23 1951

Dear momy and Ann and frona,

I hope you are are better know

after that flue. I love the

comics and are enjoying your

letters. Thank you very very

much for the lovely sweets

you sent me. The time is fly-

February 1952; half way through second year, aged just over ten

Dear Mummy and Daddy
I am sorry that this letter
is such a short one I have
been in bed just about a weak
so I have not much to say
we started hocky on saterday
but I was in bed. I have
found out I am in seventh out
of 13 or 14 I have got the Bumps

October 1952: start of third year, aged nearly eleven

we are playing marbles this tem
and I have got quite a
few in fact I have got 18
big marbles ⬤ and so small
ones ⬤. wich I will be able
to show to the gifts. We are
playing a jolly good game with
search lights. I have got
hundreds of conquers
this season, and I have
got up to a 86 Then it
was smashed. by a 4.

269

January 1953: postcard from the plane on return from India, aged eleven

Dear Mummy and Dad
I am nearly at
Rome I have had
a nice journey so
far & I am sending
another Postcard
when I get to school
and I am sending
two Broaches I hope that
everything is going well
and Mopsy is getting on.
lots of love Alan

Printed in Great Britain

End November 1953; starting the fourth year, aged nearly twelve

sir We had another lot of Scotch
dancing last night wich was
even more fun than the first
lot We are having a concert
given by all the staff who
can play an instrument
there is only about another
2½ weeks left intill the
end of term and exactly 3 weeks

February 1954; nearly half way through fourth year, aged twelve and a quarter

Dear Mummy and Daddy, we have had freezing weather And I have not played any games (except ice hockey). We have had a wizard time except for the cold as I have lost my gloves We have been doing a lot of skating lately and I am absolutely thrilled I can go quite fast, faster than most people could run. We had a very ...India

July 1954; end of the fourth year, aged twelve and a half

DRAGON SCHOOL
OXFORD
1954
18th July.

Dear Mummy and everyone at By-the-way,

By some fluke I have got my tie for cricket. There have been a lot of sports but also there has been plenty of rain, which has stopped quite a few events. I am enclosing our General Knoledge papers this years and last years. In paper ① (last year's) Questions nos 17 is personal and you would not know know it. This year nos 6 you might not know and nos 9. Please will you papers as I collect them. Packing is just going to start which is a nuiscance even though it means we are near the end of term. Our form is in about

271

Letter in late November 1954; start of final year, aged nearly thirteen

Dear Mummy,

        I spent a very enjoyable week end, and on monday I went first to the Imperial War Museum which was extremely good also I went to Harrods which was also good. There was dancing on Friday and Yesterday (saturday) there was Scottish dancing. Pallez-glyde, Roger de caveleigh Barn dance, valetta, Hoky polky and the Gay Gordons, Dashing White Seargent. There are some cartoons tonight instead of a long film. There were two matches the 2nd agianst

Letter 10 July 1955; last letter from Dragon, aged thirteen and a half

Dear Mummy and Daddy,

        I am so sorry as this letter will probabally not reach very soon but I think I might as well wait untill my results come and I have my papers back. I have played in three matches since Wednesday. Firstly I played against Cothill in which we won by about 70 runs I only made 8 runs but while I was in the score went from 44 for 5 to about 85. On Thursday

DRAWINGS AND PAINTINGS – FROM LETTERS AT
THE DRAGON

1951 Aged nine

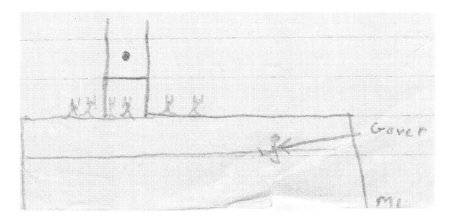

1952 aged ten

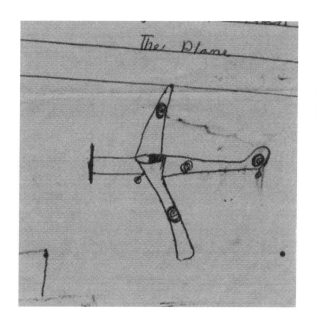

273

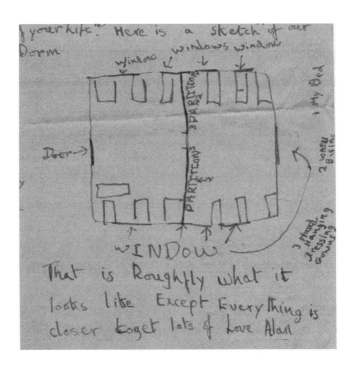

f your life" Here is a sketch of our Dorm

That is Roughfly what it looks like Except Everything is closer toget lots of Love Alan

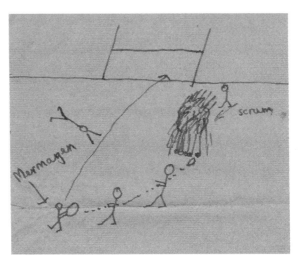

1955 aged thirteen

The last of my fortnightly reports

DRAGON SCHOOL FORTNIGHTLY REPORT

Name *Alan Macfarlane* .... Age *13·6* ...... *10 July* ...19 *55*

	Form.	No. of Boys in Form.	Place last f'night.	Place this f'night.	Remarks.
Classics *Up.*	2ᴮ	17	=12	=13	*good results in C.E.Exam.* K.M.B
English ...	A 3	17	6	=8	*Well done in C.E.E. J.A.T.*
Mathematics	A 2	18		=1	*No places. Well done.* dHS?
French ...	A 4	15	=2	=2	*v.g. FRW*
House					*good*
School					A.E.L.

276

I decided to gild the lily – a spoof report I wrote when aged 11

(spoof)

DRAGON SCHOOL FORTNIGHTLY REPORT

Name.. A.Macfarlane.............. Age. 11.2...... ..May..........19

	Form.	No. of Boys in Form.	Place last f'night.	Place this f'night.	Remarks.
Classics ...	Up1	45	=1	1	Extremely good indeed L.A.W
English ...	R1a	32	1	1	So good I can hardly believe it. J.E.B.
Mathematics	A1	24	1	1	His mathmatics is brilliant W.A.C.W.
French ...	A2	30	2	1	A real scholar C.f.J.

House **Extraordinarily** well behaved and scholarly JHRL

School **V.G.1.** REL.

A.E.L.

277

The last termly report at the Dragon; I have fourteen of the fifteen for my time there

DRAGON SCHOOL, OXFORD

Name *Alan Macfarlane* Age *13·7* **Terminal Report** JULY, 1955

Absent	days	Form	No. of Boys in Form	Place by Term's Marks	Place by Exam.	Remarks
Classics		Form Up 2B AV. AGE 13·4	17	13	11	*He has made v. good progress with v. good exams to finish up. Rest wishes. HWAG.*
English		Set A3 AV. AGE 13·0	17	=8	E H =9 =6	*A very good term's work. Don't stop using your imagination in English. Well done. S.R.S.*
Mathematics		Set A2 AV. AGE 13·3	18	=1	4	*A thoroughly good term's work HHS Good luck.*
French		Set A·4. AV. AGE 13·3	15	=3	5	*A really good term's work. well done! JRQ*
Geography		Set R3 A4	34	=10	12	*Very good DP.*

MUSIC AND SINGING		
ART		
HANDICRAFT	*Good effort*	AB
DIVINITY	*5· v.g. HWAG*	
SCIENCE	*Very satisfactory GS*	

GAMES, P.T., ETC.— *His batting improved enormously during the term, and I hope he will do really well later on. Anyway: H fielded on the field & catch almost anywhere. Performed keenly & well in the sports. Swam with zig-zag enthusiasm in the 3rd Boat. Did quite well as a drill leader.*

General Report (for Day-boys)—
House Report (for Boarders)— *Alan has done very well all round, and the smile has nearly ousted the frown! Best of luck to him at Sedbergh. It*

Headmaster's Report— *Highly satisfactory – We all wish him a happy + useful career.*

A. E. LYNAM

Next Term begins Wednesday, September 21st, 1955, at 9.30 a.m.
Boarders return before 7.30 p.m. on the day before (Sept. 20th)   Holiday Prize Work :— *Illustrated Holiday Diary*
N.B—No boy may return to School without a certificate of freedom from contact with infectious disorder during holidays

278

The Cast of *Iolanthe* in 1954, a high point of my Dragon life

Dragon School, Oxford

Iolanthe

or

The Peer and The Peri

by

W. S. GILBERT AND ARTHUR SULLIVAN

(By permission of Bridget D'Oyly Carte)

Cast

The Lord Chancellor	MICHAEL EVERS
Earl of Mountararat	ROBIN BURLEIGH
Earl of Tolloller	ALAN BROWN
Private Willis (*of the Grenadier Guards*)	OWEN BEAMENT
Strephon (*an Arcadian Shepherd*)	ROGER MOGGRIDGE
Queen of the Fairies	NICHOLAS RAISON
Iolanthe (*a Fairy, Strephon's Mother*)	ANTHONY DENISON-SMITH
Celia ⎱ (*Fairies*)	JOHN EVERS
Leila ⎰	JONATHAN BRUCE
Phyllis (*an Arcadian Shepherdess and Ward in Chancery*)	STEPHEN OLIVER

Chorus of Peers: J. GAIRDNER, R. LEES, D. WALTERS, R. WALLACE, G. STURROCK, O. NAMOUK, A. MUNRO, A. MACFARLANE, D. WILSON, P. WRIGHT, D. MILNER-MOORE, T. HUNT, W. ARBER, A. SCORAH, P. MASEFIELD, J. SCOTT, P. CARTWRIGHT, J. FLETCHER, A. BAINES, E. MOTT, G. MARSH, P. STEADMAN.

Chorus of Fairies: A. BACKUS, M. MALLAM, ALISON THOMPSON, D. SYKES, K. WYLIE, JUDITH OWEN, R. OPPENHEIMER, R. DICK, KATY MACBETH, T. WHEARE, ELIZABETH PLUMMER, R. BRYSON, J. BROWN, J. TRENT, P. WALDE.

ACT I

An Arcadian Landscape (F.E.H.)

ACT II

Palace Yard, Westminster (F.E.H.)

Date: Between 1700 and 1882.

Orchestra

First Violin: MRS. GOTCH, MRS. HOOPER
Second Violin: MRS. KINGSBURY, MRS. JOHN, MISS M. JONES
Viola: MRS. KIRBY
'Cello: MRS. LOWE, MISS ELLIOTT
Bass: MR. S. WINDSCHEFFEL
Oboe: MISS E. KITSON
Clarinet: MR. H. HINKINS, MRS. SENIOR, MISS RICHARDSON
Flute: MR. A. E. SMITH
Piano: MISS PHIPPS

There will an interval of fifteen minutes between the Acts.

Dragon School, Oxford

YEAR, 1955

PRIZE

FOR

Cricket (batting & fielding)

AWARDED TO

A. Macfarlane.

[signatures]

Dragon School, Oxford

YEAR, 1955

PRIZE

FOR

General Paper

AWARDED TO

A. McFarlane

A.E. Lynam

JHRLynam

Printed in Great Britain
by Amazon